D1376368

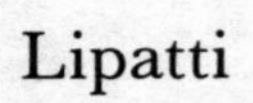

Lipatti

Lipatti

Dragos Tanasescu and Grigore Bargauanu

Foreword by Yehudi Menuhin
Edited by Carola Grindea
Translated by Carola Grindea
and Anne Goosens

Kahn & Averill, London
Pro/Am Music Resources Inc.,
White Plains, NY, USA

First published in Rumania in 1971
First English edition published by Kahn & Averill in 1988

British Library Cataloguing in Publication Data

Tanasescu, Dragos
Lipatti.
1. Rumanian music. Lipatti, Dinu, 1917–1950
I. Title II. Bargauanu, Grigore
780'.92'4

ISBN 0-900707-95-X

First English edition published in the United States in 1988
by Pro/Am Music Resources Inc
White Plains, NY 10606

ISBN 0-912483-18-0

Photoset in 11pt on 12pt Baskerville by MCS Ltd, Salisbury, Wiltshire, England.
Printed in Great Britain

Contents

Foreword

If music truly forges the bonds of human relations it is absolutely true that Dinu Lipatti was a brother to me—for Georges Enesco was a spiritual and musical godfather to us both. This analogue to the world of reality—which I sometimes feel achieves an even greater reality than that which exists—is one which by his very nature and calling a musician, possibly more than other human beings, both creates and is governed by. This spiritual realm, impregnable in its resistance to the onslaughts and the demands of life, to pain and suffering, the frustrations of "real life" is the true image of both Enesco and Lipatti.

Both suffered from irreversible progressive illnesses—Enesco's a deterioration of the spine; Lipatti's leukemia—and as unremittingly as their creeping diseases, both reached ever greater heights as much in their music as in their humanity.

Is this not a definition of civilisation itself? There is a simultaneous physical depletion and an aesthetic and spiritual restoration—a return in a different legal tender, ever less negotiable or exchangeable against a past currency, and only perhaps against some new, mysterious future one? This progression, as in all art, seems to me to be a distillation of what we come from and to what we aspire, both life-enhancing and life-consuming. Like music, it is a fleeting, evanescent vision which cannot be captured and yet is eternally compelling. Such communion with the spirit of other composers and thus equally with the spirit of everyone they encountered was the very substance of Dinu Lipatti's life, as of his mentor and godfather, Georges Enesco. It is an aspect of the man, quite apart from his great technical mastery, which made a profound impression upon me, and which is reflected in this fascinating book.

Yehudi Menuhin
London
October 1987

Preface

The Editor

This is the first comprehensive study, to appear in English, of the legendary pianist, Dinu Lipatti. It owes much to the perseverence and dedication of the musicologists, Dragos Tanasescu and Grigore Bargauanu who spared no effort in locating the cardboard boxes containing the archives of the Jora and Musicescu families.

Lipatti began his serious musical studies at the age of eight with his two great teachers and mentors—Mihail Jora for composition and Florica Musicescu for piano—with whom he maintained a weekly exchange of letters throughout his short life. Their influence was continuous during his development from the child prodigy into the celebrated artist. The authors also had access to all Lipatti's manuscripts in the possession of the Rumanian Academy and the Composers Union; to many documents relating to the old families Lipatti and Racoviceanu, Dinu's childhood and years of study in Paris at the Ecole Normale, his brilliant early artistic achievements in Rumania, concert tours before finally settling in Switzerland as professor at the Geneva Conservatoire while continuing his phenomenal career and coping with the dreadful illness which was sapping his energy.

Lippatti, 'The Interpreter', is known to many through the handful of his recordings which are considered by some of the greatest artists of our time as a model of supreme pianism.

Of utmost interest is the chapter, 'The Composer'. Apart from a few works which have received occasional public applause, very little is known of his impressive creative output. Unfortunately his many years of illness forced him to choose between his concert career and composition. The authors analyse, with much insight, every single work and emphasise the techniques he used and developed under varied influences. During his formative years he was guided by Mihail Jora, one of the exponents of the nationalist movement—led by Georges Enesco—encouraging composers to seek inspiration in folklore. Later on, when studying at the Ecole Normale with Paul Dukas and Nadia Boulanger, he tried to combine this with the neo-classical French influence, as is evident in his more mature works.

Dinu Lipatti, 'The Teacher', is a short chapter by Jacques Chapuis, one of his students at the 'Cours d'Interpretation' of the Geneva Conservatoire. It presents another facet of this great artist's personality when working with his students, whom he considered his colleagues.

The story of Lipatti's life and development emerges simply and clearly from the regular exchange of letters with his beloved teachers, family and friends. In the words of the authors:

> We deemed it valuable to present the facts faithfully *as he told them*. Our effort consists in correlating them, in establishing the different aspects which led to the shaping of his life and personality, to his work and achievement as an artist. We wanted to give the book an 'autobiographical' flavour rather than a biographical one, but with the addition of documentary interest. When writing about a contemporary personality the author has the advantage of direct information, an easier grasp of the subject, his environment and formative situations. Yet he lacks the historical perspective and the objectivity which is vital if one is to perceive the characteristic traits of that personality. We have attempted to bring to life the intense presence of Lipatti, the man and the artist, and we hope that our modest contribution to this end has been achieved. And this would be our reward.

Acknowledgements

The editor wishes to thank Ann Goosens for her help with the translation; also Henry Raynor and Ambrose Page for their valuable suggestions and help in sorting out the complicated notes and compiling the index.

1 First Steps

Music is a serious matter
Dinu Lipatti

Dinu Lipatti was born in Bucharest on 19 March 1917. That year an early spring failed to brighten the heavy atmosphere in a city where every home had been affected by the German occupation and the exodus of Rumanian troops towards Moldavia in the north. The absence of their menfolk was a source of constant grief.

The birth of a boy brought a renewal of hope and happiness to the Lipattis who had longed for a son, even naming him, well before he was born, Constantin, after his grandfather. The fairies who crowded around Dinu's cradle must have wished a vital and brilliant life for him though it turned out to be a short one and full of suffering.

Love of music was traditional in the Lipatti family. The grandfather was passionately fond of music, played the guitar and the flute and wanted his two children to receive the best musical education. His daughter Sophia was sent to study the piano at the Vienna Academy of Music, where she graduated with a *Magna Cum Laude* Diploma. Theodor, Dinu's father, studied the violin, first with Robert Klenk and Carl Flesch in Bucharest, then with the celebrated Sarasate in Paris. After his return to Bucharest he became a career diplomat but continued to play the violin for pleasure. His name was known to European dealers as an assiduous collector of rare and fine violins.

Anna Racoviceanu, Dinu's mother, belonged to an old and cultured family who founded the 'Urziceanu', a famous finishing school for girls. She was an accomplished pianist who often accompanied her husband playing the violin. Because of his parents' musical talents Dinu grew up in a home where he was able to hear good music being played from his earliest days.

Shortly after Dinu was born, the Lipatti family moved to a larger and more imposing house at 12 Lascar Catargiu Street—now, Str Ana Ipatescu—with a front garden which kept out any street noises. Today the house stands like a miniature palace, a relic from the capital city's old style of architecture before the erection of modern blocks of flats.

The birth of her son had been difficult for Anna and her health suffered as a consequence. Dinu was a delicate baby which caused his mother so much anxiety that it threatened to become an obsession. Throughout his childhood she made Dinu wear a red ribbon to ward off 'the evil eye'. The other women in the household only encouraged her in these superstitions, so it was no wonder that before long the entire life of the family revolved around the gentle and loveable child.

From a very early age Dinu showed signs of an unusual musical aptitude. At six months he was clapping time to the melodies and Czardas dances sung with fire by Ana Surcea, the maid. Daily, at the same hour, he became highly excited by the sound of a hurdy-gurdy being played by an old man passing in the street. By the age of two he could imitate any sound from

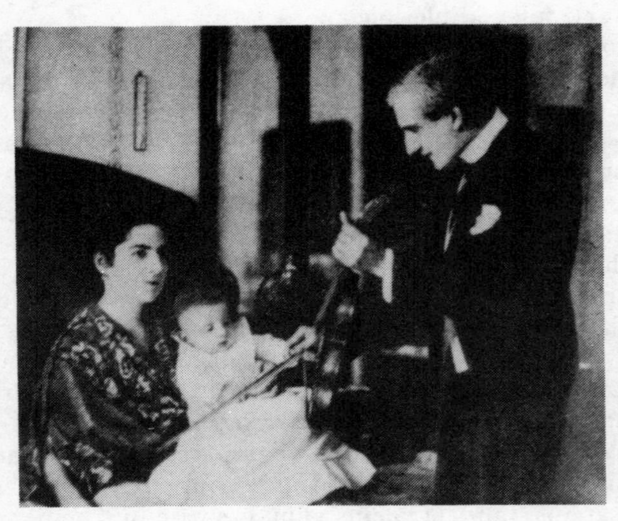

Dinu aged six months

the clinking of a glass to the horn of an automobile. His parents encouraged him by discovering all kinds of unusual musical toys, including a 'miki-phone' with tiny records. Great was their surprise when one day they found him attempting to make his own musical instrument by stretching cords across a dial to make them vibrate. He was then just three years old.

Theodor Lipatti would have liked Dinu to take up the violin but was afraid he might damage one of the valuable instruments if he touched it before he was old enough to look after it. This had the felicitous result of making Dinu turn to the piano, much to his mother's delight. He would run to the piano whenever he could to play his favourite game of picking out all the tunes he heard, or of making up his own. Gradually he developed an amazing dexterity at the keyboard.

Every morning his parents began the day by playing 'Ave Maria', Gounod's arrangement of the Prelude in C by Bach. The boy could hardly wait to jump out of bed and listen to it. His great ambition was to be able to play the piano part one day, and it was the first piano piece which his mother taught him, as a surprise for her husband. The morning Theodor played his violin to Dinu's accompaniment he knew beyond any doubt that the boy was going to be a pianist. In fact his pianistic talent was so authentic that it would be impossible to imagine a similar development had he taken up any other instrument.

At his own christening, when he was four, Dinu played a Minuet by Mozart. Among those present at the ceremony was Georges Enesco, his famous god-father, who placed a laurel wreath on the child's head as a symbol of artistic achievement. On the back of the photograph which captured this moment, Theodor wrote: "Today, 12 June 1921, Dinu Lipatti received, at the same time as his own baptism, the baptism of the art of his god-father, our great Georges Enesco."[1]

The Master must have placed the laurel wreath on the head of the prodigy with an affection mixed with some anxiety. The boy was delicate. Would he be able to carry the burden of a great talent? As though in answer to his doubts Dinu's parents photographed him when five years old dressed in a sailor-suit

[1] See footnotes page 189

Dinu aged four with Georges Enesco, his god-father

with the word 'TENACITY' on his beret. Unconsciously they must have wished this to be the motto for his future life.

Any attempts to develop Dinu's ear proved unnecessary. He had perfect pitch, and Theodor never missed an opportunity to show off his son. He would ask Dinu to name all the notes, in complicated harmonic combinations, which were being played in another room. The boy found these games amusing and he often tried to identify all kinds of noises in relation to precise musical pitch. Perfect pitch is often a sign of special musical aptitude and it certainly proved to be so in this case.

Dinu aged five

As might have been expected Dinu's first steps at the piano started intuitively, by ear. He was not hampered by having to follow the page of a score; instead, a sonorous inner world was free to grow, stimulated by the impressions received through his sensitivity and imagination. He improvised short pieces like 'The Yoghourt Hora', a protest against the daily dose of yoghourt to protect him against infections; or 'A Quarrel in the Kitchen', 'Arguments in the House', etc. Each sound, each rhythmic pattern, the use of different registers and variations in intensity began to have a definite meaning. It was clear that a sudden chord in the lower register indicated the end of a family argument when Father left the house and slammed the door. His musical portrayals of members of the family and friends were so accurate that they were immediately recognizable. Theodor encouraged his son and they often held improvising sessions, each playing his own instrument. He thought that one day it might be of interest to have a record of Dinu's early pieces, so he asked the composer–pianist

Paschil to transcribe them in a book on which he proudly wrote 'From little Dinu's Compositions.'

Dinu was six years old when his brother Valentin was born. From that moment he stopped being 'the little one' and accepted the event with all the seriousness of a first responsibility. He took particular care that the baby's delicate fingers should not be hurt, for he planned to teach him the piano.

Only a little while before Valentin's birth, when he had played some of his improvisations at a charity concert, he had received such an ovation that he now took it for granted that he would become a pianist.

Under the heading 'A Four-Year-Old Pianist' (making Dinu out to be younger than he was—as was the custom in those days), *Rampa*, the daily arts paper, announced on 14 May 1922 that: 'The most sensational part of the programme was the début of a prodigy pianist. With the lack of nerves of an experienced artist this young phenomenon played by ear a

One of Dinu's compositions, when aged five. Transcribed by Joseph Paschill

Bach Prelude and several of his own compositions, *Sweet Memories*, *Dorelina*, *Song of Spring*, *Regret*, *Sad Parting*, *March of the Imps*, *Tune for Grandma* and others, each one more beautiful than the last. This was living testimony of an undoubted musical genius which, one day in the not-too-distant future, may become the pride of the Rumanian nation....'

After his eighth birthday Dinu's parents decided it was time for him to have lessons, and they approached some of the most important musical personalities in Rumania. His real musical education began under the composer, Mihail Jora, and it was to be thorough and disciplined. From then on Dinu's artistic development took a new turn and he found himself confronted with the responsibilities of a true artist. It was this realization which prompted him to say, simply yet convincingly: "Music is a serious matter."

2 Years Of Apprenticeship

Who seeks for light must look to the heights in others, to the depths in himself.
Florica Musicescu

Mihail Jora recalls that, "One grey autumn day a frail little boy was brought to my house by his father who asked me to teach him music. When I enquired what he knew, the answer was: 'Nothing, he cannot even read music but he plays the piano by ear, and he also composes.' This was not the first time that a parent had described his offspring as a great talent, and I did not expect very much. Rather bored, I made a sign for the boy to sit down at the piano. This time it was I who felt like a fool. 'Little Lipatti'—as he was called for many years afterwards—possessed extraordinary intuition and unusual musical gifts."[1]

Jora started to teach him solfège, harmony and piano. Maria Cernavodeanu, also a student of Jora's at that time, remembers with admiration the first day this young pupil arrived in a class with much older colleagues and solved the first harmony exercise faultlessly, guided only by his intuition as he had no idea of the basic rules. This amazing ability was certainly the foundation for his future achievements.

Dinu's parents decided that he should devote all his time and energy to the study of music, and did not allow him to go to school. A private tutor was engaged, but every year he had to sit for examinations. In this way they could supervise the boy's education and at the same time take care of his health. He was a very good pupil but his love of the piano was such that whenever he had a spare moment he would run to it and "play whatever came into my head". He continued with his private education all through High School, showing diverse aptitudes.

Mihail Jora

He was attracted to literature and, at the same time, interested in science. He spent many hours working out the principles of radiophonics, and was often in the chemistry and physics laboratory which had been specially built for him by his father. He became a keen photographer, developing and printing his own photographs, and also enjoyed wood carving and even crochet work. "When I do crochet I have the impression that different voices are being woven together," Dinu told some friends.

In May 1928 Dinu received permission to play in a Festival at the 'Ateneul', the big Concert Hall in Bucharest, when he also performed some of his own compositions. One newspaper critic remarked:

> I first head this musical phenomenon when he was three-and-a-half years old. He was playing at a Charity Concert and I was amazed at his great talent. He played only by ear. Today, after three years of serious study with Mihail Jora, Dinu Lipatti has become a young virtuoso. Last Sundy he gave a very fine interpretation of *Blumenstück* by Schumann, *Arabesque* by Debussy as well as some of his own compositions for ballet, *Valse d'Une Fée* and

Danse Burlesque dedicated to the young ballerina, Madeleine Radulescu. During the second part of the programme, Lipatti played four more compositions, *Hommage à Chopin*, a brilliant paraphrase of one of the Preludes, *Fantaisie Caprice* which is a well-structured and inspired piece, *Hymne à Saint-Sebastien* and a piece full of character, *Valse Tzigane*. As an encore he played *Valse de Concert*.[2]

When he was eleven Mihail Jora coached him for the Entrance Examination to the Royal Academy of Music, and advised him to study the piano with Florica Musicescu. Theodor Lipatti wrote to her: "My son is a genius, and I beg you to accept him as a pupil." Parents often overestimate their children's abilities. Such a letter might have had a negative reaction but, after hearing him play, Florica Musicescu was immediately struck by the unusual talent of the boy. She said later, when recalling their first lessons: "What was so impressive, apart from his power to assimilate ideas and his stamina, was his amazing pianistic dexterity. He could instantly reproduce any musical idea with uncanny precision, without the slightest hesitation, in its entire harmonic structure. A feat which would normally require hours of work."[3]

Convinced of his son's unusual talent, Theodor Lipatti sent an application form on 27th October 1928 to Ion Nona-Otescu, Principal of the Royal Academy of Music and Drama in Bucharest, asking that Dinu be accepted as a student under Professors Jora and Musicescu.

Perhaps the proud parents should be forgiven for exhibiting the photograph of Georges Enesco placing a laurel wreath on Dinu's head in the window of the music shop, Jean Feder. It displeased Enesco who disliked all forms of cheap publicity. "I must say," he declared, "that Dinu's father did take advantage of me at that time...."[4]

From then on a certain coolness existed between the Lipatti family and Georges Enesco; it culminated in a most unreasonable decision that Dinu would not be allowed to go to any of the Maestro's concerts. When Florica Musicescu heard this she refused to give him any further lessons until Theodor withdrew this 'artistic boycott'.

"Just imagine," said Musicescu, "that you live in a village where your neighbour owns the only cow and your sick child desperately needs milk. Would you refuse to buy it from your neighbour because of a quarrel? This is the same as forbidding Dinu to drink from the magic source of Enesco's art!"[5]

Two main influences were at play during Dinu's development throughout his childhood and adolescence: that of his parents, and that of his two teachers, Mihail Jora and Florica Musicescu. His parents never stopped talking about their son's genius and their wish to see him launched as a pianist as soon as possible. Dinu's teachers, on the contrary, with almost rigid intransigence, were determined to make him realize that one cannot achieve anything of value in art without arduous discipline and continuous study. They forbade him categorically to appear in public before reaching a certain artistic standard. This is why his only public appearances during his student days were at Academy concerts or examinations. Thanks to this attitude Dinu developed an acute sense of artistic responsibility which made him continually dissatisfied with his own achievements. It may also have created that need for perfection which characterized the high standard of performance which he attained in later years.

Caught between two strong influences whose only common

Florica Musicescu and her pupils: Dinu Lipatti and Corneliu Gheorghiu

ground was the harmonious development of the youth, Dinu—guided by his true artistic temperament—took from each only what was best for him. An extraordinary self-discipline and a striving after perfection were enhanced, in his case, by a total inner conviction of his own worth, which provided the necessary impulse to develop his natural gifts.

'The loving tyranny' of Florica Musicescu—as his mother so aptly described it[6]—did not hinder the growing relationship of mutual respect and love between pupil and teacher. The pupil was overwhelmed by his teacher's dedication as she guided him through the complexities of her teaching towards a luminous path of artistic fulfillment where there is no room for superficiality or lack of precision. The teacher was enthralled by the talent, seriousness and humility of her pupil. Yet many times Dinu left his piano lessons on the verge of tears, and his parents were on the point of asking for a change of teacher, or at least hoped for 'an exchange of prisoners', as this was known among students when Florica Musicescu arranged a temporary exchange of pupils with her colleague, Muza Ciomac. The two professors, though totally different in temperament, shared similar teaching methods. They adhered to the admirable pedagogical principle that a reciprocal 'borrowing' of pupils for

A pupil of the Bucharest Conservatoire

specific periods can lead to a genuine exchange of ideas and experiences.

Dinu was allowed to make his first appearance as a soloist, while still a student, at a Festival at the Opera House. He played the Concerto in A minor by Grieg, conducted by Professor Dan Simonescu. He was immediately hailed as the 'star' of the Music Academy. After four years of studies he obtained his Diploma of the Royal Academy of Music and was awarded the important 'Paul Ciuntu' Prize. He also finished the courses in harmony, counterpoint and chamber-music given by Dimitrie Dinicu and Mihail Andricu.

During the summer of 1932 Dinu Lipatti took part in the concert at the Lyric Theatre given by that year's finalists of the Academy. He played Chopin's Concerto in E minor conducted by Constantin Nottara. The press notices agreed unanimously that the young artist's standard of performance placed him well above all the other performers. According to the critic Romeo Alexandrescu: "The very young pianist Dinu Lipatti has a rare and already highly developed talent. Besides possessing an unusual comprehension of music and a mature mastery of the instrument, his gifts are sustained by a sensitivity and temperament which make him an accomplished musician. Generously endowed and admirably guided until now—judging by his fine pianism—the prospect of a brilliant career lies before Dinu Lipatti."[7]

In *Adeverul* of 12 June 1932, appeared the following notice:

> The young musician, Dinu Lipatti, gave a performance of an unusually gifted and well-prepared pianist in the Concerto in E minor by Chopin. Indeed, it is rare to find such authoritative musicianship and pianistic perfection at fifteen years of age. An impeccable technique, instinctive rhythm and grasp of nuances are the qualities most needed by any brilliant professional pianist . . .[8].

In order to give their son every possibility to broaden his mind Dinu's parents provided him with a library rich in books on general knowledge, as well as on music.

> I am studying instrumentation from books brought from Paris, and am trying to learn about the intricacies and technique of every instrument. How happy I should be if I could write a piano con-

certo for orchestra this year...At present, if the inspiration comes, I am planning a little Suite as a preparatory step before embarking on any large orchestral compositions.[9]

On 10 February 1933 the young Licentiate of the Academy appeared again in public to play the Concerto in E flat by Liszt, under the bâton of Alfred Alessandrescu.

"With the pianistic foundation displayed last night, young Dinu Lipatti will not need to learn much more about the technique of the pianoforte, no matter how distinguished an Institution he may choose to enter in Western Europe. I believe, indeed, that from now on he should only concentrate on studying the piano repertoire," wrote one music critic.[10]

The musicologist, George Breazul, wrote: "I had heard about the *pupil* Lipatti, but had not expected to hear Lipatti, the *artist*. This youngster is not only a brilliant Licentiate of the

Dinu aged fifteen when he finished at the Conservatoire

Piano Class but he is also a true artist; serious, dedicated, seeking to understand what he is doing now and what he will have to do in the future. He possesses a rare gift, considering the number of 'small geniuses' invading our Music Academy year after year. Lipatti, who is on the threshold of maturity, appears to be endowed not only with a splendid technique, but also with spiritual qualities, a fine grasp of the works performed, and a great desire to achieve the correct interpretation. There is great and intense poetry, coupled with virility, in his rendering of the Liszt Concerto—qualities which will develop and deepen with serious study, and which will help him to grow into Lipatti, the *virtuoso*."[11]

The following month he appeared with the Philharmonic Orchestra in the Concerto in E minor by Chopin, conducted by George Georgescu. This marked the beginning of a lasting collaboration with this leading conductor, and together they gave many concerts in Rumania and abroad. The chance to play this work occurred when a Polish pianist who had been engaged to perform it fell ill. At a few days' notice Dinu agreed to take the pianist's place, a feat to daunt the most experienced of performers. The occasion provided further proof of the serious foundation of his musical training.

In his criticism, Romeo Alexandrescu wrote: "A second public appearance, after such a short while, can only add to the conviction that this young pianist is a musician of exceptional talent, endowed with magical qualities. In Chopin's Concerto in E minor he mastered the difficult solo parts, not only with assurance and technical brio, but with an artistic refinement, a sentiment of rare purity and a clarity of expression that can only serve to emphasize his precocious musical intelligence."[12]

Parallel to his development as a pianist Dinu achieved remarkable success as a composer. His early compositions, mainly exercises, showed the strong influence of his favourite composers: Schumann, Chopin and Liszt. The Sonata for Piano from this period received a 'First Mention' at the Georges Enesco Competition for Composers in 1932.

Mihail Jora's constructive advice was not limited to the technique of composition, for he tried to guide Dinu towards a more valuable orientation. This helped the young student to discover the beauty of Rumanian folk music. Later on he came to feel that it was his duty to study this subject thoroughly in order to make it better known. The Sonatina for Violin and Piano belongs to this period.

In one of his interviews with the authors Jora described the day when Dinu first brought this work to him. Standing behind his pupil in order to hide his emotion, he listened enthralled to the sounds evoking the atmosphere of the Rumanian plains in all its noble and nostalgic simplicity. The work received the 1933 'Georges Enesco' Second Prize for Composition, the Jury having decided not to award a First Prize. They considered that to award him the First Prize would place too heavy a burden on the shoulders of the sixteen-year old composer. The same year, 1933, brought another triumph when Lipatti won the Second Prize at the International Piano Competition in Vienna.

Accompanied by his mother, Dinu walked through the streets of Vienna overcome by his feelings and by a sense of

awe. Every corner of the city recalled one of the great masters of the past. The Competition was to last three weeks (26 May–16 June) with over two hundred candidates from many countries, taking part.

As soon as they had settled in at the Hotel Krantz-Ambassador, the first concern of Dinu and his mother was to find a decent piano. In this respect the organisers of the Competition failed to show enough consideration for the candidates by providing only small cubicles with very bad pianos, for practice.

"The noise was like an inferno and my pieces were getting muddled up with my neighbour's," wrote Dinu.[13] But his determined mother managed to find better conditions in a studio offered by the Bösendorfer Piano Factory. A few days later Florica Musicescu arrived, anxious to witness her pupil's success, which she never doubted.

In the Jury were a number of musical personalities: Wilhelm Backhaus, Emil Sauer, Alfred Cortot, Felix Weingartner, Pancho Vladigherov, George Georgescu and others. The Chairman was Clemens Kraus, director of the Vienna Opera. The first stage, the 'Eliminatory', went very fast. As Dinu reported; "It passed in a feverish turmoil with twenty candidates each day." Dinu was asked to play the Adagio from the Tocatta

in C by Bach, but was stopped after the first few bars of the Fugue as the Jury found this sufficient.

The first movement of the Sonata in B minor by Chopin followed. The hall 'Musik Verein', where the Competition was held, was packed. Dinu's entrance passed unnoticed. He was the fifty-second pianist and the last to play that day. The audience, which was beginning to grow tired, had already begun to discuss who might be the winner but, after only a few bars, Dinu's playing conquered them and from every corner of the hall one could hear, "Wunderbar ist der kleine Rumäne!". In deep concentration, Dinu appeared not to hear the Jury when told to stop the first time.

When he finally did so it was as though he had woken from a trance and was disturbed by the interruption.[14]

Afterwards Dinu wrote to his friend Miron Soarec: "Imagine, my dear friend, being stopped in the middle of a movement by the ringing of a bell—like at Court—just when I was most involved in my playing."[15]

There were three more eliminatory stages before eleven candidates were chosen for the Finals. Among these were two Rumanians, Dinu Lipatti and Maria Fotino, both students of Florica Musicescu.[16]

The Jury was faced with a dilemma as to who should win.

The choice was between the first two candidates—Dinu Lipatti and the Polish pianist, Boleslav Kohn. Alfred Cortot made it clear that he considered Dinu as the more outstanding of the two, while other members of the Jury were of the opinion that the Pole should get First Prize because his age put him close to the age-limit, whereas the Rumanian candidate, at 16, barely fulfilled the entrance requirements. In the end, Dinu received the Second Prize. Cortot resigned from the Jury in protest because his artistic integrity did not permit him to accept such a criterion in judging a competition.

Writing to the same friend, Lipatti added, "I was awarded Second Prize. The First went to a Pole who possessed great experience, assurance and calm."

Such an objective attitude towards a rival whose merit remained in dispute, the sincerity with which he described his qualities and his total lack of envy, only serve to underline Dinu's basic honesty and integrity.

"Now I am free, so free that I can hardly believe that I managed everything so easily. In fact I have only played five times, including the Gala Concert. As I write to you now I am waiting for a reporter who is coming to interview me. Can you believe it—I have become an important person! The prizes will be awarded this evening but just at that time Alfred Cortot is also giving a recital so I shall have to cut myself in two, one half to go to his concert and the other to the prize-giving."[17]

In the end Dinu decided that he could not afford to miss the recital given by the great Romantic pianist whose style of playing was so different from the other pianists. Dinu's choice was revealing since he had always shown less inclination towards reverie but rather more towards disciplined sobriety. And, in a sense, it could be said that this recital was the first lesson that Cortot gave to his future disciple.

During the autumn of that year Lipatti appeared for the third time as soloist with the Bucharest Philharmonic under George Georgescu, playing the Grieg Concerto in A minor, (the work which he performed for his final concert at the Academy).

Some press notices considered that Dinu did not achieve the same degree of artistry as when he had played the Liszt Concerto. Constantin Nottara* even accuses him of exaggerated sonorities at the end of the Adagio. A. Petrovici observes, more kindly, that the young pianist has made some progress. Only Romeo Alexandrescu believed that the orchestral accompaniment benefitted from the subtleties of Lipatti's playing.

Another critic, R. Han, however, dismissed the whole concert because of the quality of the programme, "Nothing but sheer entertainment...nothing else!"[18]

Dinu, on the other hand, was convinced that the Concerto contained passages of rare beauty due to its spontaneity and innate inspiration, but that these demanded a very subtle interpretation.

"Only those who have a superficial grasp of the work are in danger of slipping into cheap dilettantism when playing this concerto and to belittle it is proof of their lack of understan-

*'He knows how to make a work interesting even when its basic structure and ideas do not demand much insight.'

ding." Dinu continued to study the Concerto more and more profoundly and in later years he made a memorable recording, with Alceo Galliera conducting, which remains a collector's gem among the classical discs of our time.

Lipatti gave the first performance of his Sonatina for violin and piano on 25 April 1934 with the violinist Anton Sarvas at a Concert of Chamber Music given by the Association of Rumanian Composers. Later, the same year, he received First Prize at the Georges Enesco Competition for Composers for his symphonic suite *Satrarii* (The Gypsies). This was the first major composition in which he made a masterly use of Rumanian folk-music motifs.

While Dinu was still a student at the Bucharest Academy, Anna Lipatti was making plans for him to go to Paris to further his studies. She, herself, had an unfulfilled longing to travel.

She wanted her son to enrich his inner life by becoming acquainted with the masterpieces to be found in the major museums and by travelling in different countries and absorbing great music in its own climate. Instinctively she echoed Mozart when he said that if you do not travel you are to be pitied; a person of mediocre talent will remain so if he travels or not, but, if someone is highly gifted, he may never broaden his mind and progress if he stays in one place.

As soon as they returned from Vienna with Dinu, the winner of such an important Prize, Anna Lipatti tried to convince her husband of the need to move on. In fact his consent was simply a formality since the determined lady had already sold her house in 'Soseaua Bonaparte' and bought a small apartment in Paris. She had also obtained passports for herself and her two sons through influential friends. She took complete responsibility for this initiative, and Dinu was now ready to fulfill his ambition to study with Alfred Cortot in Paris, a city which had fascinated him since childhood because of the many stories which his mother had told him.

Paris—1934–1936
Success and Misgivings

After a journey through Hungary, Austria and Switzerland, lasting three days and nights, the three Lipattis arrived in Paris early in August 1934. A group of friends had gathered at the Gare de l'Est to welcome them, adding further excitement to the start of their new life. They stayed with friends for a few days as their new apartment was not yet ready. This gave the two boys time to explore the many quarters of the great city, so full of unexpected charm, and they travelled by métro until saturation point. The time-table set up with such minute care by their anxious mother could not be postponed indefinitely, and the remaining part of the holiday had to be spent differently. The family left Paris to spend five weeks at Samois-sur-Seine, near Fontainebleau, to rest and prepare themselves for the months of hard work which lay ahead. Dinu wrote to Florica Musicescu:

> We are so thrilled that our dream has been fulfilled, and we hope

that by the autumn we shall be intensely busy. At the moment we are staying at Samois-sur-Seine, a beautiful place near Fontainebleau, which has plenty of fresh air and absolute peace. We are at a big hotel which has everything, even a piano. This holiday is most welcome because of the year of exhaustive study which lies ahead of me. The hotel is on top of a hill, and down below runs the Seine. The view is magnificent, and I hope that here I shall be able to compose with the same freedom as when I lived in the village at Fundateanca.

I'm getting on well with the piano. I have started to practise again and hope to be back in form within a month. I shall not play to any Maestro before I feel that I'm ready. I completely agree with you that I should go directly to Cortot from whom I'm bound to borrow, no doubt, some of his tonal and colour palette. For the moment though, Cassadesus might be better for technique. But I must see what Cortot will say. It would make me so happy if you could send me, from time to time, some pianistic blessings to help me now that I am on my own....[19]

At the same time he wrote to Mihail Jora: "I think of you with nostalgia, and remember with emotion those beautiful moments when we worked together, and you gave me invaluable advice."[20]

Dinu never wanted to interrupt the close bond with his teachers back in Rumania, not from any sense of conventional good manners but because he felt a genuine need to share with them all his new experiences and plans for the future. One can follow his development, with all the problems facing him during this period of his life, by reading their correspondance. For their part his teachers were writing letters full of wise and valuable pedagogical counsels. Here is a fragment from a letter from Florica Musicescu which could be considered as her 'profession de foi':

I believe that once a pianist or violinist knows his *métier*—which means that he had perfect control over his instrument which he uses to interpret the music—then, if he be a *true artist*, and not one content with a faithful reproduction of the musical text down to its minutest detail, he will seek to express the *quality of emotion* which a particular work evokes in him, and he will succeed in doing this without even being aware that he is doing so.

He will not be satisfied until the sounds he produces will have the right quality and relationship to what he hears in his imagination. Just as a painter looks away from the canvas to the landscape which he paints *as he sees it*, in the same way a musician must *listen again and again* to make sure that the light and shadow, the colour, make a perfect match with what he hears in his inner ear.

A musician is not only a painter, he must be an architect and a sculptor as well. As in all the arts, he must learn to maintain an equilibrium of values and never lose sight of his ultimate aim which is to create a harmonious whole.[21]

Back in Paris Dinu followed a rigorous programme of study until "one beautiful autumn day" he presented himself at the Ecole Normale, Boulevard Malesherbes, to play before Maître Cortot. Recognizing him at once, Cortot introduced him to M. Mangeot, the Principal, in glowing terms. He made it clear that he wanted the young Rumanian to appear in a performance with the orchestra as soon as possible. He also advised Lipatti to study with Yvonne Lefébure whenever he himself was absent from Paris and at the same time Dinu was to study composition with Paul Dukas.

These three new professors realised immediately that they were dealing with an exceptional young artist of great calibre and maturity, who only required their help in order to 'expand'.

"When I first met him", recounts Yvonne Lefébure, "although he had an exceptional piano technique for a youth of seventeen, an unusual musical sense and highly organised mind, Dinu turned out to be a most industrious, modest and obedient student."[22]

For his part Dinu wrote about Yvonne: "From our first lesson I realized that she was an extremely cultured and fine musician, as well as being a first-class performer."[23]

Just as Elsner introduced his pupil Chopin in the most glowing terms, so Paul Dukas, after only one term's work with Dinu, declared: "He is exceptionally gifted, and all he needs now is to work in order to reach, through personal experience, a complete mastery of his talent".[24] Alfred Cortot introduced the young Rumanian at his Interpretation Class in the following words: "Here is a young *maître*, not a student!" After Dinu had finished playing, Cortot added, "Has anyone anything to criticize? Because I have not, it was perfection!"[25]

These unusual praises were, at the same time, an appreciation of the high standards of musical training in Rumania. Dinu was following in the footsteps of other famous Rumanian artists, performers and composers. One can say that the foundation of Lipatti's art, both as pianist and composer, belonged to the Rumanian school of music. This remains true despite the important influence on his artistic personality from his later mentors and teachers: Paul Dukas, Nadia Boulanger and Alfred Cortot. And there were many others with whom Dinu had close contact, such as Stravinsky, Arthur Schnabel, Charles Munch, Wilhelm Backhaus, Edwin Fischer, Ernest Ansermet and Arturo Toscanini. In an interview Lipatti declared: "The lessons which began after may arrival in Paris were a natural continuation of my musical foundation which I owe to Florica Musicescu and Mihail Jora."[26]

In spite of a full programme of studies as pianist and composer and regular attendance at concerts, Dinu always kept one hour free for his correspondence. After less than a month he wrote again to Musicescu:

> Today I received your postcard dated 4 October, and I sincerely thank you for recommending those piano exercises which I shall buy immediately. Do you think they can ever replace, even for a moment, the studies and exercises we did together? My practising is coming along well. Since 3 October I have rented an Erard upright, and am satisfied that at least I have a good instrument, and can now start to do some serious work. Actually, it is a brand-new piano.
>
> I've decided on the following programme to play to Maître Cortot —Bach Toccata, Chopin Sonata, Liszt Concerto, the *Waldstein* Sonata, four Chopin Etudes as well as four Intermezzi by Brahms. What is your opinion? Do you think this a good programme?[27]

In his letters Dinu often asked for news of musical events in Rumania, about programmes of music prepared by some of his former colleagues at the Academy and in particular he wanted to know about Florica Musicescu's classes. About Corneliu Gheorghiu, who was only ten years old at the time, he wrote:

> I'm very pleased to hear about little Gheorghiu's progress; we all have such high hopes for him. May God bless him with good

health, he lacks for nothing else.

About Maria Fotino, his former fellow-student:

I'm glad to hear that Cuca has begun to work again, and I send her my best wishes for a speedy recovery to her injured arm. Such a sincere and modest, (perhaps too modest), artist with so many admirable qualities...

As for myself—as far as concerts go I cannot complain of any lack of choice. Since the first week we arrived there have been very interesting programmes. For instance, this season opens with a series of Festivals of French Orchestral Music, conducted by Pierre Monteux, Albert Wolff, Branco etc. At the 'Pasdeloup Series' we shall hear Lazare Lévy in the Symphonic Variations by Caésar Franck, and Prokofiev's 3rd Piano Concerto. So far there are no piano recitals, but we hope there may be some next week.[28]

In Paris Lipatti met a compatriot, Filip Lazar, the composer and pianist, who had settled there a few years earlier. A warm friendship developed, based on mutual admiration. Filip wrote a letter to Jora expressing his enthusiasm; "I am amazed and confounded by such talent as Dinu's...I believe he is a genius. I congratulate both you and Florica on the way you have trained him. I promise to help him in every way possible within my limited means. I've told him to look on my home as his, and on me as an elder brother who only wishes to be of some use."[29]

It was through Filip Lazar that Lipatti met a whole *pleiade* of French musicians which included Ferrould, founder of the 'Triton' group, Florent Schmitt, Honegger, Ibert and others. They would spend many hours talking about music, art, literature, or about the doubts, joys and dissatisfactions in their own creative work.

On 19 November 1934 Dinu Lipatti entered the Composition Class of Paul Dukas. On the same day he wrote to Jora: "At the first lesson I played my Suite. He found it very good except for a few criticisms. He thought the first part rather clumsily orchestrated, with too much use of the trombones; one passage is repeated too often; the form is not sufficiently sustained etc. The second part—*Idylle*—he found very much better. He added that the material is of very high quality but that the structure is not always consistent. He preferred the Third

Movement which he found better orchestrated, and well constructed."[30] After his second class, Lipatti wrote:

> I played the Sonatina. Dukas found it excellent, saying that it shows a mature conception with solid structure. He particularly liked the third variation (Andante). He preferred this work to the Suite which did not stop me from sending it to Bucharest, although with my enthusiasm somewhat dampened. But I did make some revisions. For instance, in the *Idylle* I replaced several bassoon passages with the piano. I strengthened the strings, and where there are some long notes I brought in the woodwind.
>
> With regard to what work I shall compose this year, I have returned to the idea of a Piano Sonata. The *Maître* heartily agrees. He believes that I have finished with my 'schooling' in composition and that there is nothing further for him to teach me in this respect. He wishes to congratulate my Professor for the way in which he introduced me to the mysteries of the art of composition. Dukas says that in future his role can only be that of critic—an extremely severe one—of any work which I shall bring to him. So far as 'severity' goes, he is indeed not far wrong when he says it will be extreme. [31]

Although enjoying the life in Paris, Lipatti missed his home in Bucharest, the park at Fundateanca, the meadows in the melancholy light, the richly wooded hills, his friends and teachers who had made him feel so protected. These longings were to be reflected in his musical compositions and provoked long discussions with Dukas who did not approve of the 'Rumanian atmosphere' in his musical ideas. He considered this to be too primitive for the 20th century. "I maintain, on the contrary" wrote Lipatti "that if the composer integrates the 'atmosphere' into his work with great care, this can be universally valid."[32]

Dinu continued to be the same devoted disciple of his old teachers. He wrote to Jora; "I carry your counsels deep inside my heart and shall always try to be worthy of them. 'Try to be true to yourself' is the most valuable one, and the same which Georges Enesco used to give young composers." And later, "Actually, I have begun work on the Piano Sonata, but am afraid of any outside influences, particularly of Enesco's piano sonatas. Still I must try...'to be true to myself' as much as possible."[33]

Many young interpreters are eager to perform in public as soon as they are allowed to. This is proof of artistic immaturity when they have not yet had time to master their work thoroughly, at least from the technical aspect. Although winner of an International Competition and highly commended by Cortot during his Interpretation Class, Lipatti declared:

"As to making an appearance before the Paris public, I can assure you that I shall do so only when I am absolutely ready, both from a musical and technical point of view. It will not prevent me from continuing to work seriously and to learn from my professors' advice."[34]

The search for perfection continued to dominate Dinu's life, and his torments while finding himself as a composer became a leit-motif in every letter. "I still have not written anything. Either I am too severely critical, or else I lack any inspiration. Until now I have only sketched out, then torn to pieces, several themes for a sonata which is exasperatingly slow in coming...."[35] Yet this dissatisfaction with his work was not shared by Paul Dukas who considered Dinu his most brilliant student. As to any 'lack of inspiration', this remark can only be looked at from his own point of view. At the same period he also writes, "Every time I see Dukas I show him either a Fugue or some simple, or varied Chorales...."[36] He never refers to the extraordinary praise and appreciation bestowed on him by his professors as to an 'equal'. A letter from his father, Theodor, written on 18 January 1935 tells a different story.

> Very esteemed and beloved Miss Musicescu,
> I arrived in Paris on Christmas Eve desperately anxious to see my wife and sons. I found them all well. What can I tell you about Dinu? Here, in Paris, he is considered by all those whose opinion carries any weight, as a very fine pianist with rare musical and pianistic training, a true virtuoso! With his usual modesty and desire not to appear vain, he prefers not to tell you about such praise and chooses to remain silent. But I see no reason to do so myself because I am convinced that Dinu's successes are not entirely due to his own efforts, but are also very much the result of your own splendid work. Cortot thinks very highly of him, and this I know from Mlle Léfebure and Monsieur Mangeot. Paul Dukas tells everyone that 'the little Rumanian' is his best pupil as well as being a distinguished virtuoso of the piano. He also said, 'Your young compatriot will become a second Enesco'. Everyone admires Dinu, and no one is surprised at his success as they all know that he is Florica Musicescu's pupil.
>
> Dinu is proud that his magnificient musical gift was nurtured in his own country. And it is his noble ambition to show the 'enlightened West' that we who live near the Gates to the Orient are also capable of producing first-rate artists—'*di primo cartello*'—and this inspires him to work even more assiduously.
>
> As to myself, profoundly aware of these facts, I kiss your hand in gratitude, with affection, and, at the same time, wish to express my homage and admiration.
> Your devotedly,
> Theodor Lipatti.

To Mihail Jora he wrote:

> I have always believed that from early childhood Dinu has had the good fortune to be in the most capable hands possible so far as his

musical education is concerned. Today, in Paris, this belief is vindicated at every turn in eloquent and valuable endorsements by the greatest European masters.

To you all our gratitude and love. May God bless you with a long life.

Theodor Lipatti.[37]

On Christmas Eve Dinu performed Liszt's Concerto in E flat at a concert given at the Ecole Normale de Musique. His self-criticism was not affected by the tremendous reception he received from an audience who heard him play for the first time. He wrote:

I played rather nervously, yet Cortot liked it very much. He told me on different occasions that it was a 'remarkable performance'. At the end of the concert he opened the score and made some interesting remarks. He would have liked bars 22–23, in the Third Movement (Scherzo), played a little more freely, more capriciously. Also in the Scherzo, bars 141–161, he suggested I play a tremolo (similar to the one which precedes the last scale-passage in the Coda) instead of a trill, as only in this way will it sound clearly and powerfully. The same applies to bars 70–72 in the Finale.

As to bars 80–85, he suggests I play them in the version given as 'ossia', not in their original form, for the same reason. He also showed me several changes in the score made at a later day by Liszt himself. Then he said he would like to hear me play a new work, one which I have only recently studied. On 23 January I shall play him Schumann's *Carnaval* at which I am working feverishly. Afterwards I shall definately start Beethoven's Sonata in D minor, Op 31, No 2 and perhaps one of the Bach Concertos.[38]

Discussing the studies for piano technique, he says, "I am putting aside the '*Principes Rationnels*' for the moment, and turn instead to '*L'Etude Consciente*' by Emile Frey. Dear old Czerny's turn will come later, though I never really leave him."[39]

The Ecole Normale de Musique held its 47th concert on 25 February under the bâton of Alfred Cortot. Georges Enesco was also invited to participate as conductor. When asked to play one of his own works Enesco suggested that Dinu should perform his Piano Sonata in F sharp minor for its first Paris

Maestro Cortot and his favourite pupil

performance. "This way one of my dreams came true sooner than I could have ever expected," commented Dinu.[40]

"The young pianist Dinu Lipatti," wrote Mangeot in *Le Monde Musical*, March 1935, "though completely unknown to the Parisian public received six enthusiastic calls after his performance. The ovation was as much for him as for the composer. There is not time enough, nor space, to do justice to the Piano Sonata in F sharp minor as we should like to, but we shall do so very soon. Now we can only state that this work merits a place of honour among the most beautiful contemporary works for the piano, and that it requires a Lipatti to perform it. Is not this eighteen-year old artist, both as interpreter and composer, the spiritual heir of Enesco? The date, 25th February, which saw them united in the same triumph will remain memorable."

None of this praise equalled Dinu's profound delight when Enesco told him, after the concert, "Your interpretation recreated all my intentions, and even I could not have said more."[41]

About this time Lipatti made the acquaintance of the great German pianist, Edwin Fischer. "I am thrilled to have met this generous artist, and look forward to working with him when I have the opportunity of going to Berlin."[42] With characteristic respect, Dinu played to Fischer part of the programme which he meant to give in aid of the 'Association Amicale de l'Ecole Normale de Musique'. It was to be his first piano recital in Paris. To Florica Musicescu he wrote:

> Edwin Fischer found the Toccata excellent, but he told me to play the Brahms more like a 'bear'; in other words, not to play with too much fire. He liked my playing on the whole, and said he would be very happy to work with me if I went to Berlin. He also gave me an important piece of advice which I've already heard several times from you.—'Do not use the same palette for Bach as for Chopin; vary the touch, attack and intensity of nuances according to the style of the composer and the type of composition'.—For instance, Fischer insisted that in Brahms' Intermezzo in E minor, Op 118 No 6, the theme in the middle needs to be played more majestically and in the same *primo tempo*, which I was not doing. He told me that my style of playing is perfectly suited to Bach and Scarlatti...

About taking lessons with Yvonne Léfebure, and studying Beethoven's Sonata Op 110, he wrote in the same letter:

> Mlle Léfebure has a very special and deep feeling for this Sonata. The other day she played it admirably for me. She believes that this Sonata, the Concerto in G for piano and the *Variations on a Theme* by Diabelli are the most sublime pages of all Beethoven's works. She suggested that I should create a warm intimate atmosphere in the Sonata so as to express, as closely as possible, Beethoven's sentiment of benevolence towards the whole of humanity, a sentiment which possessed him all the time while writing it. How difficult it is to express this, particularly in the Adagio. Mlle Léfebure also mentioned that for a long time she had not dared to perform the work.
>
> Afterwards she played Schumann's *Novelette* much faster than I take it, and with sonorities that swell and die away like a blowing wind. This is where she imagines an impressive cavalcade approaching and then disappearing at fantastic speed The idea is not bad, but to bring it off at this tempo requires some vital technical changes which I have adopted.[43]

In May the musical life of Paris suffered a great loss. Paul

Dukas died after a long illness. By a sad coincidence Lipatti's recital, organized by the Ecole Normale on 20 May 1935 fell on the same day as the funeral of the great musician.

"This was a great blow for all of us. With a heavy heart I had to carry on with the recital which had already been arranged...[44] As a tribute to the great composer, the recital opened with the Chorale in G from Bach's Cantata No 147. The entire audience stood up as a mark of respect while the work was being played. This Chorale was to reappear like a leitmotif in nearly all of Dinu's future recitals, as a first 'encore' and, symbolically enough, was to be the last piece he played at the final concert of his short life. Lipatti seemed to find in its sober and even rhythms a climate which allowed him to express his deepest personal thoughts and feelings.

This first Paris recital was a great event in the city's musical life. The critics surpassed themselves in describing the appearance of this new pianist on the horizon. "It is rare to come across a marriage between first-rate technical achievement and the finest qualities of musicianship," states one of the notices. "But this is so in the case of Dinu Lipatti, the young Rumanian pianist who made his Paris début in a serious programme which drew the attention and admiration of all our leading musicians. He gave an admirable interpretation of the Toccata in C by Bach-Busoni. The Fugue, in particular, was played with such clarity, mastery, and a remarkable sense of polyphonic progression and architectural balance that we may safely conclude the interpreter reached the peaks of grandeur. Next came Brahms, with the exquisite poetry of the Four Intermezzi recreating a sensitive and marvellous atmosphere. Lipatti's pianism is endowed with extraordinary sonorities which are never superficial even when playing a most subtle *pianissimo*, nor ever harsh in *forte*, retaining a constant and carefully controlled richness of tone." The same notice remarks on his truly transcendental virtuosity. "At the same time, none of his fast movements betray a laboured execution but, on the contrary, seem to arise with the spontaneous abandon of an enchanting virtuosity."[45]

The success of this recital, given under the auspices of the Ecole Normale, attracted the interest of all the great impressarios. The unapproachable Kiesgen, who was famous for his flair for spotting the commercial value of any artistic talent, immediately suggested a series of concerts which he proposed to launch in time to coincide with the opening of the Paris musical season. Soon afterwards Dinu received the following note from the Director of the Ecole Normale (M. Mangeot)— *Maître Cortot, wishing to show his appreciation of your pianistic qualities, invites you to join the Jury of the Ecole to adjudicate the Diploma of Virtuosity.* Dinu wrote:

> Next day I arrived at the Ecole, and found Maître Cortot in his study. He introduced me to the other members of the Jury in this way; 'Lipatti plays like a Horowitz, and will be one of the most brilliant pianists of tomorrow!' (Just imagine how cross poor Horowitz would have been!) The Jury consisted of five: Cortot, a professor from the Conservatoire, the Director of the Hochschule of Bayreuth, another professor and myself. Cortot advised us to be quite strict in our marking as regards virtuosity because the same candidates were also going to sit for the *Licence de Concert* later on, and were destined for virtuoso careers. As for myself, I was very strict. The marks went from 0 to 20, 6 being a failure. The highest mark I gave was 18, I don't know what the others did. Except for three or four good ones, the rest of the candidates were rather weak and did not count for much. The exams lasted from 9 am until 5.30 pm. After it was all over I played my Suite[46] to the Maestro, who liked it very much, and was very surprised it had not been performed in Rumania. He wanted me to leave the Sonatina with him so that he could take it home to look at it undisturbed, as he had no time to do so at the Ecole.
>
> He emphasized, several times, that he has heard many pianists and is able to judge at once when he meets an outstanding one, and that it is a great joy for him to see how well I have been working since I came here. Next day I went again to the Ecole where the Maestro introduced me to Charles Munch, the conductor, in the warmest terms, specifically recommending my Suite for Orchestra. On the third day I assisted at Cortot's *Cours d'Interprétation*. The works played were Concerto in C minor by Saint-Saens, Variations by Pierné, some pieces by Ravel and *Nuits dans les Jardins d'Espagne* by De Falla. These were remarkably well performed by Nadia Desouches, while I played the orchestral part from the score. Then I had a meeting with M. Munch to play my Suite, which he liked very much, and said that when he had the opportunity he would certainly remember the work.[47]

In spite of Lipatti's respect for Paul Dukas and his undoubted value as a teacher, his first year of studying composition was one of struggle and obsessions about his inability to create, which culminated, shortly before his debut of 20 May, in a letter to Mihail Jora which gave rise to some anxiety as to his psychological state.

> My very dear Professor,
> I have been waiting every moment, day after day, to be able to give you some good news. Unfortunately this has not happened. I find myself, as regards composition, 'bogged down in a deep morass' due to a complete lack of perserverance and discipline in my ideas. I began a few pages of a so-called Fantasy for Piano and Orchestra only to find I could not carry on; then I sketched out in a few minutes another theme for a piece for violin and piano. This is the sum total of my work, after spending nearly one year in the best musical environment. So, there we are...I miss you and that strong iron hand with which you have guided me up until now.
>
> No one has been appointed by the Ecole to replace Paul Dukas, out of respect for the memory of this great musician, although M. Mangeot has asked Mlle Nadia Boulanger to finish the course for the current year.[48]

The death of Paul Dukas created fresh obstacles for Lipatti in his search for a new master to help him, as there were so many contradictory opinions about the criteria for choosing a professor of composition. On 22 July 1935 he wrote again to Jora: "I am glad that you've advised me to study with Nadia Boulanger. I had the same feeling after my first lesson with her. Yet there are several musicians here who think it would be better for me to work with a creative composer. They are afraid that I might end up getting caught in Nadia's web and, under her influence, start to write cold and cerebral music. And so on and so forth... I did not believe a word of what was being said. I was much too enthusiastic after my first lesson to pay any attention to such comments."[49]

His enthusiasm for his new teacher was increasing steadily as several of his letters demonstrate. "I see Nadia Boulanger twice a week at the Ecole, and again twice at her home. These lessons give me so much joy that I never miss a word of what she says. She is an extraordinary person from every point of view."[50] His admiration did not stop at his appreciation of her professional qualifications. He was also amazed by her stamina and unremitting activities both as teacher and lecturer—she spoke at many Cultural Centres—and as pianist and conductor, always trying to bring to the public eye important works which had not been published before. Indeed her influence was instrumental in developing Dinu's taste for what was new, and his dislike of any form of stagnation or of what might seem to be merely common-place. The following, in a letter to Florica Musicescu is very revealing. It refers to a concert conducted by Nadia Boulanger which consisted mostly of unknown works of the 16th century and of contemporary composers. "Mlle Boulanger is more and more admirable. The other day she conducted L'Orchestre Philharmonique de Paris in an extraordinary programme. At such moments I want to turn against all those conductors who have the possibility to present great works and do not do so. They prefer to limit themselves to that narrow répertoire 'from Bach to Debussy'. Nothing before Bach, nothing from our own times".[51]

In turn Nadia Boulanger showed great concern for the young Rumanian, watching over his musical development and activities with the greatest care and affection. Later on, when remembering her lessons with Dinu, she admitted that:

> When Dinu arrived in Paris he was already an accomplished pianist, the product of that admirable Florica Musicescu for whom he had a real cult. And he was already a serious composer with a solid foundation and knowledge, thanks to Mihail Jora. Far from being satisfied with what he had already learned, his mind was perpetually preoccupied by what he thought he had yet to learn. One could read his soul by just looking at him. His serene face, with its dark velvet eyes seemed, alternatively, lively, kind and serious; his beautiful white hands—all these were but the visible signs of a delicate but forceful being from whom emanated an impression of extraordinary purity. He had kept intact all the joy and gravity of childhood. And what a passion he had for the piano! When occasionally, I used to tell him to allow himself more time for composition, he would smile, 'I know this very well, but I cannot tear myself away from the piano. If you only knew how much I love 'him''.
>
> His ear was sensitive to the finest nuances of every sonority, to the most subtle inflexions of any rhythm. Only his wife,

> Madeleine Lipatti, could tell us with what sort of precision he worked to obtain his fingering, pedalling and the refinement of his touch. The 'craft of his métier', as he loved to call it, was his one continuous preoccupation. His compositions—whose worth has not yet been properly established—bear the same signs of a profound musical intelligence devoted to endless search for perfection in their realization. They are proof of a real creative gift and deserve to remain alongside those few recordings which will continue to keep alive the memory of his great interpretations.[52]

Apart from Musicesu and Jora, no other professor had a stronger influence on Lipatti than Nadia Boulanger. She helped him to give full expression to his artistic and emotional potential, and this was very soon to earn him a place among the great musicians of our time.

How important is the stimulus of such a teacher in the art of pedagogy? The truth is that a teacher—no matter how erudite or methodical—who fails to arouse any passion or enthusiasm is useless. "Nadia Boulanger is not only my teacher of composition, she is also my musical guide and spiritual mother." With these words Lipatti makes clear the debt he owed to her.

It was through working with this great teacher that the previous year's suffering, caused by his doubts about his talent for composition, began to disappear. After less than two months of classes, he wrote to Jora:

> My dear Professor,
> I have not answered your letter before because, at least this time, I wanted to keep my word. I am composing again! And high time too! I have started a concerto for piano and orchestra. I have only finished one page, but this time I am determined to complete the work, no matter what happens. I began with the second movement which I see as a Scherzo because I think this part will be the easiest to work out at present. I have a complete plan of the structure of the concerto in my mind; afterwards I mean to work out the detail and 'to hear' the whole work before putting it down on paper. The First Movement (in B minor), although it should be the most clearly defined, is still unclear; I am not quite certain what it will sound like. I see the Second Movement as lightly ironical in tone, that is to say, an irony verging on burlesque at times, but sometimes more refined. I hope this will give the solo instrument the possibility to decide the proper technique to use.

However, I see the Finale, an Adagio, taking on a completely different colour from the Scherzo. I imagine something majestic, like a cathedral, or a hymn swelling in grandeur with a kind of inner exultation. Nadia Boulanger tells us all the time, better turn to Bach than to the Romantics! So, I shall think of Bach when writing the Finale. Now I must not waste a minute; the plan of the work is ready, I have sufficient time and the necessary peace of mind. All I have to do is to sit down and write a work which should have been written a year ago. God help me to finish it well...

At present I am writing short pieces for string orchestra. Mlle Boulanger had asked me for a Suite for piano which I have to finish as soon as possible, although I have started on one for strings. We have agreed that I should bring to my lesson a complete work every week. I have finished the Prelude for tomorrow, and today I shall start another piece for next week. In this way I shall soon have about ten pieces to show. And it won't take long to get into the habit of working every morning on counterpoint in four, five, six, seven or eight parts. Composing 'to order' is an excellent idea for someone as stupid as myself.

Apart from composition I am also busy with the orchestration of the Suite. I have neglected to do so until now because those who heard it made various suggestions about the orchestration, and I was dreading the thought of making even more changes after all the parts have been written down. Finally, I came to the conclusion that no matter how many musicians I asked for advice, each one would make a different suggestion... That's why I have only made a very few changes.

I must finish now, but thank you once more for your letter which gave me such joy and hope.[53]

So ended Dinu's first year of studies in Paris; a period of intensive work and many doubts which all true artists experience; it had also included unexpected joys and some great successes. Cortot once told him, "If you decide to dedicate your life to this art you must be armed with patience, and be ready for many sacrifices."

The first vacation in Paris provided a chance to concentrate on his work and to keep pace with the increasing artistic demands being made upon him. Anna Lipatti was busy organizing her sons' lives down to the minutest detail. This is how Dinu describes their family life:

> My brother, who is mad about the cinema, is watching Stan and Ollie across the road, at the Pathé Cinema. He collects film stars' photographs, eats in a hurry, and wants to lose weight. Mama never stops moving about—one moment inside the house, next off to the Châtelet to buy concert tickets—she's everywhere all at once. As to myself, unable to keep up with such *tours de force*, I remain sitting at my table and compose, or else I play the piano.[54]

And later:

> We came to Duingt a charming place on Lake Annecy on 10th July. We have a panoramic view, and the mountain air is very pure—some peaks are higher than 2800m. A splendid place to rest though there are plenty of distractions—tennis, ping-pong, boating, fishing, climbing etc. The hotel is attractive and nicely situated. I have a miserable tin-trap of a piano which I have to use, for better or for worse.[55]

At Combloux, about 80 kilometres from Duingt, Filip Lazar was staying at a hotel-sanatorium because of his poor health. He made several visits to Duingt and the two friends would spend their time playing the piano, discussing problems of composition or going for walks. He often described Filip Lazar as a cultured, witty and very nice person, in his letters to Jora: "He played us some of his compositions and, before leaving, gave us some of his works inscribed with marvellous dedications" (to M.J. 6 Aug 1935; Duingt).

After a month at Duingt, the Lipattis moved on to Aix-les-Bains for a fortnight. They accepted Cortot's invitation to visit him at Annecy, and joined him one Sunday when he took them all out to lunch. He was even more charming than usual on this informal occasion and regaled them with some of his reminiscences and interesting experiences. Afterwards they took photographs and in the evening attended his recital given in Annecy. Dinu wrote about this event, "I was deeply impressed....His playing is extraordinary. I shall never forget the way he played Schumann's *Etudes Symphoniques*."[56]

The family ended their holiday by driving along the Côte d'Azur through Cannes, Juan-les-Pins, Antibes, Nice, Beaulieu, Grasse, Bar etc. They wanted to remember every corner of this part of the Mediterranean, from each splendid olive, fig or orange-tree, down to every profusion of lovely flowers growing in the brilliant sunshine. It had been a glorious vacation. "I dread going back when I think of the smoke of Paris," commented Dinu.

At the end of October he was invited to Geneva to give a recital on the radio. "I shall play Beethoven's Sonata in C, Op 53, *La Vallée des Cloches* and *Alborada del Gracioso* by Ravel. Then on Monday 28 October, at 21 hours at the Conservatoire, Bach's Toccata in C (arr.Busoni) in a programme shared with the Manhattan Quartet, and on Tuesday 29th

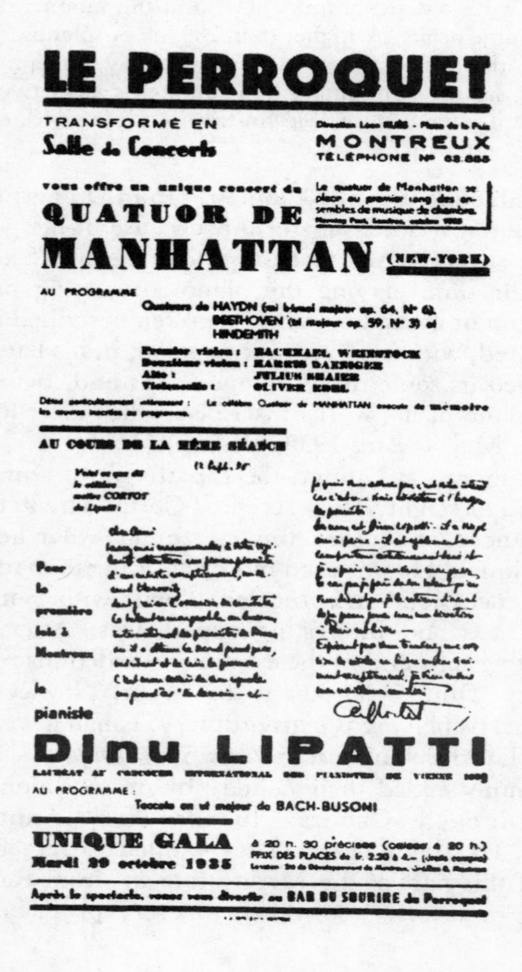

October I shall repeat the Toccata at Montreux, when I shall play again with the Manhattan Quartet."

After the Montreux recital, Cortot wrote to a well-known impressario introducing Lipatti, and praising his high interpretative qualities. In a fashion similar to Schumann when he wrote about the unknown Chopin in a famous article: 'Hats off, gentlemen, a genius has appeared!', Cortot declared:

> Dear friend, allow me to draw your attention to a young pianist with exceptional gifts, a second Horowitz, whose remarkable talent I was able to judge at the Vienna International Piano Competition. He won Second Prize although it was obvious he should have been awarded a First. It is my duty to bring to your notice a great 'ace' of the future, and to assure you that this will be to your advantage because I am writing about a real revelation on the horizon of pianists. His name is Dinu Lipatti.[57]

In spite of the prestige of the famous Manhattan Quartet, the press devoted most of its attention to the artistic personality of the new Rumanian pianist. The *Tribune de Genève* wrote on 30 October 1935:

> Without diminishing the excellence of the American Quartet which appeared for the first time in Geneva, it must be admitted that the real surprise of the evening was the pianist Dinu Lipatti. He played a most interesting Bach-Busoni transciption which proves that in the hands of a master a transcription can become a new creation. The rendering of this masterpiece by the young Rumanian pianist was perfection itself; one could not find the slightest fault with the conception of his interpretation. Cortot is right: Dinu Lipatti is 'one of the great pianists of tomorrow, if not already one of today!' Well served by a very good Steinway, the pianist gave a display of incomparable technique and strength in the service of a constructive intelligence which could rightly be the envy of many an experienced master. We hope to hear him again soon in a programme covering a wider range.[58]

The newspaper *La Suisse* wrote: "Lipatti appears to be endowed with an amazing technique, with a precision and evenness reminiscent of José Iturbi." By contrast, here is Dinu's own subdued report:

> The tour in Switzerland passed off quite well. The public gave a good reception both to myself and to the Manhattan Quartet with

whom I appeared on that same evening. The Quartet (although American...) is admirable. The audience recalled me about six times but I was afraid to play an 'encore' as I did not hear anyone say 'bis'. After the concert Mr Verleye asked me why I did not give an 'encore' and that in Geneva people do not shout 'bis'. I consoled myself thinking that it was better to present the Toccata alone and in an honest execution than a poor 'encore'. Before these two concerts I played on the radio, but my performance was not outstanding. You know very well that I have a real revulsion if I have to play in front of a microphone. I feel so hindered and this does not happen in a concert hall. I was sad that I took the first movement of the Beethoven Sonata Op 53, the *Waldstein*, too fast and that I did not play it in the tempo which I have taken in the past few days.[59]

His reserve when faced with enthusiastic notices is unusual, but Lipatti remained sceptical about what was written of him. In the same vein he commented that an adulatory interview in *La Suisse* had appeared with questions and answers rearranged, not as they had been given in conversation, but to suit the taste either of the interviewer or of the editor.

These new triumphs marked the beginning of Lipatti's second year abroad. "Dearly beloved Maestro," he wrote to Florica Musicescu, my motto for the coming year's work will be your own:

> "Whoever seeks for light
> Must look to the heights in others,
> To the depths in himself."[60]

Georges Enesco's presence in Paris helped Dinu to feel less of a stranger and more at home. His homesickness for the peace of Fundateanca was compensated by the knowledge that the 'Master of masters' was close at hand. His veneration for Enesco was encouraged by his two Rumanian teachers. "Now, more than ever," wrote Florica Musicescu, "we must show the Maestro our infinite admiration and offer him what is best in us as homage."[61] Dinu wrote back:

A few days ago I wrote a short note to Maestro Enesco asking if I could play to him the Beethoven Sonata, Op 53. He invited me yesterday which gave me immense joy. While I was playing he was conducting all the time, and I found myself hypnotized by his splendid interpretation, and had the feeling that I was playing a new work for the first time. What feeling, what generosity of spirit in every phrase... For me this was one of the most illuminating lessons I have ever received. The Maestro told me that I could come to him for advice whenever I wanted to, either about interpretation or composition... I shall certainly take advantage of this and play the 'E flat' to him. God knows what he will bring out in that!

A similar appreciation is found in other letters which show that, at the time, Enesco's overwhelming influence did not consist in giving technical advice regarding craftsmanship so much as in stimulating a young musician to discover for himself the profounder meaning of a work and the structural order underlying the art of interpretation. It is this which leads to an understanding of the emotional content of a work. [Yehudi Menuhin, had also remarked that the essential elements of Enesco's teaching and guidance were not about fingering or bowing but about the discovery of the living soul of a particular work]. From a certain aspect, Georges Enesco's suggestions were completing the valuable advice which Florica Musicescu had given him all the years. In fact, Dinu himself admitted: 'I owe my entire pianistic art to Miss Musicescu'.[62]

The beginning of 1936 brought Dinu another artistic satisfaction. His Symphonic Suite, *Satrarii* (The Gypsies) received its first performance on 23 January in Bucharest, conducted by Mihail Jora, at a concert devoted to Rumanian music. It included Filip Lazar's *Concerto Grosso*, *Divertismentual Catanesc* of Paul Constantinescu and Enesco's First Suite. Dinu's reaction to this concert was expressed in a letter to Mihail Jora:

I don't know whether I shall ever be able to thank you enough for what you have done for me...You have fulfilled one of my most ardent wishes—to have the Suite performed.

I was able to pick up Bucharest Radio quite clearly, and we could have heard the smallest details of the transmission clearly if it had not been disturbed by interference every time the lift moved inside our house. We were all sitting together in my room, Mr Lazar and myself were close to the radio on my desk. First we heard Mr Ciomac, and I was very pleased to hear his beautiful

words of praise for Lazar's Concerto and my *Satrarii*. We could hear the Concerto Grosso very clearly and Mr Lazar was most enthusiastic about the excellent performance of his work. Afterwards came '*Satrarii*'. The first part, and half of the *Idyll*, was clear but afterwards the transmission deteriorated. I regret not having been able to hear *The Feast* better. But your admirable execution filled my soul with joy. I doubt whether *Satrarii* could ever again have the opportunity of being conducted so splendidly. As to its orchestration: I noticed some aggressive trombones which I must rearrange without fail; I also noted that the strings demand a smoother interweaving... I am anxious to know what happened to the piano? Although I was 'all ears' I could not hear the piano in the Suite, although Mr Lazar maintains that he could. We shall see who was right.[63]

On the 4th March 1936 the 58th Concert of the *Association Amicale de l'Ecole Normale de Musique* took place, arranged by Alfred Cortot. The programme consisted entirely of Rumanian music: String Quartet by Ionel Perlea; first performance of

Lipatti's Sonatina in E minor for Violin and Piano with Lola Bobescu and the composer at the piano; first performance of Enesco's Sonata for Cello and Piano, Op 26, No 2 with Diran Alexanian and the composer at the piano. To end the concert, Georges Enesco played his Suite for Piano, Op 10—Toccata, Sarabande, Pavane and Bourée.

This is how Dinu described the event:

> Last night I played the Sonatina at the Ecole. Lola Bobescu played beautifully, and the Hall was packed. We were well received and got about four calls from the public. Maestro Enesco gave an admirable performance of his Suite, and I told him how happy I was to hear it from 'the horse's mouth'. Unfortunately his partner was not up to the level of the composer's extraordinary performance in his Sonata for Cello. This work, for those who have time to explore its profundity, is a gem. Sadly enough there will be few capable of so doing on a first hearing. Such a work requires at least three hearings to begin to be understood and appreciated. The Maestro received a long ovation... I forgot to mention that Perlea's String Quartet was very beautifully played, and also well received by the audience. We all thanked Mr Mangeot who had the initiative to arrange the Festival of Rumanian music.[64]

In an article entitled 'Festival of Rumanian Music', A. Mangeot wrote in *Le Monde Musical*:

> Without any doubt Dinu Lipatti is the brightest hope of the younger generation of pianists. At twenty he is already a brilliant pianist and composer. Paul Dukas was greatly impressed with Lipatti who was his last pupil. And now both Nadia Boulanger and Stravinsky show their great appreciation of his compositions. Although the Sonatina for Violin and Piano is not a large-scale work it is of the highest calibre, in particular the Variations in the Finale. The composer's presence at the piano allowed the audience to express their warm affection for him and young Lola Bobescu who is making her mark among other famous Rumanian violinists...[65]

The music critic of *Le Courier* noted:

> ...Dinu Lipatti, appears to be a pianist of great calibre... His relaxed manner of playing, complete mastery of the keyboard and the luminous sonorities which he produces are only a means to an end which permits his artistic temperament and rare musical

understanding to express themselves. His success, with that of the illustrious composer, Georges Enesco, was brilliant and well-deserved.

A fortnight later, on 17 March 1936, Dinu gave another concert at the *Cercle Interallié* which was also broadcast. Afterwards he wrote:

> I believe the Intermezzi by Brahms were good. I took Chopin's A minor Nocturne too fast, and had the impression that because of this it lost some of its grandeur. I was playing at the same tempo I used to take when I was younger. Mlle Boulanger could not be present, but she told me that several people who know something about music had thought the sonorities were admirable, but they had the impression that I had begun the piece in one tempo but finished by playing slower. This surprised me, because I usually have contrary tendencies. Finally I realized what had happened—all the Intermezzi and the Nocturne are marked *rallentando* at the end. The piano was a splendid one; the same instrument on which Maître Cortot makes all his recordings; the hall was packed.[66]

Early in June the 'Triton Group' organized a festival dedicated to Georges Enesco's works: Suite No. 1 in F sharp minor, played by Dinu Lipatti; Sonata for Violin and Piano, with Szigetti; Cello Sonata, with Alexanian and the composer at the piano. When asked to play his Piano Sonata, Enesco answered: "I should like to have Dinu Lipatti perform because he plays it so much better than I do."

According to Dinu, "I was in a good mood and played as on one of my best days. The Maestro never stopped praising my performance all through the evening. At the end he told me he had only one regret—that I had not played the whole programme! How kind he is"[67]

The highlight of that year's musical season in Paris was the first performance of Enesco's opera *Oedipe*, the sublime result of a whole life's work. "First and foremost *Oedipe*! This is a great moment in musical history," wrote Dinu to his teachers in Bucharest, "and let us hope that our dear Maestro will live at least another hundred years so that we can rejoice many more times as we did the evening when *Oedipe* received its premiere"[68]

Every important event was a new incentive for Dinu. Another letter to Florica Musicescu:

> I have finished the *Finale* of a Concertino for Piano and Orchestra in nine days. I'm pleased that at last I have managed to 'conquer myself' and break the habit of writing only one bar per week. I can hardly wait to copy out the work and show it to Mlle Boulanger so that I can get on with the First Movement.

To Jora, he adds:

> I was only waiting to finish the Toccata so as to write you with a clear conscience. I've already done two fugues for this Toccata, but felt dissatisfied with both. So at present I'm studying Gedalge's *Le Traité de la Fugue*, and after a serious study I hope to be able to write a more interesting one. On 23rd March I began the Finale of a Concertino for piano and orchestra which I finished on the 31st. The orchestra—two oboes, two bassoons and strings. The orchestral score of the Finale is 44 pages or, to be more precise, 272 bars in 2/4 time. You will certainly ask why I began with the Finale? I cannot answer this question with any certainty. All I know is that the idea came to me suddenly, and I immediately tried to 'fix it'. I am now writing the first movement, an Allegro maestoso, and hope, unless I alter the plan again before finishing, to follow this up with an Adagio, then a Minuet. I see the Concertino as classical in style. This is an area which, for the moment, offers me unsuspected resources. The Toccata is written in the same style. I showed it to Stravinsky who said he could give me no better advice 'than to continue in the same direction.[69]

Again he writes to Musicescu: "A few days ago I recorded the second part of Enesco's Sonata. I showed the discs to the Maestro when he visited us. I should love to send you the recording, but do not dare as it has a small technical fault."

By now the Paris musical season was in full swing. Posters abounded with the names of Toscanini, Stravinsky, Enesco, Cortot, Prokofiev, Horowitz, Rubinstein, etc. On some evenings several concerts were held in different halls but Lipatti never missed any of the great events. There were also many marvellous musical soirées held in private 'salons' belonging to well-known patrons of the arts such as the Princesse de Polignac, the Gouins, Rothschilds, or in the homes of the great financiers where Lipatti was often invited. Yet he remained keenly aware of very different and menacing events sweeping across France at the time "The political situation is serious" wrote Dinu. "All the shops and factories are out on strike. Everyone is afraid there may be a revolution. If only we could get away earlier."[70]

This was the other picture of Paris in 1936; side by side there existed glamour and misery, enthusiasm and depression, spiritual quests and mercenary pursuits. Then Dinu, enriched by his two years living and working in France, decided to return home to his country house at Fundateanca.

Back Home

Dinu returned to the scene of his childhood at Fundateanca in the summer of 1936 and immediately found himself part of the village life. He met old playmates now working in the vineyards. At first they were shy with the young man returned from abroad but, with his usually spontaneity, Dinu soon broke the ice between them. Chatting together during the long evenings he soon found out all about their lives. He told his friends about his plan to settle in the village for the rest of his life and to build a house in which he could work and rest. He would then spend six months of every year there like the legendary Antheus, gathering the strength and drive needed for his artistic pursuits. "The rest I allowed myself ended on the 1st September and since then I have been working without a break."[71] "I shall stick fanatically to the programme of work which I set myself if only God gives me the strength", he wrote.[72]

The first recital he gave after his return to Rumania was with Georges Enesco. "I am thrilled that I shall appear on the same programme with our great Maestro"[73] But the excitement of this collaboration was overshadowed by the tragic news of Filip Lazar's death at the early age of forty-two.

Emanoil Ciomac wrote: "The sober, elegant and dignified figure of Filip Lazar was but a façade hiding a ruthless malady attacking his very life. Three days ago, while on the way to a lesson, he suffered a haemorrhage in a taxi. He managed to get back to his home where he died in the arms of his wife.[74]

On 7 November Enesco and Lipatti gave a Violin and Piano

Dinu with Filip Lazar

Recital at the *Ateneul* in Bucharest. The programme included Sonata No 10 in G by Beethoven, Sonata by César Franck and Lipatti's Sonatina. This is how Emanoil Ciomac described the concert:

> A complete fusion of musical understanding, great precision with regard to the balance of sound and the technical details, and the pianist showed the qualities of an exceptional musician, brilliant in every respect. Perhaps the only fault one could find was that, although brilliant in every detail, too intense a preparation may result in a slight lack of spontaneity, just as one may find a bride too beautifully adorned. We might have preferred less evidence of professorial control—no matter how prestigious. Perhaps this is because one cannot help wondering whether this apparent maturity might not be artificial in a youth of eighteen. In any case, let us discard any borrowed wings and allow the richness of the soul to flow freely. The same can be said about his very important composition in which one cannot fail to detect, from the beginning, the voice of the teacher who, rightly, is so loved by his pupils that his own faults are unconsciously passed on to them.

> The Sonatina, which was written when Lipatti was 16, and was awarded the 'Enesco Prize', is much more than a promising work. Like his orchestral suite *Satrarii*—with its affinity in subject-matter to Jora's work *In the Market*—it faithfully reflects its popular Rumanian inspiration and gypsy elements. The conventional treatment of the material does not deprive the work of authenticity and freshness. In particular we find many gems in the five Variations from the Andante. For example, the third Variation, with its Christmas carol atmosphere, has a melodic simplicity and essential logic in its harmonies. Once again, anticipating a great future for this young composer, we also pay homage to an already accomplished pianist.[75]

In another press notice, written about a *milieu* which could be harmful to an artist, the same critic notes:

> When a young bird leaves the nest to try its wings, flying higher and higher, then a family chorus raises its voice in praise, forgetting that once the bird can fly it no longer requires unqualified praise, nor encouragement that can be more damaging than constructive. Thus it is time to stop treating Dinu as a school-boy who performs miracles. On the contrary, we are now confronted with an authentic talent which has crossed the threshold of maturity and which asserts itself in a serious normal way demanding respect.
>
> He is a pianist of great class. Perhaps he is the only pianist of international calibre in the country and, in this case, we have the right to expect more from him.[76]

Stanislavski made a similar observation when talking to some of his students, asking them to beware of admirers. To court them, perhaps, but never to discuss art with them. From the beginning he advised them to learn to listen, to understand and to love the cruel truths about themselves. They should find out who has the right to tell this truth and to accept the criticism only from them and this as often as possible.

It was only to be expected that Ciomac's critical notices aroused disapproval in the Lipatti entourage of admirers who could not forgive the critics' sincere and sensible advice to the young virtuoso. One of Ciomac's adversaries, a friend of Dinu's family, wrote:

> Although I was not present at the concert, and therefore not able to judge it, I should like to assure you of one thing—namely, that

> you have no need to accept useful 'advice' from any so-called 'music critics' who are not musicians themselves. These critics, before indulging in parental admonitions to Dinu Lipatti, should take a long, close look at themselves in the mirror... Your path should avoid, as far as possible, any contact with the noisy clique of national music critics.[77]

Contrary to this amiable protector's advice, Lipatti paid greater attention to unfavourable notices than to those full of praise. This reminds one of Darwin's calm objectivity when a criticism of *The Origin of the Species* prompted the following comment: "The article is masterly, and the author has cleverly chosen the weakest parts of my book, bringing out all the difficulties..." It was not Dinu himself who was upset by criticism so much as his family and friends, and when Ciomac found himself surrounded by an atmosphere of hostility, he wrote:

> We should like to underline, in passing, that our objective but affectionate notices have succeeded in upsetting those around Lipatti but not the artist himself. We wish to assure them, once again, that nothing could make us belittle his exceptional merits, nor refrain from mentioning certain reservations which we believe might then be put right.

On 12 November the Bucharest Philharmonic opened the musical season with a concert conducted by George Georgescu, with Lipatti as soloist in Mozart's Concerto in D minor, K 466, and the *Capriccio* by Stravinsky.

"I want to reaffirm," wrote Emanoil Ciomac, "that the aristocratic art of Lipatti does not bring the audience to its feet; rather it has a penetrating effect through a discreet perfection and qualities of refined musicianship which are so eloquent to those in love with what is understated and never vulgar.... The Cadenzas in the Mozart Concerto are arranged by Lipatti with the discretion and charming inventiveness which one recognizes in his work at every turn."[78]

In another article Andrei Tudor observed: "The same excellent technique and the same musicality, but with less tonal colour and power of communication. The first part of the concert underlined the particular qualities of the artist. But the

Dinu with George Georgescu

containing some fine moments, are not in keeping with the style of the composer and, consequently, are of little interest. The *Capriccio* for Piano and Orchestra by Stravinsky, on the other hand, was more suited to Lipatti's style of playing".

The critics' contradictory views about the Cadenzas were later discussed by Lipatti when he gave a concert abroad and played the same Concerto by Mozart with Beethoven's Cadenzas. As he had always played his own Cadenzas the critics presumed this to be still the case and they expressed their observations and reservations regarding their 'style'. In the few notes left by Lipatti he points out the interest he found in the conflicting points of view of different personalities.

Soon afterwards Dinu returned to France accompanied by his mother and brother, to continue his studies.

Once Again in France

The year 1937 brought more and more offers of concerts. Nadia Boulanger preferred to have Lipatti play with her whenever she was asked to give concerts for two pianos. Offers to make recordings were also coming in. At first Dinu refused them: "I was not sure that they would correspond to my conception of the interpretation."[79] But later on he changed his mind and enjoyed recording, "...only when making records can you allow yourself to replay what you consider not good enough." Indeed, as he writes, his concern to reach perfection in the recordings for HMV and Columbia was memorable. "At the last session, which lasted from 8 am until 12.30 am, we only managed to make one record, and to do so satisfactorily required eighteen retakes."[80]

Alongside his concert activities Dinu continued to attend Cortot's *Cours d'Interpretation*, where his participation was regarded as a major event. He also attended Nadia Boulanger's Classes in Analysis, and took part in the chamber music evenings.

The 'Exposition Internationale de Paris' was held during the summer of 1937 and the Rumanian Pavilion attracted great interest. One of the highlights was a famous orchestra performing popular Rumanian music with the virtuoso Grigoras Dinicu. This famous player inspired Heifetz to include *Hora Staccato* by Dinicu in his repertoire, and later he made a superb recording of it. When Dinu Lipatti visited the Pavilion he was immediately surrounded by the 'boys' of the orchestra, and Dinicu told them: "Now, all of you, let's play our very best—we all know what a good ear our Lipatti has!"[81]

A Festival of Rumanian classical music was organized for the 'Exposition'. Dinu Lipatti participated with other Rumanian musicians. Georges Enesco conducted *The Feast* from Lipatti's Suite *Satrarii*, a work which was later awarded the Silver Medal of the French Republic. Dinu performed both as soloist or in chamber music ensembles in works by Constantin Nottara, Leon Klepper, Martian Negrea and Filip Lazar. With Lola Bobescu he played the Sonatina for Violin and Piano by Paul Constantinescu, and they were joined by the Jugoslav cellist, Antonio Janigro, in a performance of Lipatti's

Three Dances for two pianos: composition of 1937
(Manuscript Lipatti)

Trio, *Fantezia Cosmopolita*. The newly-established Trio started a series of concerts, as Dinu wrote; "I don't remember whether I mentioned to you the Trio with Lola Bobescu and Antonio Janigro. We hope to give our first concert here on 20th November, at the Salle Chopin. Perhaps we shall come to Bucharest, and I say 'perhaps' because it depends on whether or not Janigro plays also with the Philharmonic. In the meantime we have announced the formation of the Trio in Italy and France, countries where we stand a chance of making our début. We are preparing the following Trios—Beethoven No 4, Schubert in B flat and Brahms in B major"[82]

In October Lipatti returned to Rumania for a series of

concerts. Under Georges Enescu he played the Liszt Concerto in E flat with the Philharmonic, then appeared in a recital with Georges Enesco. The pianist, Cella Delavrancea, wrote in *Le Moment*, 11 November 1937, a French newspaper published in Bucharest:

> It is rare that piano and violin can satisfy one when they are heard together. The qualities and defects of these two instruments are in permanent contradiction, so that if the artists are not endowed with nobility—the only quality which allows different personalities to work together—there always remains a stark contrast between the sonorous language of each performer, a contrast which numbs any emotion. However, Enesco and young Lipatti enchanted us with their Mozart, Beethoven and the picturesque Sonata by Enesco. Here they displayed an amazing clarity and colour which gave an unusual timbre to the piano...

By the end of January 1938 Lipatti had returned to France and finished the recording of Brahm's Valses with Nadia Boulanger. He then undertook a series of recitals in Italy. The one in Rome was reviewed, in the *Poppolo di Roma*:

> This excellent pianist, by making use of an impeccable technique, had proved that he is endowed with outstanding artistic qualities. I admired his lightness of touch and the mastery of his craft which reached such a high degree of perfection in all the pieces that—if we may say so—it was the interpretation of a genius. The complex Bach-Busoni Toccata gave us the opportunity to appreciate the impressive gifts and virtuosity of this pianist. Each work was received with overwhelming applause by the audience.[83]

Dinu described this concert with his usual understatement: "The concert in Rome went off quite well. Now I am having discussions with Brussels."[84]

He was hardly back in Paris when the Association Amicale de L'Ecole Normale de Musique arranged a Lipatti Recital under the artistic direction of Cortot and Charles Munch. The programme was to include Bach, Mozart, Chopin, Brahms and the first performance of works by various Rumanian composers—Enesco, Andricu, Jora, Mihalovici and Lipatti's *Nocturne on a Moldavian Theme*. About this recital he wrote to Jora:

> The recital last February went off well, (it was a triumph), and the

> *Jewish March* was much enjoyed. At present I am working on a number of piano pieces, but I have too much to do and am afraid of not finishing any of them to my complete satisfaction. I am also preparing a totally new programme for my recitals, as well as the Concerto for Left Hand by Ravel—a work which I should like to bring to Bucharest together with my *Classical Suite*. There is also work to be done on a programme for the *Cercle Interallié* concert in May, and a Sonata recital with the cellist Janigro.[85]

Dinu was also working on a new composition, the ballet sketch *Burlesque*. In the midst of these artistic successes and intense creativity an official notice arrived to remind him that he was now 21 years of age and due for military service. He was considered fit for the infantry, and "in case of absence you will suffer the legal consequences." The prospect of military service, in a world so alien to his temperament, filled him with little enthusiasm. His involvement with music left him ill-equipped for any such activity. After endless formalities and wasting much time in various waiting-rooms, he obtained, at last, a delay for one year. Since childhood he had suffered from scoliosis, a disease which made it difficult for him to practise for many hours at a stretch and which had hindered his physical growth. After another medical examination he was eventually exempted from military service.

The Ecole Normale started its Conducting Course in

February—a class which every dedicated interpreter hoped to join. Writes Dinu:

> On 15th February, I shall start the Conducting Course at the Ecole under M. Alexanian. I should be glad to have some experience of the bâton before the end of the year. I pray to God that it comes off as, so far, the students' response has been rather poor. Only three have registered so far - Pauker, a Japanese and myself.[86]

On 27th March he continues:

> With my conducting—sometimes I get on well, sometimes badly. Well—because M. Alexanian's classes are very interesting and I hope to increase my general knowledge of music. At each lesson M. Alexanian sets a quartet for us to study and mark all the important indications. In other words, he makes us work seriously with scrupulous attention paid to all the details of expression and technique. At the moment we work with a reduced number of instruments, but later on their number will be increased until we obtain a full orchestra. This is the good side of the Course. As to the bad side, the Ecole Normale holds no classes for wind-players so there is no possibility to have a full orchestra, thus we have to work only with a string orchestra.
>
> Two weeks ago, for the first time, I conducted Bach's Concerto in D minor for piano. It was a bit embarrassing at first, but now I am getting used to it. M. Alexanian thought I conducted well, making only two slight mistakes in the soloist's Cadenza in the first movement.[87]

An additional note describes a conducting class with Charles Munch:

> As a first piece we worked on the *Variations on a Theme by Haydn*, by Brahms. Charles Munch finds my movements rather too stiff. If he succeeds in teaching me something of his own smooth movements this will help me with my piano as well. Now I play the piano all day and conduct at the same time which provokes great hilarity around me, especially among my neighbours across the street. During the last lesson we studied the Scherzo from Brahms' 4th Symphony, and tomorrow I conduct the Andante. Unfortunately we can only have the orchestra once a fortnight; the rest of the time we conduct 'in the void', an exercise which I dislike...[88]

This new activity had to be abandoned despite its promising beginning. Charles Munch, like all his other mentors, considered Dinu to be one of his greatest hopes in this field. "To conduct was one of my dearest wishes," Dinu was to confess later, "which I was unable to realize because all my spare time had to be devoted to the piano or composition, and I was already finding it difficult to strike a balance between them.[89] I am now working on my Classical Suite, which I shall play at the Ecole on 30th April and then at a Festival of Rumanian Music on 10th May."[89] Charles Munch commented on this concert:

> Dinu Lipatti's pianism has great brio. The enchantment of the evening was enhanced by the composer's own performance at the piano when he unleashed a cascade of pearls, creating such enthusiasm in the audience that he had to encore the Scherzo.[90]

At the end of June Lipatti was invited to play before the Schubert Society, one of the many artistic circles in Paris eager to hear him. By now his name carried an ever-increasing prestige in France. From the most hermetically sealed doors to those of the great impressarios, all were now open to him unconditionally. Aware of carrying a great artistic responsibility he prepared each of his concerts meticulously, with the utmost attention to detail.

Dinu planned to spend the summer of 1938 working in France rather than return to Rumania. This fateful summer witnessed two prospects—one of delight from the excursions by car through Normandy, with time off to visit various beauty spots and contemplate the landscape; another of fear and apprehension at the sombre gathering of clouds heralding the outbreak of the war in Europe.

The Lipattis stopped off at Bagnole de l'Orme. Dinu, unhappy with the tone of the hotel piano, preferred to practise on a silent keyboard which he carried with him. He and his brother went off rowing, made excursions and held long discussions. From Normandy they crossed France towards the mountains in the south-east, with fear in their hearts as Dinu was driving. They spent two weeks in the mountains at Montgenèvre where the family greatly enjoyed the clean air and peaceful atmosphere and the two boys were able to follow a disciplined programme of activities.

However, Dinu had too many plans for the future for this pleasant interlude to last. Fresh engagements were pouring in all the time. They were handled by his agent Charles Kiesgen—the impressario of all the celebrities. Kiesgen wanted Lipatti to give a new series of recitals at the Colonne, Lamoureux, and Pasdeloup concert halls, and for the Société des Concerts, which caused Dinu's comment, "...indeed, I have a feeling that this year is going to be very important for my career."[91]

Dinu made a point of attending most of the important concerts given in Paris, and never missed any given by Rumanian musicians. Here is an extract from a letter to Mihail Jora:

> I had the immense pleasure of listening to your First Symphony, superbly conducted by M. Perlea. I was able to relive in my mind that memorable moment when I witnessed the composer, helped by Maestro Enesco, put the final touches to the score. Pages of pure Rumanian gold. I was particularly glad to hear it performed in Paris, and am convinced that this programme will be followed by many more.
>
> As to my own work, I am rather sad to find myself devoting all my time to the piano and none to composition. I am booked for a series of concerts up until next March, ending with three important ones at the Conservatoire, Pasdeloup and my first recital—in grand style! In December I shall finish my former ballet for which I wrote a *Finale* last month, and which has now turned into a Suite for Two Pianos.[92]

Theodor Lipatti arrived unexpectedly at the end of 1938 to join his family. He turned up like Father Christmas with a sack full of gifts and news from home. And to make the surprise complete, he had brought along Mariana Pavel, a devoted family maid who overcame her fears of a long journey to see her beloved boys again.

Dinu inaugurated the New Year with a fresh series of activities. The Association Amicale d'Ecole Normale organized a concert on 19 January, under the patronage of three ambassadors, to present the works of three new composers—Cesare Brero, Dinu Lipatti and Bernard Schülé. Lipatti played his Sonatina for Violin and Piano with the violinist André

Proffit, and his Suite for Two Pianos with the South American pianist, Nibya Bellini. About Nibya Bellini he said: "She amazes me, not so much with her interpretation but with her unlimited means for conquering all the technical difficulties in the piano répertoire. In the Suite for Two Pianos she plays more beautifully than myself."[93] With characteristic humour he concluded: "With so many ambassadors around my neck one can't even be sure that a kidnap will not be attempted. The concert will certainly have snob appeal, but I only hope the audience will be sympathetic."[94]

Now we come to the point when we must mention Lipatti's rare friendship and artistic collaboration with that great Rumanian pianist, Clara Haskil. Together they gave an unforgettable recital for two pianos. The programme included Brahms' *Variations on a Theme by Haydn*, Allegro in A minor by Schubert and Lipatti's Suite for Two Pianos.

Clara describes their first meeting during one of her Friday recitals:

> A shy young man came up to me and said 'I met you in Bucharest!' It was Dinu Lipatti. What sincerity, what kindness and generosity I was going to discover in that exceptional man! After that first providential meeting, we met almost daily. Words cannot express the intense feeling and profound respect one experienced in the presence of this great artist and musician. He often gave the impression of being embarrassed by his own genius.[95]

In an interview on Radio Cologne, Madeleine Catacuzino, who later became Dinu's wife, recalled many instances of the collaboration between these two great artists. Dinu was deeply moved by the nobility and expressive intensity of Clara's interpretations, by the poetry and tenderness which emanated from her playing, and considered her to be the 'epitome of music itself'. He found it difficult to understand how such a gifted artist could be so modest and have so little self-confidence. It is interesting to note that their mutual admiration made each one undervalue their own particular gifts. As Honegger recounts: "When Dinu, who was playing the Mozart Concerto in E flat, K 449 and heard that Clara was in the audience, he said: 'How can I play it now when no-one else in the world can play it like her!'"[96]

Here are a few excerpts, not strictly in chronological order, from the correspondance between the two artists, which continued until the end of Dinu's life:

> *Clara:* My dear Dinu, your interesting letters gave me much pleasure and I thank you for all the details about your life and career. You know how much these interest me and how happy I am to hear about your successes. Indeed, I am not surprised, as from the very first moment I met you I knew that you were destined to make a great career very rapidly. It was easily predictable with someone endowed with your talent and personality.
>
> *Dinu:* Dear Clara, you know it is not my habit to pay compliments to my friends (what is the point?). Only for you do I make an exception—you are a very great artist, and I am thankful for what you offered us last evening....

With Clara Haskil and Wilhelm Backhaus

Clara: Dear Colleague, I think my sister from Bucharest has a strange sense of humour if she told you I played well in Switzerland and that I had a great success. She must have been dreaming as it simply is not true. The only work I played beautifully was your Nocturne because I was playing with love and nostalgia...

Dinu: Dear Clarinette, I cannot find words to describe how much your performance of Mozart moved and thrilled me yesterday. I was also happy to see that you are in exceptionally fine pianistic form. With what assurance and majestic nobility you delivered your discourse, (always vibrant, never dull), as though you were speaking through every note. Once again, 'bravo' from the bottom of my heart!

Clara: Dearest Dinu, once again—I was so moved by last night's concert. In a few months you have covered an enormous distance, always remembering that you did not play so badly to begin with! (You could play a little already, could you not?) My warmest congratulations.... Sir, whenever I want to play something and remember how you played it, or would have played it, then I lose all desire to play at all. How I envy your talent. The devil take it, why must you have so much talent and I so little? Is this justice on earth? I salute you—with no feelings left!

Dinu: Dear susceptible Clarinette, you played even more remarkably than usual; it is impossible to make any criticism. You are superb, a truly great artist and exceptional pianist. If I ever need to study any more Mozart concertos I shall enroll myself as your pupil, and that's not meant as a joke.

Clara: Dearest Friend, there is no need for you to imitate my way of playing. On the contrary, it would be more proper that I should imitate you—if only I could...

Dinu: I must tell you that I listened to your performance of the *Abegg Variations* which was simply 'perfection on earth'. No one else in the world can play Schumann like you. It is truly exquisite. Again and again I want to express my profound admiration and the joy of listening to you.

Clara: Dearest little brother and Maestro, I do admire the trills in the Cadenza in the second part of your Suite, (once again you have utterly confounded me!) The Third Movement has an extraordinary eveness and refinement... You are a very great artist, and soon all your famous colleagues will be put in the shade by you. Only waiting for the joy of seeing each other again, with all my affection.

Dinu: My dear Clara, I am happy that you were able to play at least twice in my place; in this way the audience enjoyed the purest art and my sense of guilt at having to leave Holland was less heavy. I am still in bed with the same illness as last summer.... What are you doing on 14th March? Would you care to play with Balmer in Berne? You would be doing me a great favour if you could and this would make me very happy. For my part, all concerts are cancelled until October 1949. Such is life! Your old and feeble friend, Dinu.[97]

These excerpts show those traits of character which Dinu and Clara shared: generosity, affection and modesty. Not a modesty that underestimated their individual potential but one which expressed their clear perception of an ideal, as yet unattained, which it was their duty to reach. Later on, at the memorial service for Clara Haskil, Igor Markevitch described the two artists in the following words:

> These two visionaries were both children. To compare them with each other is only natural since they both possessed what can only be described as a 'Mozartian character'. Like children who can laugh and cry over a joke, Heaven blessed them, in order to protect them, with the strength to rise above their sufferings. They were continually mocking the organized disorder of our world. Beyond any doubt, this was the reason why they could play Mozart so well. With him they shared the capacity to pass from joy to sorrow as though these two emotions were sisters. As if they knew that the greatest joys arise from a deep understanding of true suffering.[98]

The recital of 29th March at the Salle Chopin-Pleyel, (described by Dinu with mock-humour as 'my first recital in the grand manner'), was unanimously considered as a great event by the Paris music critics. Previously, in all the reviews of his concerts, Lipatti had been judged as an exceptionally gifted youngster, and was compared to Horowitz, Iturbi, or other masters of the keyboard. Now he was being judged simply on his own merits and the measure of his personality was fully recognized. His name had become famous. The critic of *L'Art Musical* wrote: "We do not know what to praise most, his technical mastery or his profound musical understanding. In Dinu Lipatti the two are intimately linked, one sustaining the other. The first is overwhelmingly precise and sure. He is a marvellous, one might almost say, a dazzling technician. Whereas the second is full of nuances, phrasing and a communicating warmth of profound intensity and supreme quality...."[99]

Dozens of such notices could be quoted. We will only refer here to one by Michel Léon Hirsch who underlines in *Le Ménstrel* what Ansermet was also to describe at a later date, as the fusion between Lipatti's art and his moral being: "What attracts one towards him is the visible effort to combine meditation with honesty. He is not trying to make an impression but to recreate the spirit of the work."[100]

Another concert entirely devoted to Rumanian music was held at the Salle Pleyel at the beginning of May. Besides music by Enesco, Marcel Mihalovici, Stan Golestan, Filip Lazar, Leon Klepper, a first performance was given of Dinu Lipatti's

Symphonie Concertante for two pianos and strings, with the composer partnered by the unique Clara Haskil. As usual, overlooking the critics' reactions, Lipatti confessed, "How much I still have to learn. If only the day would come when, with a clear conscience, I could feel completely satisfied." This remark was made during a concert conducted by Charles Munch, at a time when he was being hailed as a composer and interpreter in all musical circles.

War was now inevitable and Lipatti's mind was full of frightening premonitions. He had spent an exhausting year giving many concerts, and a new series had been arranged for Belgium, Holland and Latin America. Overwhelmed by a desire to see his country again he cancelled all these appearances so that he could return to Rumania in November. His last days in Paris were spent putting everything in order so that he could start work at once on his return.

In 1939 another facet of Dinu's gifts was revealed—that of

music criticism. No one would have imagined that the brilliant pianist who paid such respect to his older colleagues, and who never made a derogatory remark about any performer, would also be capable of summing up their characteristics in one telling phrase. Even when writing about artists of world repute his own search for perfection led him to spot any discrepancies which detracted from the ideal. His remarks remain with us in his press criticisms and in letters addressed to intimate friends.

"I recently heard Stravinsky's Concerto for Fifteen Instruments. At first I was not enthusiastic but gradually I began to understand, then to accept the work; though I doubt if it reaches the perfection of his earlier works like *Le Sacre*, *Les Noces*, *Perséphone*. Still, it is wonderful to see how his craftsmanship is being continually revitalized and reborn with every single work.... He succeeds in moving irresistibly forward with everything he does."[101]

At the same time Dinu's admiration for Bartók was constantly increasing: "I believe I am not mistaken in considering Bartók' ...the great, truly greatest, composer of our time...."[102]

Dinu Lipatti sent some articles of music criticism to *Libertatea* about the musical life in Paris. As a consequence, he was made a member of the International Association of Music Critics, and given *carte blanche* to attend all concerts in Paris. "I confess this is a very attractive proposition as I go almost every day to a concert."[103] His critical notices showed great maturity of judgment and integrity. Here are some extracts, beginning with one entitled *Musical Life in Paris*:

Emil Sauer

It is a long time since I have been so moved as I was by the appearance of the venerable and illustrious Emil Sauer on the platform. The same dignified figure, the same man, the same artist. Emil Sauer stands as a symbol of the last century to our generation; his reappearance is a reminder of that rare species, the 'Eagle-Pianist', if I may use such a banal comparison.

During his recital last night I experienced so many contradictory emotions that it is difficult to define them. In the first instance, a profound joy when I realized that this artist had not altered, (and I believe he never will). Nothing in his playing or his attitude betrays his eighty years loaded with success and achievement. At the same time I felt a great sadness. How is it possible that Emil

Sauer must play in the small Salle Erard, despite his glorious past, when a Brailowsky or Uninsky can pack the Salle Pleyel? It must be due to public opinion, which remains eternally superficial, dependent on trends made fashionable by snobbery and publicity. In the case of Sauer, there may be another explanation—it is as strange as it is sad to reflect that the present generation has never heard of him, while his own generation has faded away. No matter how paradoxical it may seem this is the truth. Emil Sauer, the international virtuoso and pupil of Franz Liszt, is being forced, at the end of a brilliant career, to attempt to make a 'name' for himself. Such, at least, is the situation in France!

Here I must touch on a dangerous and difficult question for any artist, whether a great virtuoso or a simple *débutant*. The complex problem posed by mechanical music (radio and recordings) confronts the executant with demands which may sometimes lead him away from the true purpose of his art.

The result is that today we witness a tendency towards absolute technical perfection devoid of any sensitivity or *élan*. There is a further danger too: we live in an era when, in order to please a public interested in the arts, those on the platform are too often the first to seek a compromise. One of the consequences is the general lack of imagination when planning orchestral concert programmes in many parts of the world. Or, to put it another way, why is there such a lack of elementary courage to support those works which deserve to be performed instead of those which are certain to pack a concert-hall? This is why we now have audiences who are completely uninterested in any new or little-known older works. (The 16th and beginning of the 17th centuries could offer us unexpected treasures.) The same situation arises in the case of an unknown artist: the public is only interested in a few 'star' names who have become famous in America.

Let us now leave these unpleasant considerations and return to the strictly musical scene. After the Andante and Variation in F minor by Haydn, Sauer gave an admirable performance of Beethoven's Sonata, Op 27 No 2 in C sharp minor. If, in the first part of the Sonata, his playing was too 'concrete' as regards the sonorities, the rest was played majestically, the *crescendo* effects taken with great care, without hurrying the *finale*, and maintaining an exceptional vigour and clarity in the fast passages.

A small parenthesis here: Sauer's tonal palette, like Paderewski's, is certainly not as rich as that of Horowitz or Gieseking. In this respect I believe that our present generation of pianists has achieved some progress, helped on, perhaps, by the perfected action of modern pianos. Perhaps this is why Sauer did not use, in the first part of the Sonata, those '*demi-teintes*' so favoured by players like Gieseking, Kempf and even Schnabel. Nowadays the pianist is able to bring more colour to his playing than in the past, and he is compelled to listen much more carefully to his playing.

To return to Sauer. *Grillen*, by Schumann, evoked a slight fluttering of wings, and the same can be said about all the *leggiero* passages in the pieces by Chopin in the second part of his programme. There was a miraculous vitality about the Fantasy in F minor; while he brought a new freshness to that over-played work, the Nocturne in E flat, by his suppression of any exaggerated *rubato* with which, sadly, we have become all too accustomed. The climax of Sauer's performance came with the Valse in A flat, Op 42 in which he surpassed himself, bringing new life to these marvellous pages. The great pianist ended a recital which we should like to hear repeated, as soon as possible, with many encores.

Vladimir Horowitz

Nearly five years have passed since I had the opportunity to admire this magician of the keyboard. My impatience to hear him again was shared by the public, who actually assaulted the doors of the great Salle Pleyel in order to attend the Horowitz recital. I expected to hear the 'demonic' virtuoso who amazed the world at his début. Instead I found him transformed—but not for the better. He still remains the same extraordinary pianist, but I had the impression—and I hope I am not the only one—that Horowitz is trying *à tout prix* to 'purify' his interpretations, to strip them of anything approaching artificiality. Yet, he accomplishes this in such a way as to produce the contrary effect: his playing becomes mechanical and deadly artificial!

So long as he was guided by his instinct as a musician, and by the sensitivity of his youth, Horowitz remained above criticism. Today, however, perhaps influenced by his close contact with Toscanini, he is trying to explore the works he is performing to make them interesting. In fact, he is trying to transform them.

Nothing is so sad as stylized and intellectualized music where only intuition and great sensitivity are needed. I do not remember the exact words of a truism expressed by Busoni: *The fault with Beethoven was that he was too profound. True philosophy does not consist in walking through the streets of Venice in the dark during Carnival time, but in taking part in it.*

What a profound truth, and how apt in Horowitz's case when one word would suffice to liberate a great pianist from his own shadow. La Bruyère declared: *People always want to appear as they would wish to be and not as they are.* Beethoven's Sonata, Op 31 No 3, suffered most from this intellectualizing. It sounded as though the music was coming from beyond the grave. As for Chopin's Scherzo in E, whose extraordinary pages are full of poetry and the distant evocation of the old 'modes', this masterpiece was barbarously crucified by Horowitz... However, in the second part of the programme, the pianist offered us the satisfactions which the musician failed to give us in the first part. Two Debussy Etudes (though not the finest) were played more beautifully than one could ever dream of hearing them. In Chopin's Nocture No 6 the miracle occurred: Horowitz forgot that he was Horowitz and returned to being a simple musician giving us a majestic interpretation with all its poetry, and, finally, he succeeded in moving us... The Ballade No 4 by Chopin, though less inspired was interesting. The well-known Valse in A flat of Brahms, played as an encore, was out of this world, and words fail me with which to describe the magic. Everything was played *pianissimo*, with the exception of the bass and the top melody which were only slightly brought out. A lively *Capriccio* by Dohnany, played most brilliantly and with conviction by fingers of steel, electrified the audience and was followed by a series of more superb encores. Horowitz will be the most extraordinary pianist of all times the day he is content to accept himself as he is.

The Budapest Quartet

The 'Quatuor de Budapest' is certainly one of the most marvellous quartets in the world. The rendering of the works, the sure yet supple attack, which only Toscanini can obtain from the strings of an orchestra when he conducts, the disciplined *élan* and first-rate musical intelligence which these artists possess in the highest degree, explain the success which they enjoy everywhere.

The six Beethoven Concerts, during which all the Quartets were performed, cannot be easily forgotten. They never abuse the *fortissimo*—a great asset for a quartet with limited dynamic possibilities. Instead, they create a *pianissimo* which I have never heard in any other ensemble. My deep gratitude goes out to these honest musicians who could be prototypes of the genuine interpreter: one who never sacrifices musical thought to the technique of his instrument.

Kreisler

In his last recital, he charmed us most in the short pieces full of certain effects at which he remains the unsurpassed master. Certain hurrying *tempi* diminished the majestic conception of the Chaconne by Bach, and we should have preferred more liveliness in Mozart's Concerto in G. However, the rest of the programme was miraculous, particularly the Spanish pieces which Kreisler plays with such verve and rare imagination.

Clara Haskil

The Piano Concerto in E flat by Mozart, which I heard recently in a magical interpretation given by the well-known artist, Clara Haskil, convinced me once again of the grandeur and extraordinary organic structure of this masterpiece. Clara Haskil's interpretation was truly astonishing, and she surpassed herself in this performance.

The *Nadine Desouches* recital marked a fine début for this young and exuberant pianist who will certainly enjoy a brilliant career. She reached a summit in some of the sections of the much-too-long *Kreislerianna* by Schumann, as well as in pieces by Debussy where Nadine Desouches showed a great deal of sensitivity.

Only important works were played at the final concert given by the *Triton Group*—a none-too-frequent event in the musical life of Paris. First, *Les Noces* by Stravinsky, a work which is one of the foundation-stones of modern music. In spite of an apparent harshness due to its wild rhythms which interweave and sustain the score, it contains, nevertheless, a great deal of poetry. Extremely difficult to perform, *Les Noces* received a grandiose and brilliant interpretation under Charles Munch's bâton.

Interlude and Capriccio for piano and orchestra, by Marcel Mihalovici, is a lively, robust and highly spirited work which shows the composer's contrapuntal skill in his treatment of the themes. In particular the Coda of the Interlude creates a happy atmosphere. Monique Haas, the soloist, gave a highly authoritative performance.

Three very interesting works by the Czech composer, Martinu, for two pianos and chamber orchestra proved the richness of a marriage between percussion instruments and orchestra when handled by an artist of Martinu's calibre. Above all we have to admire the disciplined logic with which Martinu treats his inspiration, making it a live and passionate idiom, permanently new and sincere. The response and enthusiasm of the audience strengthens my conviction that a great work will always make a direct and immediate impact on the public.

Six extremely amusing works by Florent Schmitt received a remarkable performance by the Gouverne Choir. Charles Munch conducted the entire concert with his usual authority and passionate dedication.[104]

3 Fame

Music must be served, not used
Lipatti

Back Home Once Again

Mme. Lipatti and her two sons were met at the Gara de Nord, Bucharest, on the afternoon of 13 July 1939, by Theodor Lipatti and a large group of friends and admirers. The father was overjoyed to have a full house again and to find his family in good health. Dinu had obtained the 'Licence de Concert' after the first year at the Ecole Normale, and then he had completed the 'Cours de Perfection' and by now his professors had become colleagues and friends.

As soon as he got home Dinu went off to peaceful Fundateanca where a great surprise was awaiting him—a new Bechstein, a gift from his father who was so proud of his son's musical development. The whole of August was spent in intense and fruitful activity.

"I have the honour and pleasure to announce", he wrote to his beloved teacher, "that I have finished the Concerto for Piano and Organ which I wrote with lightning speed, and hope to perform in Bucharest next October.... From 7th August until today, the 19th, I have worked twelve hours a day, without interruption, on the four movements of the Concerto. It is full of Rumanian atmosphere.... At last! I can hardly wait to play it to you!"[1]

In answer Jora replied: "I am very happy to hear that you had such an easy delivery of the Concerto for Piano and Organ and am very anxious to hear it on your return to Bucharest"[2]

Florica Musicescu sent a message: "Dear Dinu, long live the newly-born; God grant him success and a long life!"[3] He con-

Dinu as seen by Sylvan

tinued with the piano lessons and discussions by correspondence as usual.

The Bucharest Philharmonic's opening concert, conducted by George Georgescu, featured Lipatti as soloist in his own *Suite in Classical Style*, and in Liszt's Concerto in A. The Bucharest public had already heard his symphonic suite *Satrarii*, conducted by Jora in 1936 at a concert of Rumanian music. Now they were to hear a new composition the title of which was later changed to *Concertino in Classical Style*. It was Dinu's first published work and dedicated to Musicescu with the words: *For my Maestra, my first-born, with all my love and gratitude*.[4] In fact the composition, written when he was nineteen, effectively mirrors his musical development at that stage of his life when he was still strongly influenced by his first teachers. With the accompaniment of a chamber orchestra the piano develops themes closely related to Bach and Scarlatti. Despite the characteristic clarity of the harmonic structure it betrays a certain contemporary influence. If the *Satrarii Suite* had not always received enthusiastic notices, and the *Fantasia for Piano, Violin and Cello* even less, this work aroused unanimous interest.

Virgil Gheorghiu, the pianist, wrote:

> Our Rumanian glory, Dinu Lipatti, has been consecrated with fresh laurels of appreciation as a composer. His *Classical Suite*, through its diaphanous writing and thoughtful sonorities, woven logically together, gives further proof that the old harmonies and so-called 'defunct' style are not completely exhausted. Lipatti, the composer, has succeeded in recreating new life from dead matter. His solo performance in the *Suite*, and in Liszt's Concerto in A, showed him to be not so much the virtuoso of showy fireworks as an interpreter full of understanding for the expressive poetry and symphonic development in the episodes of the Concerto."[5]

During the same month of October, a sonata recital was given by Georges Enesco and Dinu Lipatti with works by Mozart, Beethoven and Fauré. Mihail Jora wrote:

> I have spoken before about the artistic and personal affinity between these two artists in spite of their great difference in age and their few opportunities to meet. Lipatti has grown and developed away from Enesco, rarely able to be near him or to acquire any of his knowledge. So one cannot talk about the influence of master over pupil; instead we must emphasize the importance of that happy coincidence which produced in this country, over an interval of thirty-six years, two human beings endowed with similar gifts who were able to lay the foundation-stones deep in the heart of Rumanian art.
>
> What could be more useful for Dinu Lipatti than to accompany Enesco in a sonata recital? On the other hand, what joy it must be for the great artist to be able to play without the anxiety of having a dilettante at the piano... Of course, Lipatti's personality remained in the background, as was only proper, but with what intelligence and eagerness did he try to get near to the Maestro's conception and style. He attempted to realize every single idea, to move as if at one with him in every ascending and descending melodic line, to anticipate the poignancy of each accent or the *élan* of a phrase soaring into space... How difficult it is to blend the

> playing of two instruments for a concert when they are so totally different in *timbre* that a natural antagonism seems to exist between them. This did not occur during the performance, the sounds of the two instruments were joined in complete fusion and magic. It was particularly noticeable in the Sonata in A by Fauré, a splendid example of neo-romanticism, during which both Enesco and Lipatti combined to produce youthfulness, *joie de vivre* and excitement with a most unusual *brio*.[6]

This successful opening came after another achievement during the previous summer. At the New York World Fair, the critics had been full of praise, (apart from Grigoras Dinicu's and Fanica Luca's stupendous performance of Rumanian folk music), for Enesco's two *Rumanian Rhapsodies* and Lipatti's *Cheful* (The Feast) from the *Satrarii Suite* which were conducted by Enesco at a concert devoted to Rumanian music held at the Metropolitan Opera House.

After the opening of the autumn season in Bucharest, the Philharmonic Society, 'Gheorghe Dima' from Cluj, arranged for a concert to be given at the Academy conducted by Mihail Jora, with Dinu Lipatti as soloist in his own *Suite in Classical Style*. This was the first time he appeared as a soloist in a concert conducted by his first teacher. "I am so happy to play with you," he wrote.

By this time Lipatti had become an important part of Rumanian musical life. His public grew as large and enthusiastic as Enesco's and that of the great foreign artists. The Ateneul Hall was no longer big enough to seat the audience eager to attend his recital of 16 December, when he played Bach, Chopin, Fauré, Albeniz and Ravel, and introduced a new work of his own, Three Dances, with Smaranda Athanasof at the second piano. This recital was such a triumph that it had to be repeated on 29 January 1940.

Two weeks later started the first collaboration between Dinu Lipatti and Madeleine Cantacuzino (who later became his wife). They gave a concert for two pianos on the radio. The programme consisted of: Duettino Concertante by Mozart-Busoni, Concertino by Jean Françaix, and Polka de Concert by Lennox Berkeley.

In the following month Dinu played his Three Nocturnes for piano, which he had written the year before, at a concert of the Rumanian Composer's Society.

Dinu's first and last appearance as a conductor took place on 16 April in a radio concert with Smaranda Athanasof and Madeleine Cantacuzino as soloists. The programme included his arrangement for Wind Quintet of Six Sonatas by Scarlatti; Bach's *Brandenburg Concerto No. 3 in G* and Concerto for Two Pianos.

The summer of 1940 was spent as usual at Fundateanca, "the only place where unhealthy breezes do not blow, where the war of nerves does not exist...."[7] The son had now returned home to be applauded also as a composer of great gifts and it was expected that he should appear as soloist during the new season of concerts.

He was invited to play Beethoven's *Emperor* Concerto under George Georgescu. Dinu had always felt a certain hesitancy over performing Beethoven's works, a hesitancy which he conquered only a short while before his death. Unfortunately this left no time to record any of his outstanding performances. For Lipatti it was not enough to know a work, he had to understand it. Only then did he dare play it in public.

The year 1941 saw a close collaboration between Lipatti and the Rumanian conductor George Georgescu. He spend the month of January touring with the Bucharest Philharmonic as soloist, playing his own Concertino in Prague, Dresden, Leipzig, Berlin, Hanover, Frankfurt, Augsburg, Munich and other centres. The tour was a triumph for the Rumanian Philharmonic, and Dinu's contribution played an important part in making the orchestra and himself known to the German and Czech publics. "The concert turned out to be a truly artistic event, rarely equalled during the past fifty years of historical concerts held in this hall,"[8] wrote one German newspaper after a concert given at the Gewandhaus in Leipzig.

After this tour Lipatti played again with the Philharmonic Orchestra, as soloist in the Liszt Concerto in E flat. Then, with Alexandru Theodorescu, the violinist, he performed his Sonatina for Violin and Piano on 8th March. *Universul Literar* published the following notice, 22 March 1941, written by the music critic, Romeo Alexandrescu:

> Dinu Lipatti's Sonatina is a successful example of the new music presented in the evening's programme. The music of today, like that of all times, can only be divided into two broad categories: good and bad, regardless of the style it adopts. A true conception

GESELLSCHAFT DER MUSIKFREUNDE IN WIEN

GROSSER MUSIKVEREINS-SAAL

Samstag, den 4. Jänner 1941, punkt 19·30 Uhr

KONZERT der

Bukarester Philharmoniker

Dirigent:

GEORGE GEORGESCU

Mitwirkend:

DINU LIPATTI

PROGRAMM:

RICHARD STRAUSS:
»Don Juan« (Symphonische Dichtung)

SABIN DRAGOI:
»Drei rumänische Dorfbilder« für kleineres Orchester

DINU LIPATTI:
Concertino im klassischem Stil
für Klavier und Orchester
Allegro maestoso Adagio molto Allegretto Allegro molto
Am Flügel: DER KOMPONIST

Pause

PAUL CONSTANTINESCU:
Musik aus dem Ballett »Hochzeit in den Karpathen«

GEORGE ENESCU:
2. Suite für großes Orchester in C-dur
Ouverture — Sarabande — Gigue — Aria — Bourrée in Rondoform

rigourously sustained, a personal style with the power to create an expressive atmosphere, knowledge coupled with a sense of structure, have always been the foundations of good music everywhere. Lipatti's Sonatina possessed all these qualities and, at the same time, shows an interesting and ingenuous treatment of the two instruments...

The same critic noted Lipatti's recital a few weeks later at the *Ateneul*:

Each of Lipatti's appearances raises the obvious question which everyone who has followed his splendidly-sustained career must ask—what are the immediate prospects of any further development when the scale of his achievements has placed him so high right from the beginning? One answer is that Lipatti has repeatedly proved that there is no danger that a great artist can ever be hemmed in, no matter how early he is launched on a career, because in art there is always room for further development. Yet I cannot believe that any of his other recitals has achieved such a total liberation from all material elements, nor such a categorical step forward in the conception and spirituality of his interpretation. Never was the mechanical aspect more subservient, blending discreetly with the inner expressiveness of the music, than at this recital. One can clearly state that Dinu Lipatti has entered a most important phase in the expression of his personality, growing closer to the core of his own art. Oblivious, as usual, to creating any special effects to please the 'great public', he chose an essentially musicianly programme containing occasional pages which demanded a very simple technique. These never diminished him as a performer but on the contrary, were a luxury which only the true artist can allow himself when he is concerned with poetry and deep feeling, and not with the showing-off of finger dexterity. Such were Schubert's two Impromptus, the first one a perfect 'lied' of penetrating sensitivity murmured with exquisite delicacy of feeling in quiet meditation. The same can be said about the Chopin pieces shaped with such masterly grace....[9]

On 4 May Dinu appeared with Madeleine Cantacuzino under the baton of George Georgescu, as soloists in his *Symphonie Concertante* for Two Pianos and Strings, and the Concerto for Two Pianos in C by Bach. Romeo Alexandrescu covered the performance (10 May 1941) in the *Universal Literar*:

In a very short time since his last brilliant concert Lipatti, the composer, has answered the needs of Lipatti, the pianist, with a new work. This is similar to a race between the two facets of his talent, two independent developments, and it is difficult for an umpire to judge the winner in the field of his achievements. However, the two totally independent tendencies serving his art do not prevent one from seeing that Dinu Lipatti has a great deal to offer both areas—the accomplishment of this highly gifted young man is finding the same noble and vigourous expression in both domains.

The Symphonie Concertante displays a wealth of imagination. Thematic inventiveness blends with the harmonies and counterpoint creating a continuous movement and sonorous mobility, from the most capricious to the most contemplative moments, so that the whole work is never stagnating, nor monotonous. Even when a delicate elegiac *cantilena* unfolds itself in the second movement of the Symphonie Concertante the music still continues to progress, develop, and never ceases to present us with something new by a use of the most varied and polyphonic and instrumental means. This is the authentic and outstanding quality of Lipatti's music. With regard to rhythms this work is a source of permanent renewal and rich ideas. Written for two pianos and orchestra, it makes ample use of the varied resources of the modern piano... .

In the *Curentul* issue of 14 May, Emanoil Ciomac wrote:

George Georgescu had two brilliant and responsive collaborators in Madeleine Catacuzino and Dinu Lipatti. The first, endowed with intelligence and sensitivity, has shed all the amateurism of the non-professional. A finely-etched technique brings out her innate musicality. Her velvety sonorities may not blend too happily with the incisive, vibrant and crystalline qualities of her partner, but it is just the variety, contrasting tones and colours of the phrases and passages moving from one instrument to another which enhanced the expressive value of the concert. I am not sure that Madeleine Cantacuzino can master the 'heroic' qualities necessary for a virtuoso career with her subtle and feminine playing, but I believe her to be a most gifted partner for chamber music playing.

There is no need to mention again Lipatti's qualities as a great virtuoso and authentic musician. The evident desire to 'return' to Bach, Handel and Vivaldi in the first movement, with continuous fragments of theme, rhythm and aggressive chords, gave a nebulous impression from which no definite personality could emerge. But in the Molto Adagio we found atmosphere, poetry, an inspired cantilena with beautiful timbres from various instruments—the cello, the violin or the viola. There is an impressionistic quality of magical tranquillity reminiscent of the Second Movement of Enesco's Sonata for Violin and Piano written in Rumanian folk-style. The Finale, Allegro con Spirito, seemed the most accomplished part of the work with its mood of Stravinskian and gypsy fiddler humour. The entire composition shows an expert use of forms and formulae, as well as the full range of the orchestral palette.

One can see from these notices, written in undoubted good faith, that opinions differed. Romeo Alexandrescu never made negative comments nor had he any reservations because the qualities of Dinu's work were so evident that it would have been a waste of time to search for any flaws. Emanoil Ciomac, however, though full of praise for the qualities which were always evident, showed as he did before, a more didactic and

critical approach, outlining any aspect's of Dinu's work which he believed needed further shaping and perfecting.

The repertoire of the *Dinu-Madé Ensemble*,—as Dinu called it—was steadily expanding. Apart from Bach's Concertos and Brahms's Variations on a Theme by Haydn, it included the Duettino Concertante by Mozart-Busoni, Polka by Lennox Berkeley, Concertino by Jean Françaix, Variations by Enesco, Nocturne by Debussy, Valse by Ravel, Invitation to a Waltz by Weber-Corder, and many other works which both partners were performing in an atmosphere of warm and mutual affection.

On 8 May 1941 the Rumanian Composers' Society arranged a special concert to celebrate its twentieth anniversary. The programme, presented by the Bucharest Radio Symphony Orchestra, under Ionel Perlea, was devoted to works by Constantin Silvestri, Zeno Vancea, Nicolae Brînzeu, Paul Constantinescu, Ion Dumitrescu, Constantin Bugeanu, Gheorghe Dumitrescu, Dinu Lipatti, and ended with Georges Enesco's Symphony No 1 in E flat. Mihail Jora, founder and vice-president of the Society at that time, made the following speech:

> This evening's concert celebrates twenty years since the Rumanian Composers' Society was founded. It was started in 1920 by a handful of young, unknown musicians after great difficulties endured during the country's 'war of integration', their only asset being a love of beauty, enthusiasm, and an unflinching desire to create a school of contemporary Rumanian music.

With this meagre asset and with the assurance of help from our great master, Georges Enesco, we have slowly climbed the difficult path of our aspirations. When we reach our goal, when it will no longer be necessary to yearn for a distant summit, we shall have earned—on looking back—the satisfaction of knowing that a small part of our journey has been achieved. Today, a great medley of sound can be heard from down below, just as it was twenty years ago. There is a new generation of youngsters, eager to compete and climb up towards the summit. With the same love of beauty, with the same enthusiasm, they are following in the footsteps of their predecessors. They may even surpass those who prepared the journey for them. This evening marks the presentation of these young musicians by the Society of Rumanian Composers.

It is our duty to let them have their say since they represent the product of the Society's aims and aspirations. All, with the exception of Zeno Vancea, are the product of the Rumanian School created by the founders of the Rumanian Composers' Society. Most of them have never had a chance to travel beyond the frontiers of our country, and all their works are imbued with Rumanian feeling, while allowing each one to express his own individual personality. In this programme Enesco's Symphony No 1 stands, side by side, with the works of this younger generation of musicians as a symbol and as an example. It is a symbol of the ever-youthful creativity of our great Maestro: it sets an example of arduous work, faith, professional and personal integrity. He first set an example for our generation to follow which continues to be valid today to a younger generation.[10]

The same evening, after mentioning the merits of each young composer, Mihail Jora had this to say about Lipatti's work:

Dinu Lipatti is still searching for a personal style. His great talent is tormented incessantly by the need to restate old ideas in new forms. At the height of his development he is changing his manner of expression from one composition to another, a manner which is bound to crystallize decisively very soon.

Here are the programme notes about *The Feast*, the Finale of the *Satrarii Suite*: "Written in a native idiom, like the rest of the *Suite*, the Finale expresses in a lively movement all the joy of sunny celebrations in village life, the spirited gaiety of revelling folk, and the movements of dancers to the rhythm of the cembalom".

At the end of the season Lipatti returned to the tranquility of Fundateanca in order to work. In August he was interrupted by an invitation from the Bucharest Philharmonic Orchestra to appear as a soloist in Liszt's Concerto in E flat at a charity concert. War had been declared by now, and all plans for concerts and travel abroad had to be abandoned. The quiet village life of Fundateanca, however, was ideally suited to Dinu's introvert and thoughtful disposition. He was very different in character from the rest of his family. "Their daily aspirations," wrote Dinu, "are all directed towards Paris and city life, not towards a village life which they can only stand for a month at a time."[11] He attempted to build himself a studio as a place of refuge for his creativity. "I have made 3,000 bricks up until now. I only pray that God will not send us any rain as this would ruin the bricks which I must fire on 14 September... Father knows nothing about my latest activities..."[12]

He had one other secret activity. He had started to plant several acres of fruit trees. In order to avoid any fuss from his family about 'ruining his hands or his health' this outdoor work, which brought him so much satisfaction and joy, had to be kept secret. He only interrupted it to participate in the celebrations of Mihail Jora's 50th, and Georges Enesco's 60th, birthdays. He wrote:

> I have recently composed a Sonatina for left hand, a trifle in three movements which I finished in two days. It is lively, based on Rumanian themes, and written to celebrate *Conu Mishu's* fiftieth anniversary. It was Silvestri's idea and you can imagine how enthusiastic I was. To my shame I had forgotten this date, but Silvestri proposed that every student of our generation—himself, Paul Constantinescu, Bugeanu, the two brothers Dumitrescu and myself—should write a piece dedicated to Jora to be played during an intimate concert in the Exhibition Hall of the Orpheu Music Shop, and to end with one of the Maestro's major works.[13]

In another letter he described how he tested the artistic value of his composition:

> Last night I played my Sonatina to someone who does not possess a trained musical ear but who listened carefully and thought the Andante was marvellous. I believe this experiment to be a valid one since it proves that simple, sincere pieces, where I concentrate

my feelings within an uncomplicated but tight structure, are more easily understood by the public.[14]

On 12 October Lipatti played the Concerto in D minor by Bach-Busoni. Emanoil Ciomac published the following notice, in his usual vein, about 'the only Rumanian pianist of international calibre.'

Lipatti is an interpreter who penetrates inside the meaning of music. At the same time he knows how to use his intellect to structure the plan and the progressive developments of a work and to place his highly gifted pianism at the service of this realization. In our opinion Lipatti's style has more affinity with the music of Bach than with Beethoven or the Romantics; among the latter he is more at home with Chopin than Liszt. In spite of a lack of grandeur and heroic feeling, Mr Lipatti gave us an exact image of 18th century music. This was achieved through intelligence and precision, a true balance being sustained between sonorities and their qualities and by the infinite shades of his pianism; fine, supple, skilful and full of detailed subtleties, which never loses sight of the general lines. This music, apart from grandeur, has much grace and a luminous and delightful lyricism. He did not give us an abstract, ascetic, dry and geometric Bach but one which was lively and held our attention all the time. Occasionally the orchestra, under the careful direction of Mr Georgescu, tended to cover some of the fine and delicate interlacings of the soloist—a pianist who gains so much from being heard on his own.[15]

A few days later another notice appeared in the *Universul Literar* under R. Alexandrescu's signature. Here is an excerpt from this notice:

Each new appearance by the young composer and pianist, Dinu Lipatti, is greeted by the public with an interest which we are the first to recognize as being legitimate… The latest stage of Lipatti's development, heard at the Philharmonic Concert on 12 October conducted by George Georgescu with his usual supple vitality and rhythm, seemed to us to place him on a very high plane in the interpretation of music by Bach. His concentration, tonal individualisation of each sound, expressive meditation and rare artistic integrity combined with a technique which is completely subservient to the masterpiece and never used for any cheap success achieved through finger dexterity, gave us a clearer picture than ever before of Dinu Lipatti's true measure. We are convinced that he will never deviate from the artistic and musical path he has carved out for himself in the field of piano-playing in Rumania.[16]

Soon afterwards a new tour with the Philharmonic Orchestra took Lipatti abroad to Bratislava, Vienna, and Sofia. He was the soloist in his own Concertino, and in Mozart's Concerto in D minor (K.466). As on previous tours, the conductor devised a programme mainly devoted to Rumanian composers, which also included the Grieg Concerto in A minor.

The foreign press published highly appreciative notices about the Orchestra's artistic merits and mentioned, in particular, the calibre of the young Rumanian pianist.

The journey to Vienna was a delightful experience for Dinu: "The fields pass by like a gigantic musical record with the horizon, a fixed centre, radiating outwards its many loving thoughts." Once arrived in Vienna he wrote: "Here I am back again in Vienna; how many moving memories are associated with this fascinating town when I recall that famous but exhausting competition...."[17]

In Sofia, at a reception given by the Bulgarian Government for the most prominent members of the Rumanian Philharmonic Orchestra, Dinu was asked to play some improvisations. From early childhood he had shown a rare gift for improvisation which his father had consistently encouraged. But in latter years Dinu had avoided all manifestations of this kind. Despite their brilliance, which clearly showed his serious musical training and pianistic skills, he came to regard them as a form of artistic exhibitionism. For the sake of a 'surprise-turn' one was expected to sacrifice the hard-earned results of a deep interior struggle which can never be shown in public. Any true composer at the miraculous and exhausting moment of creation must stand alone. This is why, as time went on, he avoided any such performances demanded by 'miracle-seekers'.

On this occasion Lipatti improvised on a Bulgarian folk-song, a theme suggested by Sasha Popov, the conductor. He began with a prelude and fugue in the style of Bach; next an allegro from a sonata after Haydn, followed by a Mozartian minuet, an intermezzo after Brahms, a nocturne inspired by Chopin and the improvisation ended with a prelude in the style of Debussy. He astounded the audience. It demonstrated his profound mastery of the technique of composition and of the styles of these great composers. Sasha Popov embraced him with uninhibited enthusiasm, kissed his hands, and emphatically declared him to be a genius, one of the most brilliant of all contemporary personalities. "During my childhood and youth I heard the great Busoni improvise," said Sasha Popov, "but believe me, he came nowhere near the standard reached by this genius representing Rumanian music."

On his return home Lipatti had another opportunity to demonstrate great qualities of musicianship during a Sonata Recital with Georges Enesco to celebrate the 150th anniversary of Mozart's birth. "Technical perfection...elegance, crystalline transparency...spontaneous gracefulness..." are only some of the terms used by the same critics who were against 'exaggerated praise'.

During the happy days of childhood, playing in public had been a joy, but with maturity Lipatti's sense of responsibility towards his art grew stronger every year. No one would have imagined that, in spite of his calm appearance on stage, the internationally-acclaimed pianist suffered days of feverish and nervous anxiety, unable to eat anything before a concert. Even as a student at the Academy every examination or public appearance had caused him great tension—his hands would become ice-cold and he would have to hold a hot-water bottle to keep them warm. His worried family consulted several doctors and all advised him to give up a virtuoso career as his nerves could never stand up to such tension. But any such renunciation was out of the question. His love of music was inborn just as moths are drawn to the light of a candle though their wings get singed.

Paul Sacher commented: "Several hours before a concert he would put on his tails, then pace up and down agitatedly, unable to control his nerves. He often joked about giving up his concert career to become a farmer. But the moment he sat down at the keyboard all his fears and anxieties vanished at once, as if by magic, giving way to perfect control and concentration."[18]

On 10 February 1942 Dinu gave another recital at the *Ateneu*. The programme consisted of Suite no 3 by Handel;

With Paul Sacher and Arthur Honegger

three Sonatas by Scarlatti; *Le Tombeau de Couperin* by Ravel; two studies by Liszt; three Intermezzi by Brahms; three Studies Op 25 by Chopin. This time even Emanoil Ciomac, usually so difficult to please, admitted that Lipatti had attained the complete liberation of his personality:

> This refined, cultivated and intelligent virtuoso finds close affinity with the 18th century and with modern French music. When talking about the 18th century we immediately think of the grandeur of Bach and Handel and the infinite poetic grace of Scarlatti, and these composers were included in the programme. Bach was represented by a Chorale and Sicilienne (played as encores, and which we enjoyed best); Handel, by a Suite in D minor consisting of Prelude, Fugue, Allemande. Courante, Aria with variations and Presto—all in the same key and character which can become rather monotonous. Three delightful sonatas by Scarlatti, and Ravel's *Le Tombeau de Couperin*, in particular the Toccata, were splendidly rendered by Lipatti's prodigious technique, and a crystal-clear and incisive playing with fine tonal range and full of brio. These rare qualities were very evident in the two Liszt studies, particularly in *La Leggerezza*, in the Intermezzi by Brahms, (the second one in E

> flat showing deep inner feeling), and in the three Chopin Studies, brilliant in their technical execution though perhaps a shade cooler in expression. He gave several encores, including two pieces by Bach when this musician obtained the most moving effects through a serene simplicity combined with tranquil and concentrated feeling. The audience became increasingly enthusiastic, demanding more and more 'encores', and the pianist, not yet exhausted by his recital, was offering them with the simplicity and charm which adds to his youthful personality—fully liberated, at last.[19]

A few days later there was another Enesco-Lipatti sonata recital. Inserted between the Bach and Fauré Sonatas, Enesco gave the first performance of his *Impressions from Childhood* with Lipatti at the piano. Thrilled by the exceptional qualities of his young partner with whom he could perform in complete freedom, Enesco dedicated the Suite: *To Dinu Lipatti the godfather of this work, with profound gratitude and admiration.*[20]

In the following month there was a concert of the works of the two great hopes of Rumanian music : Dinu Lipatti and Constantin Silvestri.

"Lipatti follows a more traditional line" commented the music critic of *Universul Literar*; "His music is clear without any profound torment, spirited, full of luminosity and imagination. A youthful delicacy is tinged with sensitivity and tenderness."[21] Dinu played his Three Nocturnes for Piano, Sonatina for Left Hand and the Sonatina for Violin and Piano with the violinist Alexandru Theodorescu.

Later on he was invited to give a recital in Berlin and on that occasion the great pianist Wilhelm Kempff was most enthusiastic and said that he considered Lipatti to be one of the greatest interpreters of our time. Such an appreciation makes it unnecessary to mention any press notices. This is how Lipatti described his feelings when writing to Madeleine about the same concert:

> In my opinion the recital in Berlin was good, (unless I am becoming very stupid...), and I must confess this gave me much joy. What else can be expected when an audience of fifteen hundred people, all listening intently, ends up by drumming their feet on the floor and running towards the platform? I must admit that I experienced a feeling of guilty pleasure which made me play with redoubled zest. What a '*cabotin*' I am![22]

Dinu and Madeleine

In his usual witty style he also describes the next recital he gave in Vienna:

> The Vienna recital was from every aspect less successful than the one in Berlin. First of all the hall was only three-quarters full, and I could not recapture the mood of well-being which I had experienced in Berlin. I cannot say it was a bad concert, but it was not what it should have been. Far from it. Yet the piano was a much better one, infinitely so. Bach was less architectural, Scarlatti

good, Chopin slightly hurried (especially the three pieces which I had played so majestically before that I surprised myself). Finally, the Schubert was better than in Berlin, (I do admit the piano helped, having an ampler bass register). Next, Enesco: Toccata—7 out of 10; Pavane—8 out of 10 and the Bourrée—9 out of 10; whereas in Berlin I gave myself 9½ for the Toccata, 9 for Pavane and 7½ for Bourrée. What can I add to be more precise? During the evening I did not play the Intermezzi to shorten the recital, but gave many 'encores'. I also played my *Négresse*. The audience did not want to leave, although the lights went out. The public was thrilled, much more moved than in Berlin. But the standard of the Berlin concert was much higher. That majestic hall, seating fifteen hundred people, with not one empty seat, and those severe characters dressed in black who barely raised their eyebrows when they smiled—I liked them better, though I know that the worthy Viennese, in their warm enthusiasm, are quite capable of carrying an artist about in their arms if he pleases them and knows how to choose his programme, yet I felt more satisfied by warming up the icebergs."[23]

After Vienna the series of concerts continued in Italy. The inaugural concert was given at an official reception at the Rumanian Legation in Rome. Lipatti described his own feelings on that occasion:

First of all, my 'flu resembled a hurricane. 'The Devil take that handkerchief!'; George Georgescu kept on repeating half laughing and half irritated by my cold. I was dreading the awful moment when I would have to play in the afternoon at the reception. During the morning I rehearsed for two hours, as I have done every day, with few exceptions. I played the three Scarlatti Sonatas; the Schubert in E flat (which I performed better than ever); two Chopin Studies and, by popular request, the Third and Fourth Movements of Chopin's Sonata in B minor. I can say that this was the first time that I found a salon of snobs to my liking.[24]

The enthusiasm which he generated resulted in the cancellation of all concerts in other Italian towns in order to give a recital in Rome. Apart from the pieces he had played at the Legation he performed two Intermezzi by Brahms, his own Sonatina and Enesco's Suite. One cannot describe the success of this recital. He was invited to broadcast on Radio Roma, and to play as soloist with the orchestra, an unaccustomed honour for a foreigner. An orchestral concert followed at the Teatro Adriano in Rome, conducted by George Georgescu, with Lipatti playing his *Concertino in Classical Style*.

When the concerts were over, Dinu was free to wander through Rome from morning till dusk, visiting exhibitions, and marvelling at the artistic monuments which turn the whole of Italy into a museum. He left Rome and immediately received a telegram from Germany inviting him to give a series of concerts in the South. Too fatigued by now to do so, he had to refuse, but resumed his tour of Italy, playing in Pisa on 16 April and in Trieste two days later, where he also did a radio broadcast. "The audience did not want to leave..."

In Italy he met and became friends with two Rumanians living abroad: the composer Roman Vlad and the artist Eugen Dragutescu.

On his return to Rumania Lipatti appeared with the Philharmonic, then he retired to Fundateanca to prepare a new series of concerts for the coming season. It would have been inconceivable to start a new season of orchestral concerts without Dinu Lipatti opening it.

On 11 October, under Ionel Perlea as conductor, Dinu performed Grieg's Piano Concerto in A minor, the same work which he had played after receiving the Diploma of the Bucharest Royal Academy of Music. "A decisive turning-point was reached when the soloistic *brio* of the Concerto was entrusted to the steely and agile hands of Dinu Lipatti," wrote Romeo Alexandrescu. "He was able to make the fusion between a virtuosity of high calibre with truly moving moments of expressive searching. This young artist knows how to attain complete freedom of expression, allowing it to filter through his own individuality and at the same time achieving great spontaneity without hindering the formal structure of his conception of the work."[25]

In November Lipatti gave one of his last recitals in Rumania. The programme included Pastorale in F for Organ by Bach, several Scarlatti Sonatas, Sonata in B minor, Op 58 by Chopin, two Impromptus by Schubert, Debussy's *Etude pour les Arpeges Composés, La Soirée dans Grenade* and *La Cathédrale Engloutie*, two pieces from Ravel's Suite *Miroirs*, and *La Danse du Feu* by Manuel de Falla.

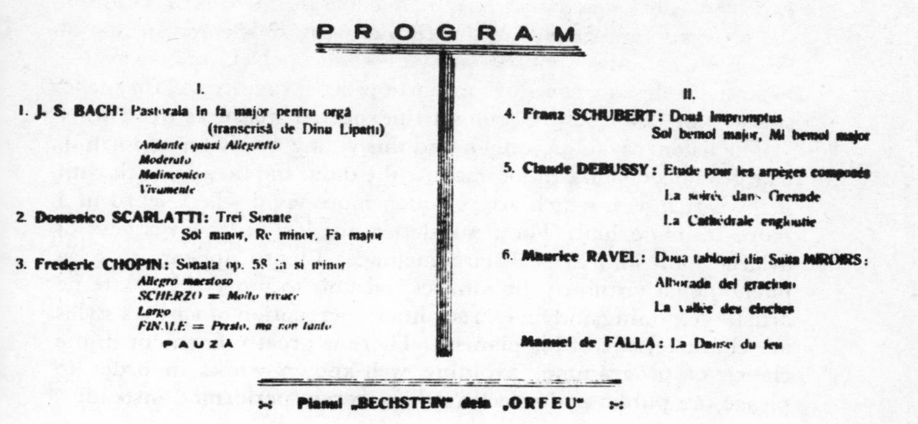

PROGRAM

I.

1. **J. S. BACH:** Pastorala in fa major pentru orgă (transcrisă de Dinu Lipatti)
   Andante quasi Allegretto
   Moderato
   Malinconico
   Vivamente
2. **Domenico SCARLATTI:** Trei Sonate
   Sol minor, Re minor, Fa major
3. **Frederic CHOPIN:** Sonata op. 58 in si minor
   Allegro maestoso
   SCHERZO = Molto vivace
   Largo
   FINALE = Presto, ma non tanto

PAUZA

II.

4. **Franz SCHUBERT:** Două Impromptus
   Sol bemol major, Mi bemol major
5. **Claude DEBUSSY:** Etude pour les arpèges composés
   La soirée dans Grenade
   La Cathédrale engloutie
6. **Maurice RAVEL:** Doua tablouri din Suita MIROIRS:
   Alborada del gracioso
   La vallée des cloches

Manuel de FALLA: La Danse du feu

Pianul „BECHSTEIN" dela „ORFEU"

Emanoil Ciomac had this to report:

As his previous performance of Grieg's Concerto clearly shows, our eminent pianist and musician Dinu Lipatti is now at the height of his development. His interpretations grow day by day in breadth and virility. I believe he is still at that stage which lies on the surface in the development of his many and diverse qualities, and the need to become more profound will come with age. We must remember that Dinu Lipatti is only twenty-five years old. If one may be excused the old *cliché*—it is only through 'living' that his playing will become enriched by an inner and more personal accent. That lyricism created from his own great conviction which is so convincing to an audience: that spontaneous, untaught lyricism, the imponderable element of deeply-felt emotion, will surely affirm itself with the passing years. The fabulous technique of this pianist is the servant of a happy temperament blossoming in the exaltation of conquered difficulties, in spacious luminosity and elegance. The darker corners of the soul, psychological turmoils and the inner searches are not yet finding the most apt interpreter in the young, lively virtuoso. But one must not think that he is lacking in authentic musicality. Only it is more like a breeze and not a storm, more like a fine brush than a thick one for frescoes. Rather than the ample tone resulting from a world of profound resonances, his tone is more incisive, almost dry. This lack of generous amplitude, of a more moving accent, whether in moments of exaltation or depression, may perhaps explain why the audience failed to be totally conquered, as one would have

> expected. This was particularly noticeable in the interpretation of the great romantics. But in the 18th century music and in that of the French contemporary masters—Fauré, Debussy, Ravel—Lipatti's refined sense of proportion and nuance, clarity and subtlety of tone-colours brought unexpected treasures to light.
>
> The listener who has only heard this young musician perform in a large concert-hall cannot imagine the thousand details, each with its own richness, which are so much more vivid when heard in a more intimate hall. These subtleties are lost in the vastness of a large hall, and in such circumstances Lipatti appears to be a phenomenal virtuoso who amazes but fails to move. His extreme artistic reasoning and an extraordinary perception of various styles are characteristic of his pianism. There is great refinement in the choice of programme, avoiding well-known works in order to please the public and selecting those rarely performed instead.

The critic goes on to remark about the manner in which *La Danse du Feu* by de Falla was played, "trying to equal the ease and brio of Rubinstein", while *Alborada del Gracioso* and *La Vallée des Cloches* by Ravel were perhaps "the finest in the whole recital".[26]

On 19 December, Enesco appeared in a sonata recital with Dinu, his favourite partner. "I believe," wrote a critic referring to the performance of Fauré's Sonata in A minor, "that not even in their own country, the France of Thibaud and Cortot, could one find a team who could penetrate and recreate so perfectly the spirit and letter of this work as Georges Enesco and Dinu Lipatti did".

The year 1943 began with another invitation for Lipatti from Berlin to make a recording of his own *Concertino in Classical Style* with Hans von Benda. "Benda seems to have a professional sympathy for me. He must be hoping to be invited to Bucharest, perhaps in April. He has commissioned me to write a violin concerto… Those cold Berliners applauded after the Minuet and I had to get up three or four times. I am now working on the Liszt Concerto as if it were the Holy Bible itself, to be performed on 15 January with the Berlin Philharmonic under Wolfgang Brückner."[27]

He continued his series of recitals in Leipzig, Vienna and Bratislava, where he made some recordings. On 16 February, after returning home, Lipatti played the Liszt Concerto in

KONSERTBOLAGET

Konserthuset, lilla salen, torsdagen den 16 september 1943

Dinu Lipatti

Program:

G. F. HÄNDEL .... Svit d-moll, nr 3
Preludium – Fuga – Allemande – Courante – Aria con variazioni – Presto

L. v. BEETHOVEN .... Sonat C-dur, op. 53 (»Waldstein»)
Allegro con brio
Adagio molto
Rondo. Allegretto moderato

– *PAUS* –

F. SCHUBERT .... Två impromptu, Gess-dur och Ess-dur

G. ENESCU .... Pavane, Toccata } ur svit D-dur

C. DEBUSSY .... La soirée dans Grenade (Afton i Granada); La cathédrale engloutie (Den sjunkna katedralen)

M. DE FALLA .... La danse du feu (Elddans)

Bechsteinflygel från Hoffmans Pianomagasin

E flat under Mengelberg. He played the same Concerto again on 25 February in Sofia with the conductor, Sacha Popov. When a well-known pianist was suddenly taken ill Dinu was asked to take his place and this involved a new tour which covered a number of cities:

3/4	March: Vienna and Linz	—concertos
6	March: Prague	—recital
12	March: Chemnitz	—concerto
14/15	March: Berlin	—concerto
17	March: Halle	—recital
19	March: Kassel	—concerto
21	March: Frankfurt	—concerto
23	March: Cologne	—concerto
25	March: Dresden	—concerto
28/30	March: Osnabruck	—concerto
		—recital

On 31 March he performed his Concertino and Mozart's Concerto in D minor (K.466) with Hans von Benda. During the tour he also played Liszt's Concerto in E flat under such great

conductors as Hermann Abendroth and Karl Böhm. On his return to Bucharest Lipatti played the Concerto in D minor by Bach, under Ionel Perlea and on 24 May he gave a recital of French music at the Institut Français which included Enesco's Sonata No 3 which he was to record later on in Bern.

By now rest was imperative, and Dinu retired to Fundateanca. "It's like Paradise; all the trees I planted are now in full bloom." But it was to be only a short respite before a further series of concerts was arranged. Before setting out on this tour he opened the 1943 autumn season.

— SOCIETATEA ROMÂNĂ DE RADIODIFUZIUNE —

ATENEUL ROMAN

CONCERT SIMFONIC EXTRAORDINAR

ORCHESTRA RADIO

cu concursul la pian al d-lui

DINU LIPATTI

Conducerea muzicală maestrul

WILLEM MENGELBERG

PROGRAM

1943

Final Departure

After cancelling all concerts arranged by the impressarios, Schröder and Backhaus, Dinu prepared himself for a tour of Vienna, Stockholm and Helsinki, a real adventure at that troubled stage of the war. His future wife, Madeleine Cantacuzino, had managed to obtain a passport to accompany him. They had become artistic partners and she was to share with him the magnificent success which lay ahead but which fate was to cut short so cruelly. In Stockholm and Helsinki they were asked to play Mozart's Concerto for Two Pianos in E flat (K.365) and they had great success throughout the opulent and peaceful Scandinavian towns. This is how Lipatti describes their journey:

> As you know we took the plane hoping there would be no stop before Budapest. But as we flew over the Carpathians the oil-pump of the left motor broke down. By a miracle we reached Arad, where we landed for repairs. An hour later we took off again. But no sooner had we reached an altitude of 1000 meters than the poor motor started to 'huff and puff' so badly that we thought it would explode. The horrified pilot managed to stop it and we had to make a forced landing in 'Stuka' fashion, with only one motor. It was lucky for us that we were flying over the military airfield at Kecskemet in Hungary. We dined in the canteen and waited for five hours for a bus to take us to Budapest. As we were no longer 'in transit' we had to go through the customs and visa fomalities, but Madeleine categorically refused to go any further in the damaged plane, which had been repaired in the meantime. The Hungarians very politely escorted us to a bus. While the more daring passengers continued their journey to Vienna by plane, we travelled to Budapest across the safe land at sixty kilometers per hour. A very beautiful city. We stayed at the Bristol, and that evening, elegantly dressed and with Hungarian gypsies playing for us, we dined by the Danube.
>
> Next day, deciding it would be a pity not to visit the city, we caught a later train. In Vienna the Grand Hotel was handsome but rather deserted. We did a radio broadcast, went for a walk and on 9 September began our journey towards Berlin (Brrh!).

Dinu and Madeleine reached Stockholm and Dinu could not fail to admire the beauty of the city, the seemingly peaceful life, the abundance of goods.

> The concerts went so well that the impressario arranged for an extra one. The audiences, rather cold at first, warmed up in the end. From here we go to Helsinki, taking the 9 pm plane on 24 September, where we shall do a radio broadcast on the 25th and a recital on the 26th. We return to Stockholm on the 28th and take the train to Göteborg, then Malmö, for other recitals. From Malmö, probably on 1st October, we shall take the plane to Berlin and go by train that evening to Basel, then on to Zurich where I have a recital on the 4th. Afterwards we shall go via Lucerne to Geneva and finish in Berne where I shall give my last recital on 11 October. In all probability we shall leave Switzerland by the 12th or 13th and be back in Bucharest by 15 October.[28]

Everything worked out according to plan except that fate stepped in and altered all arrangements. From Dinu's short accounts it is difficult to grasp the extraordinary reaction of the audiences in places where, formerly, only a Cortot or a Horowitz would create such a response. "One can only reproach him with one thing," wrote the critic, Kurt Atterberg, jokingly, in the Stockholm *Tidningen*, "Dinu Lipatti is incapable of making the slightest mistake; he possesses unusual accuracy and sonority."[29]

In the newspaper *Allehanda* another critic observed:

> What is so rare in an artist who possesses such intensity and such an extraordinary technique is the degree to which he avoids falling into the trap of empty virtuosity by placing it at the service of artistic values. He does not allow his southern temperament to interfere with the style of music, but maintains a balance of artistic passion and inner sensitivity which is expressed without any harsh moments or cheap sentimentality. Power and clarity are two qualities which characterize his manner of playing, while elegance and nobility of musical conception complete them. In the programme were two contrasting pieces: Toccata in C by Bach-Busoni, in three movements, and the Sonata in B minor by Chopin. The Master of Eisenach's work received a monumental performance with the sonorities of an organ; while the Chopin Sonata was marked by the most delicate nuances. His pianism displays unusual clarity and, at the same time, great sensibility. Indeed, I have never heard the Sonata played so nobly and with such fine intelligence. Every one in the enthusiastic audience realized that here was one of the most accomplished pianists of our time.[30]

Apart from these enthusiastic notices two appeared in the *Svenska Dagbladed* signed F.H.T. which, unable to find fault, reproached Lipatti for playing a Bach transcription. "I ask myself what reason can induce some pianists to include such works in their programmes. This is not done from love of Bach but of their own talent...[31]

Another notice, in complete disagreement with the opinion of competent musicians, seemed to be prompted by a quite different motive. The political régimes of the day were busy fostering hatred between neighbouring countries. Rumania and Hungary were typical victims of nationalist propaganda, particularly on the cultural plane.

Dinu wrote from Stockholm, 21 September 1943: "The criticisms were good, with the exception of one, obviously written in a highly subjective manner which attacked everything Rumanian."[32]

If the first bad notice maintained its discretion by being signed with initials, the next one in *Dagens Nyheter* remained suspiciously anonymous:

> Dinu Lipatti appears to be one of Rumania's most famous pianists. It is possible. In Sweden we know few Rumanian pianists of any importance so we have no reason to doubt this claim. However, when Cortot—judging by the posters—hails him as 'a second Horowitz', and an 'ace among pianists', we are entitled to express our surprise. Those in Stockholm who had the opportunity to hear Horowitz play several times realize that no such comparison can exist. It is even stranger that Cortot should make such a superlative comparison when such different aims separate the two pianists. Lipatti has nothing of the thinker, no refinement of nuances nor any of the mysterious subtleties of musical expression. When he played the Sonata in B minor by Chopin, hurling himself at the keyboard and playing with the fury of a machine-gun salvo, our thoughts returned to Cortot who plays with such poise and lyrical subtlety. Lipatti is a well-trained virtuoso who attacks the most difficult pianistic problems without visible difficulty; yet as an artist he fails to give the same impression... He also played the *Bourrée* by the well-known Rumanian composer, Georges Enesco. This piece does not represent a favourable picture of contemporary Rumanian music; it is as empty as a balloon filled with air.[33]

Lipatti had now the opportunity to understand the meaning of Cortot's words: "When you begin an artistic career you must be armed with great patience and be ready for any sacrifice".

In Helsinki, Dinu and Madeleine received a warm and enthusiastic reception. From there they took a plane for Berlin, a difficult and fearful journey interrupted by several forced landings. It was during the period of preparations for the 'Berlin bombardment'. On 5 October they went on to Zurich where Dinu gave a recital. The following day both he and Madeleine broadcast a programme of Rumanian music: Variations on an Original Theme, Op 5 by Enesco and Three Rumanian Dances by Lipatti. Other recitals followed in Berne, Geneva, Lucerne, Neuchâtel and Versoix. They spent a week in Lucerne where Dinu started a warm and great friendship with Edwin Fischer. "I played for him, he played for us, we could not bear to part."[34]

Early in November Dinu wrote from Versoix: "I left

Bucharest on 4 September for only ten days, yet today marks the second month since we became artistic nomads. I've played in Sweden, Finland and Vienna. After my first tour of Switzerland I have been re-engaged for a further series of five more concerts in Berne, Zurich and Geneva" (where he gave a recital for the International Red Cross. Ed.).[35]

Before his Geneva recital Dinu was invited to a diplomatic reception given by the Rumanian Embassy. "In October 1943", wrote the Swiss critic and composer, Frank Martin, "I was invited to hear a young Rumanian pianist at the Rumanian Legation. I don't really know why I accepted the invitation. I went full of the usual scepticism felt on these occasions. After the audience sat down the young pianist placed his hands on the keyboard and began a Bach Chorale (the Myra Hess transcription of 'Jesu, Joy of Man's Desiring'). After the first chords, I felt that something unusual was happening, that I had never heard the piano played like this. It is true that the pianist's personality appealed to me at once. From that moment on our friendship was born, one of the most valuable that I have ever been offered."

At about the same time Dinu was writing to his teachers about his unforgettable meeting with Edwin Fischer. Fischer lived at Hertenstein, near Geneva, and the visitors had to cross the Lake to reach his home. Villas and woods were reflected in the waters, the images doubling themselves in a harmonious play of green, white, grey and blue. Fischer had lost everything during the War, including his library and piano. He left Germany on foot with his eighty-year old mother whom he never left for the rest of her life. The villa they occupied was sparsely furnished and resembled a doll's house. "My house is a piano surrounded by walls!" were his first words of greeting. From the terrace of the house, where tea was served, was a magnificent view which helped to contribute to a sense of serenity and peaceful happiness. Lipatti played the *Waldstein* Sonata and other works from his repertoire.

> He listened to me most attentively and afterwards gave me his opinion, seated at the piano. From that moment the enchantment began. He played the Finale, saying that he did not like the way I played it and drew my attention to the daring way in which Beethoven indicated the use of the *forte* pedal. I believe Fischer to be correct when he maintains that, from the beginning, the C major passage, (and every time the passage is repeated in other keys) it must sound through the other harmonies because of this pedal effect. The effect appears strange at first, but the audience is caught by it without knowing exactly why. I tried out this experiment at my last recital in Berne. At the end Fischer played for us the first Schubert Sonata in A minor which he will play in Vienna. He had only recently learnt it. With great humility he asked: "Do you think it will be ready in two weeks time?". Of course we all laughed. Afterwards he played, with regal bearing, Handel's Suite in D (which I also play) and some Schubert, so movingly and intimately that it brought tears to my eyes. He often gets excited and then his mother, a remarkable musician to whom he owes his marvellous art, looks at him lovingly. So ended the day (we nearly missed the last boat back), a day we wished could have continued forever.[36]

After the first meeting Fischer and Lipatti often met, playing to one another, discussing the planning of programmes and savouring the rare satisfaction of their friendship.

Lipatti settled down in Geneva and with great difficulty

found a fourth-floor attic to live in. The Geneva musical set adopted him immediately and surrounded him with admiration and affection. A number of good friends gathered around and helped him over difficult moments. Among them were Henri Gagnebin, Director of the Geneva Conservatoire; Hugues Cuénod, the tenor who recorded Brahms's waltzes in the Comtesse de Polignac's salon in Paris and with whom Dinu often had improvising sessions; Igor Markevitch, Frank Martin, Ernest Ansermet, Nikita Magaloff and Aloys R Mooser, who actually lived in the same house. Other friends also gave support, among them artists like Nadia Boulanger, Backhaus, Fischer, Schnabel, Janigro and many Rumanian visitors who came to see them.

Above all, Lipatti hoped that he would benefit from the valuable advice of Edwin Fischer. In his own words, Fischer had opened new and unsuspected vistas for him. Another reason for staying on emerged, one which was going to keep him in Switzerland indefinitely and which made him cancel more and more concerts—a mysterious illness. The first signs of illness were occasional bouts of fever which could last for weeks. Concerts in Vienna, Bratislava, and Bucharest on 21 December had to be cancelled.

On 8 December Dinu writes:

> I continue to be ill in bed with fever; the doctors come and go, but none can tell me what it is. Everything else is normal, the tests show nothing abnormal. Yet it is not normal to have a temperature of 38 degrees every evening. This, coupled with four days of strict dieting in case it is an intestinal infection, has weakened me considerably. I am eaten up with fury that the Berne recital, cancelled on 17 December, may have to be postponed yet again... Because of this illness I have no money left. My family sent some but not sufficient. I stay at home and...knit. My one wish is to be able to work with Fischer.[37]

Dinu and Madeleine remained calm and brave throughout the medical consultations, when the great artist was like a child faced with his own physical suffering. When he realized that his concert career might be in jeopardy for a long time, Lipatti tried to find an administrative job to provide a more secure existence. He applied for the post of Cultural Attaché at the

International Bureau for Education in Geneva. "Thus, not being part of the usual offices attached to the Ministry of Foreign Affairs or Propaganda, I shall not be involved in politics of any sort. My work would be of a technical nature and should be considered such by the Rumanians, or by any foreign authorities. By giving me the possibility of remaining here I could successfully serve our national cultural interest..."[38]

After spending twenty days in bed with high fever and suffering from being 'badly poisoned', as it was thought, Dinu appeared to recover. He was able to make appearances in Zurich, Geneva and Berne, where receptions in his honour and enthusiastic reviews became commonplace. He was offered concert tours all over Switzerland including places where he had not played before: Lausanne, Fribourg, Neuchâtel, Winterthur, Saint-Gallen etc. But between 23 November and 14 December he was unable to get out of bed. He recovered for three weeks only to fall ill again. The doctors recommended several months of rest in the mountains, and fewer concert performances. Dinu and Madeleine immediately left for Montana. A letter followed:

> At the moment I am resting, at 1500 meters altitude, in a place with fairy-tale scenery, where it never rains and spring is perpetual. I am splendidly installed in a hotel built of wood whose owner was for twelve years the Maître d'Hôtel at the *Cina* and the *Chateaubriand* in Bucharest. So, occasionally, I am served 'borsht with meat balls', 'stuffed cabbage leaves', 'mititei' (a kind of hamburger), or stews, to the accompaniment of gramophone records of Fanica Luca and Grigoras Dinicu, which he jealously guards.[38]
>
> I received a moving letter from Fischer who thinks I have some lung disease like everyone else here. He tells me how upset he is that I am ill but that I should not despair because all artists who have made great efforts must rest occasionally. He promises to visit me in Montana and bring anything I need.[39]

Being kept fully informed of news by his friends and from newspapers, Dinu wrote to his teachers at home about his life, his illness and the musical life in Switzerland:

> Backhaus is actually playing all Beethoven's Sonatas in various places. He is appreciated, but sometimes criticized. Do you

> remember Turczinski? He is busy creating havoc, producing his Chopin recitals in factory quantities! As to our very dear Fischer, he has been appointed to the Lucerne Conservatoire and will be able to see me in February. I can hardly wait to spend a longer time with him than I did in October. Flesch is also at the Lucerne Conservatoire, and we made some music together. He is now 70 years old, still full of vitality, and has a fine character. I have also met a very gifted pianist, Nikita Magaloff, who hopes to play in Rumania. He liked the sound I produced very much, and I've told him a great deal about you—he wrote to Florica Muzicescu—and he is very anxious to meet you. Am trying to convince Backhaus to pay a visit to Rumania. Gieseking has already got my Concertino...[40]

On 17 January he writes: "my health continues to worry us. Every evening a temperature of 38 degrees. Had to cancel tours to Germany and Holland."

The necessary Rumanian formalities for his new appointment as Cultural Attaché were delayed and, in the end, never arrived. Meanwhile, although he had refused the offer of Swiss citizenship, the Swiss authorities approved his appointment as Professor at the Geneva Conservatoire on 1 April 1944. "It is a great honour for me to hold the same Chair as Liszt, and one where the Laureates of the Paris Conservatoire often fail." It was, in fact, an honarary appointment and, according to the rules, he was not permitted to give private lessons. The stipend was small so that his only hope for survival lay in being able to give some concerts. But a number of interventions and disputes occurred before a permit was given to Lipatti to reside and work in Geneva as Professor of the 'Cours de Virtuosité' at the Conservatoire.

This is how Dinu describes the preliminaries before his appointment:

> One day the Director of the Geneva Conservatoire came to see me and asked whether I would like to succeed Alexandre Mottu in the 'Postgraduate Virtuoso Course.' A week later the Committee held a meeting and unanimously agreed to my appointment to teach for at least three years—which moved me deeply. Afterwards the Conservatoire took all the necessary steps with the Federal authorities to get permission for me to live and work in Geneva. In the meantime, my future 'dear colleagues' at the Conservatoire

BULLETIN
DU
CONSERVATOIRE DE MUSIQUE
DE
GENÈVE

Nouveaux professeurs

Pour succéder au regretté Alexandre Mottu, le comité du Conservatoire a nommé professeur des classes supérieures et de virtuosité de piano M. Dinu Lipatti, artiste éminent. Né à Bucarest en 1917, Lipatti a commencé l'étude du piano à l'âge de quatre ans. Entré au Conservatoire de Bucarest, il en sort à quatorze ans après avoir suivi la classe de Mlle Florica Muzicescu et le cours de composition de M. Jora. Il étudie ensuite à Paris avec Alfred Cortot, Nadia Boulanger, Paul Dukas et, après la mort de ce maître, avec Igor Strawinsky.

En 1933, il a obtenu un second prix au Concours international de piano à Vienne.

Bien que très jeune encore, Dinu Lipatti a parcouru une très brillante carrière de soliste. Il a été engagé à la Société des concerts du Conservatoire de Paris, deux fois de suite (fait rare) à la Philharmonie de Berlin, à celle de Vienne, à l'Augusteo de Rome, aux grands concerts de Stockholm, Madrid et Lisbonne. En Suisse, il a remporté de grands succès à l'un des concerts par abonnement de Berne, à

got together to prevent any steps taken by the Committee becoming effective. They even sent a signed petition to the Berne Police expressing their disapproval and annoyance...and they succeeded so well that, at first, the authorities were won over. But these actions by my opponents failed, thanks to an energetic group of influential musicians who, in the end, managed to obtain my work permit. The steps taken by my friends, among them Ansermet, Frank Martin the composer and Gagnebin, the Director of the Conservatoire, resulted in their making enemies of the entire teaching staff of Geneva.[41]

The following is the text of an article published in the Bulletin of the Geneva Conservatoire of Music in April, 1944:

...Although still very young, Dinu Lipatti has already made a brilliant career as a soloist. He has been invited to play twice in succession (a very rare honour) by the Société des Concerts du Conservatoire National de Paris; by the Berlin Philharmonic, by Vienna and Rome; and has appeared in celebrity concerts in Stockholm, Madrid and Lisbon. In Switzerland his concerts and recitals have enjoyed grest successes in Berne, Zurich and Geneva, including his performance with the Suisse Romande Orchestra at a charity concert on 30 March. Dinu Lipatti is not only a virtuoso possessing a transcendental technique and a pianist with rare powers of perception, he is also a highly gifted composer who has written a Concertino for Piano and Chamber Orchestra, Three Symphonic Sketches, a Symphonie Concertante, and several chamber music works. In fact he is a man of great culture, the outcome of mature and fruitful studies...

In answer to some nationalist objections raised by some members of the staff of the Conservatoire, the same article continues:

> If almost all our Professors are Swiss, it is only normal in exceptional cases that we should make room for a foreigner with exceptional gifts. This is what the Federal and Cantonal authorities understood by granting Dinu Lipatti, after a long and careful investigation, the right to become a Professor. In the past our Conservatoire had Marteau, Berber, Stavenhagen, Szigeti and Iturbi. Today Dinu Lipatti can take his place among these eminent names adding to the glory of the Geneva Conservatoire. We wish him a brilliant career in our midst.

Dinu asked the Rumanian Ministry of Propaganda to advance the sum of 2,400 francs towards organizing six concerts in different Swiss towns to help him in his financial difficulties. This advance, which should not have created any problems, considering Dinu's prestige, was never granted. "To my surprise," he wrote, "I heard at the last moment that the request for 2,400 francs had been refused on the grounds that 'they don't need any propaganda at present in Switzerland.' This did not prevent them from building a pavilion costing about 50,000 francs, and which nobody visits."

Despite his illness, Dinu returned to Geneva at the end of April. This time the doctors were able to diagnose the cause of his illness, but told the patient that he was suffering from 'a glandular infection of a non-tubercular nature'. The thought of two months wasted in Montana was discouraging, yet it was a relief to know that he did not have tuberculosis; now he could even crack jokes about his fears.

On 16 May 1944 he wrote to Professor Bickel: "At last, after nine months of suffering and investigations, they have found the remedy. I start X-ray treatment on 1 May to burn away the famous gland that first appeared like a button on the radiograph taken in 1942, then like a nut in January 1944, and which was as big as a pear by April. Today I had my tenth session of X-rays and I feel much better."

Those close to Dinu now lived in constant fear, after being told the truth about his illness by the doctors who had joined his circle of devoted friends. At the same time the lack of any regular news from his family and friends at home were contributing to Dinu's worries. In spite of this in the Spring of 1944 he began working with increasing interest and devotion with his students at the Conservatoire.

"This appointment, which unfortunately is only quasi-honorary, has brought me an unexpected prestige in Switzerland. Every week professional pianists come to me for advice. I encourage those who are able to do so to enter the Conservatoire. Regretfully, I must refuse to give any private lessons as this is not allowed by the Federal authorities." In a letter to Florica Musicescu, on 2 August, Dinu outlines the works he had to play between then and March of the following year:

> On 5 August the Chopin Concerto in E minor with Scherchen; on the 12th, a recital in Montana; from the 28th a fortnight in Lucerne with Fischer who will interpret all the Beethoven Sonatas; a recital in Frauenfeld on 28 September; 15 October at Vevey; on 31 October Liszt's E flat Concerto and Mozart's D minor, Chopin in Fribourg, 12 November; Ravel in G, and Haydn in D, Zurich, 5 December; Liszt in Basel, 16 January; Liszt and Martin's *Ballade*, 19 February in Geneva; the same programme repeated on the 21st at Lausanne; recitals in all these towns in March: in short, a great deal to do. And on 16 September my classes start again at the Conservatoire.

He began a tour of Italy and Belgium. Then he played in Paris where he was no longer the brilliant student of a few years ago but a recognized and much-loved artist. He was given a moving reception. After his recital he appeared twice as soloist with the orchestra. As usual he only refers briefly to his tremendous success in his letters home.

> To celebrate New Year, 1946, my friends and admirers offered me a gift (and what a gift!) of a splendid piano, so I now have three

pianos in my home. And, jumping from one to the other, I make the most hellish row... But none of the neighbours has complained so far.

The recordings I made in Zurich last summer seem to be very good both from the technical and interpretative aspects, but travelling for seven weeks between Zurich and London has affected them. Walter Legge, who has become our good friend, advises me to re-do them in London next February. I work incessantly, without a moment's rest, as I must give more than sixty concerts between September 1946 and June 1947. My health, thank God, is good and I hope I have got rid of my illness this time.

On 12 February we go to Paris, on the 18th to Brussels, and to London on the 20th for two weeks of recordings and seven concerts. Afterwards back to Paris for a recital on 7 March; then several concerts in the German part of Switzerland, followed by fourteen concerts in Italy between 28th March and May 1st.[42]

This period of optimism did not last long. Dinu's health began to deteriorate again. Biopsy after biopsy were performed. The X-rays were continued but had distressing side-effects producing terrible headaches, vertigo, vomiting and a general 'cavalcade of miseries'. The idea of having an incurable illness began to enter his mind. When playing the piano his movements became more deliberate and economical. No one suspected that this was in order to minimize the pain caused by the pressure on the mass of swollen glands in his arms, and no one imagined that the beautiful tones, precision and subtleties of his interpretations were the result of such great effort. The Columbia Record Company offered him the highest fees for his recordings, but by now Dinu's concert programmes had to be planned according to his physical strength, which was gradually diminishing. He could no longer allow himself to play works like Schumann's *Etudes Symphoniques* which he put aside for some time. Nevertheless, Columbia began the recordings which represent his artistic testament.

After a long silence Dinu again received a letter from Florica Muzicescu. He replied:

When I saw your handwriting I could not think how to begin... For me you are more than ever close to my heart. How could I ever forget you when I realize that everything of value which I have achieved over the past few years is due to a wealth of experience which you knew how to communicate to me, not without great effort. This real and sincere love of music has given me the skill of an honest worker, without which I could achieve nothing today. I conduct my classes at the Conservatoire thanks to your teaching, and far from being able to give a quarter of what you gave me, I am trying to transmit an inheritance which is very dear to me. I am convinced, however, that I am a poor pedagogue because I propose instead of imposing, (it is not easy to change one's nature!), and this brings results only with those rare pupils who realize their own ideals and who emulate me. Besides... I have not got the call. I often think with sadness of the mornings, such a waste for me, which I spend trying to correct people who, for the most part, have very little in common with music, and how life is too short to be spent like that. In my first year I had twenty pupils, in the second fifteen, and now I have twelve.

The concerts, on the contrary, grow at an inverse ratio. I have appeared twenty five times this season in Switzerland alone, which has been a tremendous help from every point of view. I spent a shorter time abroad (three concerts in Paris, two in Brussels, two in Milan and Turin), but this will increase from next October. On 4th, 5th and 6 July I record the Chorale in G, 'Jesu Joy of Man's Desiring', by Bach, in the transcription of Myra Hess for Columbia, a Sonata in C by Scarlatti which is not often played, Nocturne in D flat by Chopin, Petrach Sonnet 104 by Liszt and probably Mozart's concerto in C (K 467), with Paul Sacher and his orchestra. I shall try to send you all the records when they come out. But now I have to cut down on my engagements. In two days I shall probably sign a contract for America, which I shall accept in order to take a years' rest afterwards when I shall be able to do some thinking. As regards composing, this has become a luxury which I can only afford during the summer. Much too little. Have written four songs and many sketches without really getting anywhere due to the lack of continuity[43]

The projected American tour—the accolade for any European artist considered to be of international calibre—never took place as the strain would have caused a rapid deterioration in Lipatti's health. His strength was gradually diminishing and the doctors advised him to postpone this series of concerts.

Among the events which Dinu described with great feeling, were "those on the occasion of the concerts given in July 1946 in aid of the restoration of *La Scala* of Milan," when he had the

With Nadia Boulanger and Allegra, daughter of Igor Markevich

good fortune to hear Toscanini and to get to know him well. "... His words of appreciation went straight to my heart... He attended my two rehearsals and on the evening of the concert it looked as though he was among those who applauded most enthusiastically. By attending all his rehearsals and concerts I lived through moments of profound and unique emotion and learnt great lessons."

It is well-known that Toscanini did not allow anyone to attend his rehearsals but, not only did he accept Dinu, he actually invited him. The great conductor declared that he considered Lipatti the 'greatest living pianist', to which Lipatti answered, "How can you say such a thing, Maestro, when your son-in-law is none other than Horowitz?" Toscanini may have been right as Horowitz was making fewer and fewer public appearances at that time. Dinu wrote:

> When I met Toscanini the evening before my first rehearsal at La Scala, I asked him if he would listen to my playing and give me some severe criticism, which he readily agreed to do. Votto, the conductor, had done everything possible to cover my playing by doubling the number of strings and taking the lid off the piano under the pretext that he could not conduct behind the instrument. Madeleine was very upset. When I mentioned this to Toscanini, he reduced the orchestra by half, (I never expected as

much as that!), and ordered the piano lid to be replaced. After the first rehearsal he congratulated me, and said: 'At last we have a Chopin without caprices and with the *rubato* to my liking. The great majority of musicians want to re-write compositions written by others and interpret them.'

He attended my second rehearsal and was friendlier than ever; at the evening concert it looked as though he were leading the *claque*. At the end, after several recalls, I took the advice of those around me and played 'Jesu Joy of Man's Desiring' as an encore. Afterwards Toscanini congratulated me on the Chopin, but gave me this important advice: 'You must not give an encore. Never play encores at a symphony concert. Keep them for recitals, though if I were a pianist I would not play them even then.' Ashamed of myself I wrote him a letter trying to explain the reasons for my behaviour. In reply he invited Madeleine and myself to spend the evening with him. From then on we often went to his house, and I was allowed to assist at all his rehearsals. One week we went twice to La Scala where, seated in the darkest corner of a box, we listened intently and watched how, under our very eyes he transformed a second-rate orchestra into one of international standard. These were rare moments of joy and encouragement for me. Particularly as I sensed, at certain moments, a similarity in conception, feeling and manner of conducting with our beloved Enesco, to whom Toscanini felt very close as a musician. In his opinion Enesco was 'Europe's greatest musician'.

The last rehearsal was a stormy one with scores thrown about, shouts, insults, threats, until we did not know where to hide ourselves. It was on the day he celebrated 50 years of marriage, 60 years of musical activity and his 79th birthday. That week spent at La Scala will always remain a most important event in my life. We met Toscanini again in Lucerne and when we dined together after the concert he expressed great concern about my future.

Madame Toscanini gave me good advice about my trip to America. It seems that Horowitz is quite ill again. He can give only ten concerts a year in the United States, and is afraid of travelling in case he should die. Good for him! Rubinstein is in full swing, and so is Serkin, but the younger generation has little to offer.

We went recently to the Engadine, at 2000 metres altitude, and happened to stay at the same hotel as Schnabel. I am very sorry to say that he heard me play the Mozart Concerto in E flat (K271) just barely prepared for this small concert in the mountains. I

> never expected to run into any 'crocodiles' there. But Schnabel was very kind and we went to see him every day until we left. I played Enesco's Sonata in F sharp to him, which he liked, and my cadenzas for various concertos; then he played me his cadenzas for the same concertos, pointing out a great many interesting things.[44]

During the latter half of October Dinu and Madeleine left for a tour of Belgium, to give recitals and play with the orchestra, while Madeleine was to accompany the well-known tenor, Hugues Cuénod. A close friend of Dinu's, he remembers with deep emotion the admirable 'Schubertiades' which took place at Lipatti's home during the artist's moments of relaxation. The evenings were inspired by displays of his verve and his many gifts. He would play with gloves on, or with a cover over the keyboard. He would place paper over the piano strings and imitate in an amazing fashion the sound of the zither. Often he would improvise, using all three pianos in the house. Cuénod recalls, in particular, the unforgettable improvisations they did together. These 'séances' took the following pattern: Cuénod would read poems from various authors and Dinu would play a few chords to create the right mood and a harmonic framework, then Cuénod would start singing and from then on the two artists were carried away, stimulating each other and creating a magical world of music. Without the slightest hesitation the songs and the accompaniments flowed as though the two artists had studied them together for a long time.

After the Belgium tour Dinu and Madeleine spent a few days in Paris, then returned to Switzerland for a series of concerts and to make some recordings. On 12 December he gave a recital at Neuchâtel; a week later, Lausanne, then Zurich where Dinu played the Concerto in D minor by Mozart; then Lucerne on 27 December.

Switzerland had adopted Lipatti by now and he felt very much at home there. He was in great demand and was received with great affection everywhere. In the small towns where he played he tried out new pieces, giving 'first performances', so that he could attack them with confidence at future concerts. In the beginning of 1947 engagements from all over the world

With Enesco in the Rumanian Broadcasting studios

were pouring in. A tour of the major European centres was planned. He arrived in Paris on 13 February where he spent the first two days visiting his friends and professors. The concert took place on 16th February at the *Société des Concerts* when he played Grieg's Concerto in A minor, which was an unparalleled success.

On his arrival in London a fresh crisis in his illness forced Lipatti to cancel all his concerts. The Albert Hall was sold out, and the London public waited anxiously for his recovery. With great effort he only managed to make a few recordings for Columbia: Nocturne in B flat and Sonata in B minor by Chopin, Bach's Chorale in G, 'Jesu Joy of Man's Desiring' (Myra Hess' arrangement) and the Scarlatti Sonata in D minor, (L413). The Chopin Sonata alone took him no less than three days to record, and was later awarded the Charles Cross Academy Prize by a unanimous and enthusiastic jury. Dinu wrote:

> My desire to work is greater than my physical stamina. And although my general state is satisfactory, three days ago I had a fourth crisis with my glands... Once again I had to have X-ray treatment, which tires me greatly... I have a mysterious ailment which is defeating the competence of all these famous doctors. They treat the effects but at the same time the cause should not be ignored. After my Paris concert I realized that my illness does not help the technical side of my playing but artistically it is of

> great help. I can't tell you how many moving letters and telephone messages I have received. I can hardly believe it as I was far from satisfied with my performance.[45]

Despite pressing advice from the doctors, Dinu's feverish activities continued. He formed a new trio with the cellist Janigro and the young Belgian violinist and Enesco's pupil, Arthur Grumiaux, planning a series of concerts in various Swiss towns, and a separate tour of Switzerland and Italy with Janigro alone.

> I want to plan a new programme for a piano recital: Bach English Suite in C minor; Beethoven Sonata Op 31, No. 2; Bartók Sonata or Sonatina; six Chopin Etudes and three Preludes; ending with two Albéniz pieces and two by Liszt... Ansermet has engaged me to give the first performance of Bartók's last Concerto, No 3, a marvel of extraordinary purity and feeling. I can't tell you how Rumanian it sounds. I read the score with real emotion and accepted the offer with enthusiasm... I hope to play it about six times in Switzerland, then perhaps in Paris, Brussels, London and Rome.[46]

Dinu's doctors urged him to spare himself, to give up his tours, to cut down his hours of study, to reduce the hours of teaching. They stressed the need for his co-operation if his state of apparent well-being were to continue and if they were to be successful in combating a 'malignant lymphogranulomathosis'. This new diagnosis was now revealed to him. Dr Sarasin and Dr Dubois-Ferrière became Dinu's close friends and stayed by him until the end of his life, doing everything possible to alleviate his sufferings.

On 30 March 1947 Dinu writes: "I am tired and am sitting in my dressing-gown and slippers thinking with melancholy of the beauty of the spring in Milan where I cannot go now. Both Madeleine and the doctors have been very firm and forced me to 'clear up' this end of the season which, through greed and love of work, got cluttered up with too many concerts."[47]

His undaunted courage, or perhaps an urgent need to give was the source of new strength. Between 18 and 20 April he continued his concerts in Rome, Turin and Milan. He also remained faithful to several Swiss towns where the public worshipped him and where he often gave away his fees to

Lipatti with Paul Hindemith

charity. When the doctors advised him at least to cut out these small concerts he answered that he was never more moved than the evening when he heard that a very poor young man had walked all the way from Paris to hear him play. He added that he would go gladly to play, no matter how far, even for only one person if that person listens to music with all the heart.[48]

In May he played with Janigro in Lausanne, Berne and Zurich. Dinu wanted to help his friend gain recognition from the Swiss public.

At the end of term Lipatti's class at the Conservatoire earned a marked success. "Today my most talented pupil passed her Diploma exams very successfully. In the morning she played works by Bach, Rameau and the *Waldstein* Sonata exceptionally well; in the afternoon she played the Mozart Concerto (K467), *Allegro Barbaro* by Bartók and the Handel Variations by Brahms in an outstanding manner and like a great artist so that all my efforts have been amply rewarded. She is a Polish girl, only thirteen years old and absolutely remarkable. Has excellent fingers, already possesses the technique of an accomplished pianist and has great sensitivity and a lively intelligence."[49] One member of the jury telephoned to congratulate Lipatti on the standard of his class. Thus he proved that he could also be a great teacher.

On 22 June 1947 the sad news came from home of his father's death. As often happens after the loss of someone very dear, Dinu was overwhelmed by the pain of his loss, as well as by a sense of guilt and deep sorrow that he had not been able to lighten Theodor's last moments. He wrote: "My head is empty, my heart is heavy. I move about the house like a sleep-walker, I don't know what I'm doing or thinking. Above all I regret that I never saw him since I left the country and that my absence must have added to his suffering during the past years."

A Rumanian friend wrote advising Dinu to return to Rumania where his great talent would find the recognition it deserved without preventing him from making international tours. He replied:

> Your suggestion arrives, by a strange coincidence, during one of the most poignant moments of my life and cannot but increase my longing for my dear ones, my friends, my country, our common past. If it depended on my inner wishes alone, the answer would be a categorical YES! without the slightest hesitation. Unfortunately my situation is such that I cannot undertake a project which I might not be able to sustain. If I make you my confidant you will understand better why, for the first time, I feel my courage faltering. You know very well that since 1943 my health has suffered from a ganglionic infection which I have not been able to get rid of. Last February, when I was preparing for the most important concert of the London season, I fell ill again with a high fever, for the fourth time. All my concerts had to be cancelled. The doctors shrugged their shoulders, all they could recommend was rest, and again rest. As if I could ever do this. I was most depressed, realizing how feeble my body is and how tenacious this illness. Back in Geneva I cancelled many concerts, in spite of serious financial losses, and followed the doctors' recommended treatment. Now I am worse than ever, as another nucleus of ganglions has developed under my left arm, and the doctors dare not treat it with radiation because of my too recent treatment last February.
>
> I had planned to do fourteen concerts in Italy but, for the same reasons, could only do four, fortunately with great success. The other ten towns expressed their disappointment and even tried to coerce me by insisting that a vote by ballot should be taken to decide which towns should be without a concert; but when they

understood the reason they gave up. Czechoslovakia and Hungary also made concrete offers, but I had to give them the same answer. Not to mention tours to other continents, which are very important for me, but which I dare not attempt since I dread any relapse. Life is difficult, journeys are fatiguing and the work, once home, would be enormous—I could not bear not being able to travel from one corner of the country to the other to bring music to the hungry ones. If, by doing this, I were to fall even more seriously ill than I am at present, far from my doctors and their treatment...what good would my returning home accomplish?

The fact that, without consulting me, you have managed to obtain the proper authorisation, in principle, for me to enter and leave Rumania whenever necessary can only give me joy. On the other hand, I cannot understand why I should not get this official permission anyway since I have never been mixed up in any kind of politics.

There is one other difficulty. Assuming that next season will not produce more surprises, nor illnesses, than this year—this is my programme from 21 July till 10 August: four concerts in Siels-Maria and St. Moritz, solo and with orchestra; 23 August, Lucerne, Mozart's D Minor Concerto at the International Festival conducted by Hindemith; also at Lucerne, in early September, a Chopin Gala Recital in aid of our needy and starving back home, as well as some recordings (Grieg Concerto); 1–9 October, a tour of Holland; 21 October, another Chopin Gala Recital in Paris, also in aid of our starving people.

Back in Switzerland I shall begin a season of concerts with Ansermet, playing Bartók's last Concerto on 19,20,21 and 25 November in Geneva, Lausanne, Chaux-des-Fonds and Fribourg. Recitals in Switzerland in December; the same in January; 8 and 9 February, concerts with orchestra in Berne; 27 February, with orchestra in Neuchâtel; in March a new series of recitals in Switzerland with new programme (Bach's English Suite, No 3, Sonata by Stravinsky, several Chopin works and Iberia by Albéniz) Next April—England; Recital in London on the 11th; the Concerto No 3 of Bartók at the Albert Hall on the 13th; then Belfast, Northern Ireland, and other English cities. On my way back to Switzerland I shall give two concerts for the *Société des Concerts* in Paris, and one recital in Brussels. In May and June I shall be tied up teaching my students, so will stay at home and give only a few concerts. Afterwards, God willing, I shall try other continents. I am sending you the programme of my concert with Ansermet given in aid of Rumanian children, and you will see for yourself that I am not idle here... I believe I can be more useful from here than at home, when you realise that the Lucerne concert along could buy medicines worth 6000–7000 French francs.[50]

After the final exams at the Conservatoire, in the spring of 1947, Dinu started to suffer from 'X-ray sickness.' He left for the Engadine, where he gradually recovered and was able to prepare himself for the autumn season, with London as the starting-point. He gave two recitals at Samaden and Silvaplana, in an enchanting, small Romanesque church where the number of music-lovers greatly surpassed the seating capacity.

Madeleine describes the two events: "There were so many people that Schnabel, the great pianist, was waiting patiently outside the church to get a seat. When I saw him there I was furious at this involuntary lack of politeness from the organisers and offered him my own seat. He refused, jokingly 'What do you expect? The impressarios made a great mistake; for Lipatti they should not have hired this tiny church but St. Peter's in Rome' In the end everything was settled happily, and though the end of the concert was greeted in silence, the atmosphere in the church was charged with emotion." She also mentions the moving interpretation of the Haydn Concerto with Dinu's own cadenzas, conducted by his friend, Paul Sacher.

Dinu returned to Geneva to prepare for the concert tour beginning with the International Festival in Lucerne with Hindemith conducting. Madeleine had this to say: "Mozart's D Minor Concerto was more than a mere achievement and the critics did not hesitate to underline that it was the highlight of the whole Festival. For the first time Dinu played the Beethoven Cadenzas which are not often played because of their revolutionary spirit, but which are of great beauty. It seems that only Busoni used to play them."

In Geneva Lipatti gave a Chopin Recital in aid of the distressed Rumanian people. In his own home he organized a private concert and played Bartók's Third Piano Concerto. This was the Hungarian composer's last work, and 17 bars of the composition remained unwritten at the time of his death. "Fortunately, these had been sketched in pencil," commented

Dinu. It was the first European performance of a masterpiece which was to be repeated in several Swiss towns and afterwards in London. Also in London Lipatti recorded Bach's Chorale in G, the Scarlatti Sonata in E (L23), the *Petrarch* Sonnet of Liszt, and Grieg's Concerto in A minor, conducted by Alceo Galliera.

About this last recording session Dinu writes: "It was hard work. I think we had to repeat each side five times in search of perfection, the slightest slip by the pianist or the orchestra being unacceptable. While this went on I was thinking about my adolescence, my parents, and all those happy days which are now gone forever." Madeleine continues: "We have only listened to the first side which seems very good. Schnabel, whom we met a few days ago in Amsterdam, says he listened to the Cadenza and found it magnificent."[51]

In England Lipatti played twice on the radio:

> The BBC is a marvel of precision, seriousness and inventiveness. They have wonderful Steinways in every studio, and the care which they take with every broadcast, whether a recital or a symphony concert in the studio, amply rewards an artist for all his efforts.[52]

He gave a concert in Norfolk which electrified the audience and moved people to tears. From England he went on to Holland where his triumphant tours—reminiscent of those made by Liszt—continued. In Hilversum he played Bach's Concerto in D minor and Ravel's Concerto in G. In the Hague, where he was also asked to give a recital, he played the Mozart Concerto in D minor. The love he inspired in the Dutch public was such that he was urged to settle in Holland. On his return to Switzerland he met with a similar success. However, his feverish activities coupled with his rapidly-failing health compelled him to remain in bed for some time. Aware of his fate, Dinu tried to spare those around him and began to conceal the deterioration of his tortured body. No one was going to know about the new glands swelling under his left arm. "Oh God, why must one live with the knowledge of death when life could be so beautiful from a creative point of view," he wrote.[53] The doctors, in their endless efforts to find an antidote, resorted to a new treatment using the dangerous

Yperite (mustard-gas). The injections, which Dinu bore with great fortitude, produced serious side-effects. A thrombosis developed in his left arm which became so swollen that only expert tailoring to his dress-suit managed to disguise if from the audience. Severely handicapped by this arm and in great pain he nevertheless continued to play and thrill even the most severe critics. Most of the recordings which continue to amaze us as examples of unsurpassed heights of interpretative art were made during this time.

The end of the year brough new crises and sufferings with the resumption of radiation treatment. Even in those crucial moments Dinu retained a sense of humour and cracked jokes about his swollen arm. "It gives me such formidable sonorities in the bass that even Miss Musicescu would be satisfied!" The New Year, 1948, found him back in bed, but he gathered sufficient strength to give a Chopin recital in Brussels. By now his recordings made in London had been released, and the demand, from all over the world, surpassed all expectations. Dinu writes to Florica Musicescu:

> The London notices about my Grieg are wonderful. "Columbia want me to record the Schumann Concerto with Herbert van Karajan, (I studied it during the summer of 1945). If such an opportunity thrills me, as you can well imagine, the Concerto itself fills me with apprehension. I'm afraid of not being sufficiently

Jianu, Lipatti, Silvestri and Enesco

'Schumannian'. Do you think that I am making a great mistake? I know perfectly well that I can always refuse to have it released if I am not satisfied. But, would it not be more honest to say 'no' before recording it? As to the technique—I know it well; the music—I love it profoundly but have never played it in public. Have I the right to make a recording under these conditions? I am afraid not. You once told me a truism: 'Don't play only the music you love, but play the music which loves you.' Does Schumann love me? That is the question.

I have asked the organisers in Basel to let me play the Schumann instead of the Grieg, on 16 March, to 'try it out' before London. I only hope they will agree[54]

Dinu toured Switzerland in February and March, receiving enthusiastic acclaim. He also had the joy of meeting again Georges Enesco in Geneva. "Enesco's recital was a great success in Geneva. An exceptional evening, both of us being greatly moved: so many memories, so many unique moments lost forever!"

At this time a great friendship began between him and Igor Markevich. Dinu had already noted this distinguished musician in 1936 when he was a student at the Ecole Normale in Paris. Markevich's Cantata on Milton's *Paradise Lost* had been presented by Nadia Boulanger. "What an extraordinary person" wrote Dinu then, "at the age of 24 to conceive a work of rare grandeur based on one of the most profound themes and give it the treatment of a great master. I was fortunate to have studied the work before so was able to appreciate its magnificent orchestration. Markevich himself adapted the libretto from Milton. It appears that the more he advanced in his work on the Cantata, the more he departed from Milton's text. In the end the composer took many sentences from Goethe and Dante. The public received well the work which was conducted by Markevich himself. Maestro Enesco, who was also in the audience, told me that he liked it very much"[55]

Ten years later, in another letter he wrote: "Igor Markevich has become a fine orchestral conductor since the end of the War and has had many successes in Switzerland. We have grown very close lately and we shall work together almost everywhere during the next season. He is a remarkable musician who will have a brilliant career, his health permitting."[56] Dinu's prediction came true. The following incident which occurred one year later shows the quality of their friendship. Igor Markevich and his wife were expecting a child and long before the birth they had asked Dinu to be god-father. As he was suffering from deep depression at the time, Dinu refused, with the excuse that it was not a good thing for him, in his state, to act as sponsor to a new life. Their mutual friends tried to reassure him that he would get better and that nobody else could be god-father to the child but him. The baptism became a sort of alliance against death which had to be conquered thanks to the love of all those close to Dinu and through his own will to live. The christening of the child, a little girl, symbolically called Allegra, eventually took place with Dinu as the god-father.

In March, April and May Dinu gave concerts in England, Holland and France. His life had become a continuous journey across Europe, bringing new friendships, emotions and crises. In London he recorded the Schumann Concerto under Karajan, as well as Ravel's *Alborada del Gracioso*. The latter is perhaps the only recording with which he was ever totally satisfied.

He also played in Glasgow and did three radio broadcasts of the Concertos by Schumann, Chopin in E minor and Bartók No 3. Two recitals, one on the radio and one at Wigmore Hall, are described by Madeleine: "The Hall was packed with a public anxious to hear the pianist who was already well-known through his recordings released a year earlier. The audience's reaction and his success were a great reward after the sufferings and fears which had been his constant companions during the past four years."

From London Dinu wrote:

> Before leaving London we spent an unforgettable evening at a charming lady's house where we met Ilona Derenburg, an 82-year-old former pupil of Clara Schumann, and intimate friend of Brahms. She was keen to meet me and hear me play. I have always avoided the type of person who passes on the so-called 'tradition' of the great masters, over the years, and ends up with a completely distorted version of their personal messages. Great was my surprise to discover, on the contrary, that in spite of her age, this woman plays the piano divinely and has a prodigious

> memory. She kept us spellbound for more than three hours playing many pieces by Schumann, Brahms, Scarlatti and others. I was surprised by the freedom in her playing, despite using very little *rubato*. I played to her Schumann's *Etudes Symphoniques* and she told me some very interesting things. She was in London during the whole of the Blitz. Her house was hit by a bomb, and she was saved by a staircase under which she had crept clutching her only treasure—the letters from Clara Schumann and Brahms! Very moving![57]

The triumphs continued in Holland and then in Paris.

> The Paris recital was my best this season. The Salle Pleyel was full. The audience sat in complete silence. I offered them fifty minutes of Bach: Toccata in D, four Preludes and Fugues from *The Well-tempered Clavier* and two Chorales. One should never do this, yet I did so without the slightest hesitation. The audience appeared to be so moved that I had to repeat the Bach. Next came Chopin: two Etudes and the *Barcarolle*; and Schumann's *Etudes Symphoniques*. A famous North American impressario came specially to see me and offered me some engagements. He is returning to New York and hopes to present me in the United States at the end of 1949...[58]

Dinu also received offers of contracts for South America, Egypt, Australia, Scandinavia, Spain and many European countries. If one remembers his continuing Swiss tours and his commitments as Professor at the Conservatoire, his activities at this time 'were sufficient to kill a horse!' Despite the turmoil of work Dinu was devoting greater attention to his teaching, having learnt from his own teachers to be very conscientious. He found out a great truth, one which he would not have become aware of but for his work with his students, that 'you learn from teaching'. Later he was to declare: 'Teaching is part of my life.' Indeed, as Madeleine noted, a teacher like Dinu does not have pupils, he has disciples. The essence of his teaching could be summed up in one sentence as he told one of his students: "You have found the spirit of this work, now have the courage to say it aloud and with confidence."[59]

"I have such a deep longing for a quiet and uneventful life. This shows how ungrateful and inconsequential is human nature" writes Dinu to Florica Musicescu during this period. "I believe I have made some progress in musical expression.

I feel that I am freer, more sure of myself and make better use of my time. What else can I say? I am getting older and would love to have finished with these concerts, to get away somewhere in the mountains and have a 'pianistic spring-clean', to learn new works and take a breath before continuing on with my travels."[60]

His health was getting worse again. The colleagues at the Geneva Conservatoire, now his fervent admirers, found a diplomatic solution to lighten the burden of his work. They suggested to Dinu to take an assistant, Professor Louis Hiltbrand, a young colleague with a real teaching vocation, who had been slightly underestimated because he did not have the reputation as a performer. Lipatti, who held the proposed assistant in high esteem, gladly accepted the suggestion and the collaboration proved a fruitful one. Alfred Cortot was to say later on: "We cannot overlook—now that we are trying to emphasize the many aspects of Lipatti's activities which inspired our affection and admiration—the importance of his courses given for several years at the Geneva Conservatoire, when he proved himself an eminent professor of his instrument, as well as a true animator of the musical conscience..."[61]

Dinu Lipatti's appearances on the European musical scene—with resounding echoes in other parts of the world—began to assume a legendary character. It was generally known that he was suffering from an incurable illness, and sometimes a journalist eager to report sensational news actually announced his death. Yet Lipatti's face on publicity posters continued to confront the world with the same calm, serenity and integrity with which he met each audience. His appearances, sometimes unexpected but always welcomed, were interpreted by music-lovers who were his fanatical fans as a hope that his illness might be some sort of macabre joke. No one, except those closest to him, could imagine that he was slowly being destroyed by his illness. The fatigue of his many journeys exhausted his energies, but his total involvement in the unforgettable interpretations, which brought happiness to thousands of music lovers, reached a new spiritual level. Yet in the summer of 1948 he played again in Engadine, as if urged by the same inner need to give as much as possible of himself before leaving this world.

The doctors' orders, which had not always been respected, had to be taken seriously when Dinu's fever refused to abate and the slightest effort left him exhausted and suffocating attacks became more and more frequent. He entered a clinic in Geneva where he underwent seventy sessions of X-ray treatment, and the usual blood transfusions to clear his blood-stream. The summer became a mixture of nightmare alternating with hope. September found him miraculously calm, and he went off to Siels-Maria, in the mountains, but this respite was short-lived. A treatment with a new vaccine failed to yield any results.

On 8 October Dinu wrote to Paul Sacher: "During the past two weeks my health has again been endangered. One evening I discovered two ganglions under my right arm. I did not mentioned this to my wife for about ten days, and was tormented by all sorts of depressing thoughts. I shall finish with the radium treatment on 14 October and will know then whether to despair or not."[62]

"He suffered a small relapse which was caught in time," writes Madeleine on 28 October 1948: "He is taking advantage of this to do some serious work. His illness has matured him and his playing has become even more profound. Each single note contains so much meaning that I have the feeling I can hear him speak."[63]

Inspite of his ordeal Dinu continued to keep in touch with the main musical events in Switzerland: "Segovia playing the guitar gave me one of the greatest emotions of my life. Extraordinary musician and virtuoso." He still had the modesty to believe that his own musical activities were not sufficient, as though sixty concerts planned for the immediate future were an easy feat. Towards the end of the same letter he adds: "It's a strange madness, but I cannot give up... I feel that I have grown in sensitivity during my illness. I do not regret this, but the physical cost has left me permanently weak."[64]

Agents were pestering him all the time. Long tours were proposed in Australia, and no less than three years' work in the United States, without mentioning many European offers. "When I was healthy, I lived from hand to mouth; now that I am ill everybody wants me," declared Dinu with his usual humour. "As to my personal work, eighty percent of my time must go to preparing seven recital programmes and six concertos for Australia, leaving me twenty percent for a composer's ambitions which are continually being thwarted by concert tours and my illness..."[65]

The year 1949 found him in Montana surrounded by devoted friends, including Backhaus. "Exchanges with Backhaus, thousands of new ideas. It is indeed wonderful."[66] At this time Madeleine was, at last, free to marry Dinu when her husband finally granted her a divorce.

Lipatti's inner energy, coupled with his desire to share the radiance of music with his friends, made him feel better. At the very time when his physical resistance was diminishing, he was preparing a less tiring programme: Bach's Partita, Sonata in A minor by Mozart, Two Impromptus by Schubert and all the Chopin Waltzes which he was to record in June. At the same time he was 'warming up' concertos by Mozart, Chopin, Bartók and Schumann to have them ready at his fingertips whenever needed. On 20 January he writes, at the beginning of a tour of the Netherlands: "Health delicate, but quite good. Success everywhere... Next week I play Bartók with Markevitch, and do several recitals. I keep to the same programme of rest so that I can face up to any blows. Have forty concerts to do between now and 2 May."[67]

That evening he suffered a relapse which "was much worse than any previous ones." He left Holland immediately on a train with a special carriage attached to make his journey as comfortable as possible. All concerts were cancelled until November, and he remained in Geneva for the next two months, returning to Montana on 15 April.

The Committee of the Geneva Conservatoire, in the Minutes of 4 April 1949, recorded with great regret the resignation "of this eminent Professor." The Annual Report of the Conservatoire noted: "Fortunately Dinu Lipatti will not leave the Conservatoire altogether since he has promised to hold an annual course for one month devoted to the works of a specific composer. In this way the Conservatoire will still be able to benefit from the art, prestige and fame of this artist, one of the finest musicians of today. For the past five years Lipatti has been one of the glories of the Conservatoire, and thanking him profusely for all he has done we send him our very best wishes for his good health."

Meanwhile, writing to friends from Montana, he comments:

> 29 April 1949... How we despise health when we have it! I have been unable to recuperate during the past year. I must have swallowed all the medicines marketed in the past twenty years. All in vain. The last hope, Yperite, is slow in showing any results. I still have a fever every evening, and cannot work more than half-an-hour every day. I am unable to appear in public for another five or six months, so I console myself by composing. I have finished the Aubade for Woodwind Quartet and, before starting a trio which is running through my mind, I want to put some order into some of my old works. How I wish I could have recorded a series of Chopin's and Bach's music before the autumn. But it does not depend on my will alone....[68]

A letter to Paul Sacher, 1 June, says, "It is not the suffering which eats me up but the constant relapses which never stop. No one can imagine the strain. In this state I cannot play, compose nor even write letters. All I do is read and listen to the radio."[69]

A slight ray of hope made him write, 16 June, to Florica Musicescu:

> My health is improving, and I have started to play and walk a little. No doubt I shall need many months of patience but the treatment does appear to be efficacious, and hope is returning. Many thanks for your valuable words about the Grieg. I'll try to send you the Schumann, but I am sure you will have pages and pages of reproaches to make. In fact I want to remake these recordings next year. Although they are in great demand this does not mean very much. You talk to me of Brahms when this is all I am waiting for. Alas, for the time being, I am not allowed to play anything with heavy dynamics for fear of getting pleuresy again. That is why I'm doing *The Well-Tempered Clavier*, Mozart, a bit of Chopin, and that's all... Have been asked to record the *Indian Fantasy* of Busoni, which I don't really like, and several other pieces, fortunately more interesting, like the Mozart Concerto in C (K467)... My next season will be a quiet one as I have refused all orchestral concerts. The American plans have also been postponed. Maestro Enesco is back again giving his course, as indefatigable as ever. Nikita Magaloff is now my successor at the

Conservatoire. During the next few days my abandoned pupils must sit for their exams, Madeleine helped them with their studies during the month of May.

On 20th August Dinu writes again from Montana:

I have been feeling so well during the past fortnight that I hardly dare believe I may be cured. If the next crisis, which is expected with much trepidation towards the end of the month, fails to materialize, then I may consider the battle won. I can play the piano for three to four hours and do many other things as well. Every morning I run through my sixteen concertos, and go over one of my six recitals so as not to get rusty. In this way I keep my repertoire on the alert. One thing I dread is that as soon as I return to Geneva all my friends, acquaintances and ex-pupils will want to see me, and this will be exhausting. This is why we shall return end of September. I am allowed to give one concert a month...still better than nothing. I shall mainly be making recordings. I am filled with the desire to work and I have many new ideas.
17th September—As was feared, a new crisis has left me immobilized in bed. My artistic projects could be so magnificent if it were not for this miserable health which I must drag around with me. I accept this as a trial which will have served its purpose if I could only learn something from it.[70]

After a slight improvement in his health, Dinu received a visit from his old friend, Cuénod. Together they started to improvise on *The Fables* of La Fontaine in the hall of the sanatorium in Montana. There was no longer any talk of a cure by now—and as though from despair or perhaps as a compensation, he would use up all his creative energy at the first hint of any respite. His art and work gave him no rest and he continued to make plans for studying works and for concerts.

New complications set in: decalcification of the vertebrae with its painful consequences, the blood transfusions had to be increased and the X-ray treatments rose to more than one hundred sessions.

In September 1949 he heard that a visit from his mother, whom he was longing to have near him, had been delayed. This saddened and depressed him and he started to show his bitterness. But the moral strength of his close friends helped him to maintain his self-control. They arranged small intimate concerts to give him a feeling of activity. In a most tactful manner a group of admirers and friends offered him a substantial grant, together with a 'Golden Book' with the signatures of all those who had contributed. The editor of the book refused any fee on the grounds that one could not talk of money when paying homage to Lipatti, the man and artist.[71]

4 Finis Tragediae

Music has lost one of its finest crusaders.
Emil Vuillermoz.

In spite of his exhaustion at the beginning of 1950, Dinu continued to work with dedication. A slight recovery after some desperate measures were taken in his treatment permitted him to return to Geneva and play the Schumann Concerto with Ansermet at the Victoria Hall. Under the headline, *The Return of Dinu Lipatti*, a critic described the event:

> This tenth concert of the season will remain a memorable one, not only because it marks the return of Ernest Ansermet from the United States, but because it also marks the unexpected return of Dinu Lipatti. It is well-known that an insidious illness has kept him away from us for far too long; the absence of this artist from Geneva, which has adopted him, was deeply felt in the concert halls where he had become one of our familiar performers, and at the Conservatoire where his departure created a great void. Lipatti offered us not only the brilliance of a miraculous pianistic technique but a rich personality sparkling with something very pure and radiant. This is what I found again last night while listening to his Schumann Concerto which he interpreted, not only with his usual control and extraordinary crystalline touch, but with a nobility and dignity of feeling which communicated an infinite depth of emotion to the entire audience. It is not difficult to imagine the endless ovation which greeted Dinu Lipatti who, we hope, was fully aware of the unanimous wave of admiration, gratitude and love going out towards him.[1]

More concerts followed in Lucerne, Zurich and Berne. From now on Lipatti's doctor and close friend, Henri Dubois-Ferrière, was always in close attendance. New hopes for recovery occurred in the summer. Lipatti described in various letters sent to Rumania, "the miraculous American drug which was brought specially across the ocean" for him, the first European to try the treatment. Lipatti then proceeded to sketch out his pedagogical ideas during several pianistic consultations and in the project for a 'Course of Interpretation' in which he formulated some of his artistic beliefs resulting from his life-long struggle to reach perfection. These pedagogical notes were to be published posthumously.[2] At the end of May Dr Dubois-Ferrière told Columbia that the moment had come to go ahead with making the recordings, which Dinu had had to postpone so many times, as he was in very good form, but that this could not be expected to last for long. June coincided with the appearance of the new drug—Cortisone. At the same time friends were surpassing each other with offers and proofs of their friendship. He received a new Steinway concert-grand, 'never touched by another hand', and a house was placed at his disposal in a picturesque area near Geneva, with trees and gardens, to remind him of his childhood.

A team from Columbia, headed by Walter Legge, arrived in Geneva with a fully-equipped van. The interval between 3–12 July was like a fire whose flames grow in brilliance before exhausting themselves. Dinu put into these recordings all his love of truth and beauty, all his respect for music and striving for perfection. He recorded, cut, re-recorded, only to start again, dissatisfied, from the beginning. It was exhausting, only to watch, for all those around him. For Dinu, however, the work was like the search for the source of living water in the fairy-tales of his childhood, which the Handsome Prince drinks in order to acquire magical powers with which to overcome the giants. No detail was too small to pass unnoticed or be left to chance. He recorded all the Chopin Waltzes, Bach's Sicilienne (transcribed by Kempff from a Sonata for flute and harpsichord), and Partita in B flat, Mozart's Sonata in A minor, a Chopin Mazurka, several Bach Chorales including the one in G, 'Jesu Joy of Man's Desiring,' which was the last work he ever performed. After these recordings Walter Legge wrote: "He has such a complete physical mastery that he was by nature the 'cleanest' player I have ever worked with."[3]

A letter sent by Dinu from Geneva, on 14 July, was full of optimism. Thanks to the new drug he had been able to com-

An optimistic moment

plete more than half of his recordings. He planned to record Beethoven's *Waldstein* Sonata in October, but this was never carried out.

He spent the summer of 1950 in the little park at Chêne-Bourg where his villa was situated, leading an orderly and concentrated life, planning future programmes, although his seeming good health and vitality started to fluctuate. Fever recurred with exhausting bouts of suffocation. On 23 August he appeared at a public concert, and Madeleine Lipatti wrote to Florica Musicescu:

> He played Mozart's Concerto in C in Lucerne with von Karajan. If you had been there you would have been as moved as I was by the reception of an enthusiastic, almost delirious, audience only a few days after he had been feeling so weak, and the nearness of this concert had only added to his sufferings. He is preparing now for the Besançon recital at the International Festival on 16

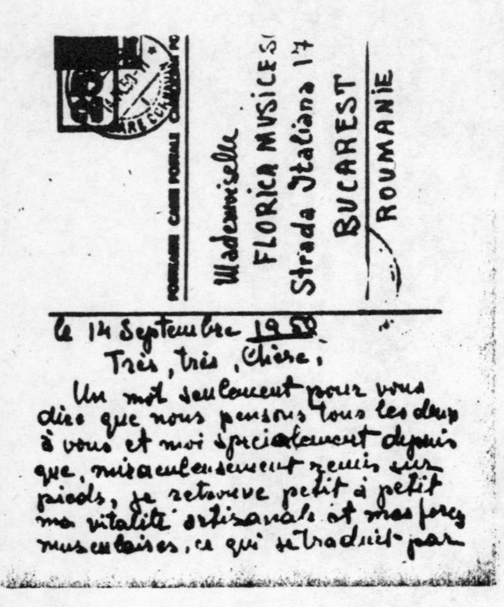

Mademoiselle
FLORICA MUSICESCU
Strada Italiana 17
BUCAREST
ROUMANIE

le 14 Septembre 1950
Très, très, Chère,
Un mot seulement pour vous dire que nous pensons tous les deux à vous et moi spécialement depuis que, miraculeusement remis sur pieds, je retrouve petit à petit ma vitalité artisanale et mes forces musculaires, ce qui se traduit par

His last letter — dated 14 Sept 1950 — addressed to Florica Musicescu

September at 4.30 pm—a concert to be broadcast on all the French stations. We are waiting for pressings of the July recordings: the Mozart Sonata and Bach Partita in B flat which will appear on 'long-playing' discs lasting about thirty minutes each side. This is the first recording of its kind in Europe. It is arranged that we go to England at the beginning of October to record the Concerto in E minor by Chopin with Galliera. There will also be a concert at the Albert Hall, Dinu playing the Schumann Concerto with Furtwängler. There are other projects as well, but everything depends on Dinu's health because one cannot make long-term plans for him. One can only hope.[4]

Dinu's optimism continued, and on 9 September he writes to his mother:

My health is better, I shall continue with the Cortisone for another three months. I finish with the X-ray treatment next Monday and then take the drug sent from across the ocean which is curing my illness. With these three treatments I hope to overcome this illness in two or three months... I have an enormous amount to do. The only trouble with the Cortisone is that it prevents me from sleeping. I go to bed at 11.30 pm and wake up at 5 or 6 in the morning, like you. I do my correspondence, at 8 I have breakfast, at 9.00 I take a short walk, and then I go to my piano. At 12.30, lunch. Another walk in the park, then from 2—4.30 I sleep, make a few visits or go into town; evening meal at 7.30 and back at the piano from 8.30—10.00... We chat or listen to the radio. Nadia Boulanger came for forty-eight hours just to see us. Next April we shall give a course of five public sessions at the Conservatoire. It will be splendid; she will talk, we'll listen to the students, I shall make comments and, afterwards, play to show how the faults should be corrected.[5]

Two days before the Besançon recital Dinu wrote to his teacher, full of hope: "Splendidly back on my feet. Little by little my vitality and my muscular strength are returning. This means using more ample sonorities; it also gives me the hope that in a year's time I shall be able to play those bravura pieces which I thought this accursed illness had forbidden me, forever.... I hope to play about twice a month..."[6]

The Besançon recital—Dinu Lipatti's last concert—could be compared to an ancient rite of sacrifice on the altar of the gods. No one could better describe the atmosphere in which this final concert on 16 September 1950 took place, than his wife, a devoted witness of all his happiness and misfortunes.

Though very ill, he insisted on respecting the Besançon engagement. The doctors tried to convince him to give it up but in vain; he was determined not to break his word. For him giving a concert was proof of his devotion to music which he took very seriously; at the same time he considered it his duty to produce, through music, joy in the souls of those who wished to listen. On the eve of the Besançon concert he arrived in a state of utter collapse and could hardly drag himself to the concert hall to try out the piano. Back at the hotel his state worsened so much that the doctor who accompanied him again tried to persuade him to give up the attempt to play. 'I have promised, and I have to play!'. Several injections were given to revive him. Afterwards, like an automaton, he put his coat on and walked slowly towards the car which was taking him to the hall. There, climbing the stairs was a real calvary as he was choking and on the point of fainting. The public, having arrived from many different places, was overwhelmed with

> emotion. They had come to listen for the last time to this young genius who, everyone knew, had only a short time to live. He gave only one sign of weakness, and this a very moving one—he had no strength left to play the last of the fourteen Waltzes. Broken by fatigue and hardly able to breathe, Dinu had the courage to offer them the Bach Chorale in G which became his swan song...[7]

Music must not be used, it must be served! Dinu Lipatti was serving music for the last time.[8]

A week later Dinu had the joy of seeing his mother again, and of being spoilt and looked after as she had done during "those happy years now gone forever!" His death occurred in an atmosphere of warm family tenderness. The morning of 2 December was calm. A blood transfusion was received with resignation. As Dr Dubois-Ferrière was about to leave, Dinu gave him a disc, with the Bach Partita, recorded in July but only just issued.[9] One of Beethoven's quartets could be heard on the radio as if the genius whose music Lipatti had approached with such deep respect was now coming towards him to lighten his last moments. In the cold silence of that beginning of winter music lost 'one of its finest crusaders'.

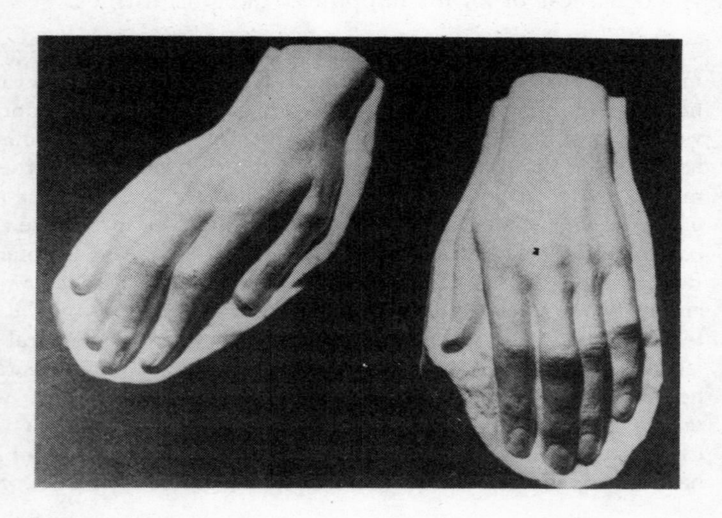

5 The Interpreter

I never asked myself if he was the greatest
because I was convinced he was the best!
Roland Manuel

The development of recording techniques led to musical interpretations being treated as a subject-matter, like composition or aesthetics. Dinu Lipatti's interpretations do not share the fate of Bach, Mozart, Liszt or the great performers of the last century—which remain legends based on hearsay or written testimonials, often arbitrary or vague—but survive today thanks to the micro-grooves of records.

The study of musical interpretation has produced a wealth of information. Complex and sensitive apparatus has tried to measure, analyse and record the most diverse aspects of the vibrations and the sonorous components of a disc in the hope of discovering, like the alchemists of old, the 'elixir' of musical life. The more precise these instruments, the further from the truth are any conclusions as to the laws governing musical interpretation because every interpreter has his own aesthetic principles and these cannot be controlled by laboratory tests nor can they be determined by them.

On the other hand the infinite number of concepts which can be included in the musical phenomenon proves the impossibility of translating it into concepts alone. In the same way any attempt to explain a word does not include its own content which is the *idea* and not the *object*; just as the translating into words of a musical message deprives it of its true meaning. Nonetheless a description in words, of an act of interpretation, does not mean that analysis is futile.

Many detailed analytical studies of each piece recorded by Lipatti have been written. The critic HL de la Grange, in the commemorative *Album* produced by Columbia in 1955, apart

A!

Jeudi 6 Septembre - 20 h. 45

Théâtre Municipal

HOMMAGE A DINU LIPATTI

Musique d'Europe Centrale

Orchestre National de la Radiodiffusion Française
Direction : Georges ENESCO
Solistes : Madeleine DINU LIPATTI et Bela SIKI

PROGRAMME

Première Partie

Allocution par M. le Dr BIDAULT, Vice-Président du Festival

1. Symphonie Concertante pour 2 pianos et Orchestre	**Lipatti**
2. Rapsodie N° 2 en ré majeur	**Enesco**

Deuxième Partie

3. Musique pour cordes, batterie et célesta	**Bartok**
4. « Tziganes », 2e et 3e Mouvements	**Lipatti**

from certain remarks regarding synthesis, noted some important details: the use of pedalling in some fragments, certain pizzicato effects, retakes of phrases in different moods, pregnant rhythmical passes or the emphasis of some modulations, etc. No doubt such an analysis will become more and more useful in later studies of comparative interpretation. In his annotated editions Alfred Cortot writes about the beauty of an interpretation which seems to elude any analysis. This is because the integral value of an interpretation does not depend on any of the various isolated elements of execution but is the product of a general view, of the ensemble of all the means of expression whose equations have the same X's as in any original artistic creation. Yet certain explanations are necessary, not so much to discover the value of the performance but to underline the characteristics of a masterly interpretation.

In Rumanian culture, Lipatti exists on the same plane as Enesco, Brancusi or the poet Eminescu. But his greatness is also universally acknowledged.

His exceptional musical gifts were complemented by a great capacity for work and power of assimilation and by extraordinary physical qualities: unusually large and supple hands reaching, like Bach's, a twelth. He had the fortune to be nurtured in the right musical environment under the guidance of the two teachers, Florica Muzicescu and Mihail Jora, who were both playing decisive roles in establishing a Rumanian school of piano and composition. Through this Dinu received the German musical tradition, both his teachers having studied with Teichmüller in Leipzig, and later on came under the influence of the French tradition while studying with Nadia Boulanger and Alfred Cortot in Paris.

Over the years Lipatti's musical experience was enriched by his contact with the great artistic personalities of the time; Schnabel, Fischer, Toscanini, von Karajan and in particular Georges Enesco, 'the Master of Masters', as he called him. Thus Dinu developed a mature conception about what art is and what varied and complex qualities are expected from a pianist today.

From a technical aspect, as Honegger said, Lippatti was "above all a musician and, secondly, a pianist." Nevertheless, he paid great attention to technique throughout his life, studying specialized treatises on the subject, having endless discussions with his teachers or finding his own ways for perfecting it.

The same attention to detail and the same analytical spirit are found in the preparation for his repertoire and in the approach to the solution of technical problems according to the precepts laid down by Alfred Cortot: by analysing the difficulty of a particular passage rather than the passage itself. To achieve this with as much freedom as possible he paid great attention to fingering, the starting point in any contact with a work. We find in his scores the minutest details and directives with many possible variants. Moreover, similar indications can be seen in the first draft of his own compositions. It is evident that this scrupulous attention to detail was not to reach any simple mechanical solution but to find the best means of artistic expression.

Photographs reproduced in the Columbia Album show Dinu Lipatti in special postures of various movements of the hands or body depending on the work being performed. One cannot talk about the pre-established manner of execution of certain musicians, but about 'a spontaneous reflex action emerging from a true fusion of the inner movements' created by the emotional climate of the piece with the technical pianistic gesture resulting in the actual sounds produced. Dinu Lipatti confesses in a letter that only "the sincerity of the *élan* counts," and admits that during a performance he sometimes notices how he unconsciously 'sheds' all manner of studied physical movements in favour of others more suited to his emotion at that moment. These movements and expressive gestures appear as spontaneous organic growth of the artist's personality and his artistic conception of the work.

In Lipatti's few notes, published posthumously, one sees an attempt to formulate his principles on the art of interpretation. A new aspect of his personality emerges from some of his letters—that of the aesthete and pedagogue. Although these few excerpts do not indicate any definite aesthetic concept or a well-structured method, they express with great sincerity his artistic credo, his scruples and aspirations; above all, the efforts to formulate his own artistic intuitions on a theoretical plane. Only a few months before his death he prepared the outline of a project for a course on interpretation which he was hoping to give at the Conservatoire with Nadia Boulanger. Here are those few pages:

> It is mistakenly thought that the music of any epoch must maintain the characteristics and even the failures prevalent at the time of its creation. The interpreter who adopts this view does so with a clear conscience and thinks himself safe from any dangerous deviations from the truth. But what an effort is needed to rake through the dust of the past and how many useless scruples are necessary before confronting 'the one and only object of our attention'. Trying to bring it to light in a too faithful manner we only end up by drowning it in a flood of prejudices and false data. We must never forget that great and true music transcends its time; moreover, it never conforms to the setting, formulae and rules accepted at the time of its conception. Bach demands the electric organ, with its many devices for playing his organ pieces, Mozart

demands the piano and a different style from that of the harpsichord; Beethoven vigorously calls for the modern piano which did not come in use until Chopin who was also the first to lend it more colour; while Debussy went further by allowing a glimpse of the 'Martenot wave' in his *Preludes*.

The desire to reset the music within the framework of its epoch is similar to dressing up an adult in adolescent clothes. This may appear charming when thinking of a revival, but it can only be of interest to those searching through the dead leaves of the past, or to the collectors of old pipes.

These thoughts came to mind when I remembered the amazement I provoked when playing Mozart's Concerto in D minor, with Beethoven's magnificent Cadenza, at a major European festival some time ago. There can be no doubt that the same themes sounded very differently when fresh from Beethoven's quill! The importance lay precisely in the interesting confrontation between two such different personalities. I must add that, apart from a few enlightened minds, no one understood much about this confrontation; what is more, many accused me of having written that anachronistic and unacceptable Cadenza.

How right Stravinsky was to say that "music lives in the present". Music must be alive in our fingers, eyes, hearts and minds, with everything we have to offer.

Far be it from me to advocate anarchy or scorn for the fundamental laws which govern, in general terms, the co-ordination of any true and valuable interpretation. However, I do believe a grievous error is committed in any search for useless detail as to the manner in which Mozart would have played a certain trill or made a certain turn. The very different indications, often contradictory, left to us in some excellent treatises—already considered dated—lead me firmly along the path of simplification and synthesis. I abide inflexibly by those few basic principles which we all know (or should know, I suppose); but for the rest of the time I rely on my intuition, (that second and most valuable intelligence), as well as on that power to penetrate deeply into a work which, sooner or later, is bound to yield up its own particular truth.

Never study a work with the eyes of the past or of the dead; you may end up with no more than poor Yorick's skull! Casella put it aptly when he said that "we must not be satisfied with respecting great masterpieces, we must love them!"[1]

Lipatti's attitude, so clearly expressed and so often repeated, is that inherent in the creative interpreter whose sincerity is a condition *sine qua non*, is a quality which can only manifest itself by living in the present. As a performer Lipatti approached the works he interpreted with the detachment of a scientist and the intuition of an artist. In this way he realized in his interpretation a fusion between reason and feeling, between premeditation and spontaneous action, a synthesis between the objective character of a musical text and the subjective conception of the work. He expresses his ideas in an interesting letter to a friend, a young South African pianist, who had asked for his advice.

> Our true and only religion, our only unshakeable landmark, must be the *written text*. We must never stray from the text... This must always be *our Credo*, *our Bible*... We must study it, confront it with other editions so that ultimately we can bring to light that image which corresponds with uttermost faithfulness to the initial thought of its creator.
>
> Once this is well established we must never forget that the text, in order to acquire its own life, needs to acquire our life as well. Just as when building a house we must place on top of the concrete foundation of our scrupulous respect for the text everything else required to finish the house: the *élan* of our hearts, the spontaneity, the freedom and the diversity of emotions, and so on.[2]

Dinu has always shown great respect for the works he had to interpret. "He knew what risks he was assuming when approaching a masterpiece," wrote Nadia Boulanger, "and he was always afraid of not being sufficiently prepared to serve it with his whole being, or not to have listened deeply enough to understand its meaning, and perhaps not being worthy of transmitting it as it deserves..."[3]

In a letter to Aloys R Mooser, Lipatti expressed his doubts:

> How is it possible to play without departing from the work to be interpreted? What can one do to avoid being carried away and taking slight liberties which gradually, stealthily, may become unpardonable deviations.
>
> Because of this, there is only one way: to begin again and again, forgetting everything you have done before—phrases, accents, nuances, dynamics, movement, and reconsider the study of the text as if you had never seen it. Surely a certain phrasing tends to deviate more and more from the original thought; an accent or nuance receives an importance which had not been intended when

we first started; the contours of a rhythm become blurred... and these transgressions grow worse with time...[4]

What could have been more edifying than Enesco's amazement, after a concert when Lipatti played his Sonata in F sharp minor: "Dinule, you have interpreted this exactly as I had intended it. I could not have played it better."[5] There is no greater praise for an interpreter than when the composer admits to an exact translation of his own intentions.

To the synthesis between thought and intuition should be added another aspect: the unity between the whole and its components, between striving towards a complete grasp of the work and the care of presenting its structure with the utmost clarity. His continuous preoccupation with detail was mingled with a monumental vision of the work as a whole. When discussing the piano concertos of Grieg or Schumann, he insisted, that "every note must live by itself, contributing in this way to a significant recreation of the work as a whole."[6]

When analysing the musical language of Lipatti, the interpreter, we find that its beauty consists in the simplicity, essence and purity, which is nothing but the reflection a superstructural plan of the artist's personality. In Ansermet's words, "The qualities of this musician are nothing else but a reflection of his moral being."[7] The simplicity of his manner of interpretation does not mean that it is objective or cold, but on the contrary has immense expressive power, all the more poignant because of the economy of its means. These qualities of Lipatti's art never appear as an aim in themselves but as the result of an intuitive response to the essence of the musical phenomenon and of an artistic imagination. Lipatti's musical language is stamped with an authenticity so characteristic that it can be identified from the first few tones. One can even talk of a 'Lipattian timbre' the specific sounds in the context of a given work 'matching' the quality of tone produced through his 'touch'.

Continuing the letter mentioned earlier to his friend, a young pianist, Lipatti points out certain simple and essential 'laws', fundamental to any interpretation:

1. Study of solfège, particularly the rhythmic solfège.
2. Accentuation of the weak beats. (To insist and stress the

strong beat is to commit one of the greatest errors in music because this is nothing else but a diving board towards the weak ones as *these* bear the real weight.)

3. The ignorance of many pianists about the immense possibilities obtained through the independence of various attacks and touches in the same hand being able to produce *different timbres*. By attaining such independence the interpretation immediately stands out in unexpected relief and the playing reflects the timbrual variety and plasticity of an orchestral execution...[8]

Dinu Lipatti's own interpretations are a true demonstration of the principles formulated above. First of all, one must underline his perfect rhythmical precision which seems to reflect the characteristics of his own personality: precision and clarity. Let us recall the Finale of the Schumann Concerto, or Ravel's *Alborada del Gracioso*.

The accenting of the weak beats is illustrated in several ways. Sometimes this is achieved by a definite accent demanded by expression or phrasing which cannot take into account the strong beats in the bar. The metric accent and the measure are useful theoretical conventions, but these sometimes hinder the expressiveness of musical language. We find such an example in the theme of the first Movement of the Schumann Concerto, or in its recapitulation in C major, where the measure appears 'displaced' because of the rhythmic accent. (Accents and other markings in parenthesis do not exist in the score but *represent* Lipatti's own interpretation).

In the second theme of the Finale, especially in the concluding phrase with its characteristic rhythm, Dinu Lipatti gives its true acentuation and phrasing, transforming the $\frac{3}{4}$ measure into $\frac{3}{2}$:

The same type of accentuation is noticeable in Mozart's Concerto in C. Here is a fragment of the Finale:

In other places, weak beats are slightly prolonged, taking on an important expressive role. This device is often met when his playing of Chopin's works achieves that fine *rubato*, simple and sober, which cannot be marked on the score. Occasionally he makes use of this device in Grieg, Liszt, Schumann, Schubert and even Mozart (see *Andante* of the Sonata in A minor.)

On the other hand, when he considers that the interpretation demands a perfect equality of duration for each sound, this is achieved with amazing precision. A simple experiment will confirm this: if we listen to any rapid passage, (for instance, the *Allemande* of Bach's Partita in B flat), played at a slower speed than that of the recording, the evenness of every single note remains perfect throughout the passage, a rare occurrence with other pianists.

Finally, the accentuation of weak beats must be understood as a continuous expressive faculty of the beats, each sound being imagined as an anacrusis of the following one. This is how Lipatti realized that unique continuity in the melodic lines, like the human voice; a difficult feat to achieve on the keyboard. To this he adds his perfect knowledge of the laws of resonance resulting in a refined and careful use of the pedals.

The refinement of Lipatti's pedalling allows us to feel the growth of the sounds produced, and more importantly, he makes us hear them as though they belong to the human voice. In fact, it becomes a process of integration of sounds created by the intended emotional climate when the actual tones lose their individuality and become part of the whole work. The cantabile quality of his touch can be explained by the science with which Lipatti makes use of dynamics and the relationship between nuances. The intensity of sounds, with their *crescendi* and *diminuendi*, is realized with an exactness of scientific proportions: nothing is vague, everything is chiselled in detail, note after note achieving such a well-proportioned relationship to various intensities that one cannot believe a piano with hammers is being played. It is more like the continuity obtained by stringed instruments with one movement of the bow. Claude Debussy's ideal is realized when Lipatti makes one forget that the piano is a percussive instrument. This is what a graphic representation of the sounds in the fragment of a melodic line from the Chopin Valse No 2 in A flat, would look like:

One notices that the last sounds achieve a continuous succession as regards dynamics, the intensity of the vibrations of each sound fading away towards the next note. This type of dynamic treatment, with the same exactness, is often met with in Lipatti's interpretations. The pianist achieves a dynamic range of rare elasticity and richness without ever making use of exaggerated nuances.

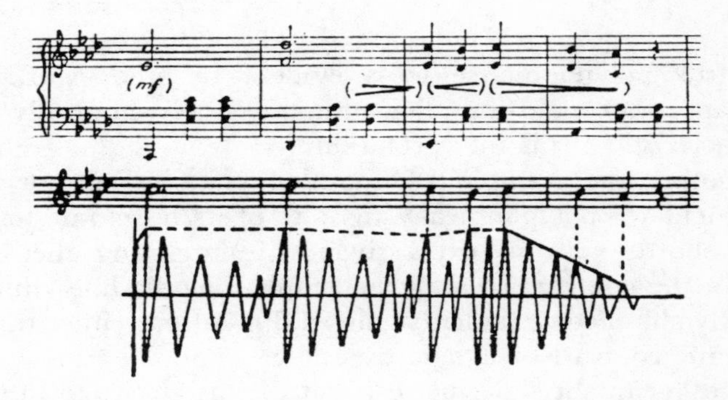

Furthermore, it is known that through dynamic-agogic treatment the piano can produce certain effects of subtle differentiation of timbres. This is the 'third law' mentioned by Lipatti when he refers to the possibility of creating a variety of sonorities and colours. For instance, in the interpretation of Ravel's *Alborada del Gracioso*, he creates authentic orchestral sonorities and it seems that each instrument has a completely different colour emphasized with amazing clarity. The same effects occur when bringing out the different voices in Bach's polyphony. Consider the three sonorous plans in the Chorale in F minor:

or the Chorale, 'Jesu Joy of Man's Desiring',* where the main voice 'meanders' unhindered through all the other voices.

Lipatti's polyphonic sense is evident in other works and perhaps one could say that thinking 'polyphonically' is a characteristic of his interpretation.

Another fine example is Chopin's Sonata in B minor which he elucidates polyphonically in spite of its harmonic texture. The chords gain in expressiveness, integrating themselves within the context, creating an ample melodic line while the equally chiselled ornaments gain in dimension, either through dynamic contrast or agogic treatment.

Another quality specific to Lipatti is his ability to interpret styles and works of great diversity with equal competence. As convincing in Bach as in Brahms, in Scarlatti as in Schumann, in Schubert as in Ravel, he was also an outstanding Mozart player as well as a rare interpreter of Chopin. From his motto: "If you wish to approach a work it is not sufficient to love it,

* In G, No 10. Finale of the Cantata BWV 147. Transcribed for the piano by Myra Hess

it must also love you"—we realise that this capacity to grasp different styles of music sprang from deep roots. This explains his amazing improvisations which, according to witnesses, sounded like authentic works by Scarlatti, Bach, Chopin and others, so perfect was the integration of each style with its particular emotional climate.

Looking at the recordings left by Dinu Lipatti we discover that only a fraction of his vast repertoire remains but what exists is of immense value. Bach's music was loved, studied with passion and hardly ever absent from his recital programmes. He would bring out the profoundly human element in the music, often creating organ or harpsichord sonorities. Perhaps no other composer has ever demanded such freedom within a disciplined framework as Bach. In his sober music, Lipatti displays profound sensitivity, his objectivity is only on the surface. He is discreet and full of awe and one can realise that when listening carefully to the inflexions in the dynamics, it is evident that Lipatti makes use of a great and intense 'affect' with minimal means of expression.

The first great work to be discussed must undoubtedly be Bach's Chorale in G, 'Jesu Joy of Man's Desiring', which became the leit-motif of Lipatti's life. He played it at his first recital in Paris and at his last concert in Besançon, which was recorded, but not released until he had listened to several different versions, shortly before his death. When studying Lipatti's interpretations one cannot help thinking of Tolstoy's remark, that it was not the sound that one heard but that into everyone's soul poured a marvellous torrent of poetry as though known by all for a long time and only expressed for the first time.

Returning to the Bach, we must mention the extraordinary rendering of the Siciliana of the Sonata No 2 for flute (in Wilhelm Kempff's transcription), or the Gigue of the Partita No. 2 in B flat, totally liberated from the usual Bach interpretations. The decrescendo on a broad line is remarkable and its dying away follows parallel with the emotional intensity.

Scarlatti is played with perfect evenness and crystal clarity. Full of brilliance and with incisive rhythms, Lipatti's pianism shows at the same time an extraordinary spontaneity. He always felt especially drawn towards Scarlatti and actually made several successful transciptions of his Sonatas for Wind Quintet.

Mozart is represented by two important works: Sonata in A minor K.310, written in Paris during a period of distress and disillusionment in which the dramatic torment heralds Beethoven, while the lyrical and passionate development contains the seeds of romanticism; and the Concerto for piano and orchestra in C major K.467 (with Lipatti's *Cadenzas*) which equal in importance the D minor K.466, A major K.488 and C minor K.491 Concertos. All were written in Vienna in 1785 and 1786, a few years before the composer's death and are examples of Mozart's new style of composition, more intimate and profoundly dramatic, after he became obsessed with the thought of death and could only maintain his equilibrium through the joys of creation.

The Sonata in A minor exists in two different versions: one made in July 1950, and the other in September of the same year when he played it at that memorable last concert in Besançon.

If we compare the recordings we observe the same treatment of the dramatic structure and general conception. But, somehow, the later one seems inspired with a more authentic and convincing participation. Both interpretations reflect certain characteristics of Lipatti's pianism. The *appogiaturas* are slightly slower with varied and subtle expression and a very discreet *rubato* emphasises melodic lines without ever falling into any sort of romanticism which he studiously avoids. This is even more noticeable in the Andante of the Concerto in C; the repeated notes acquire varied dynamics, trills are like a *vibrato* with inflexions of nuances of amazing agogic evenness and the use of polyphony is exceptionally well realized. We could talk of a 'polyphony of dynamics', no matter what the structure of the work, when following the precision with which the intensity of each sound is achieved.

In all the works which appear in several versions, as in this particular Sonata, we observe a similarity in execution, noticeable in the smallest details. Far from being the result of any prefabricated interpretation this reflects the degree to which Lipatti would go in order to attain his conception of a work, 'resting' on his ideas without ever becoming detached.

Yet there is always a renewal of the freshness with which he approaches the same piece, each time.

In the Concerto in C the same characteristics are evident as regards Mozart's style—dramatic accents are given with extreme precision in contrast to the moments of serene expression. Here is a fragment from the *Andante* where Lipatti, in the last year of his life, smiles to us through tears of pain like Mozart, his brother in suffering.

"It is no longer the sound of a piano", said von Karajan, "but music in its purest form."[9]

Among the Romantics it appears that Dinu had a special affection for Chopin, judging from his concert programmes, recordings and projects for future programmes which he sketched out as late as 1957.

Contemporary musicologists consider Lipatti as one of the most representative interpreters of this great Romantic composer. All annotated discographies unanimously describe Lipatti's recordings as unsurpassed. The French musicologist, Robert Aguettant, in his book on *Chopin*,[10] had this to say:

> Lipatti's recordings head the list of Chopin discography and should have the first and foremost place in the entire history of the disc. The age of these records, from the end of the "78's" era, does not detract from their musical perfection—they are incomparable and exemplary. What matters here, where age is immaterial, is an absolute pianistic perfection serving a conception in which stylistic

purity and divine intuition become one. Never was the union between freedom and discipline, between poetry and a majestic and transcendental virtuosity better realized.

After one of Lipatti's concerts Toscanini exclaimed: "At last we have a Chopin without caprices and with the *rubato* to my liking;" and a French critic, after listening to a Lipatti recital wrote: "I listened to Chopin himself interpreting his Sonata in B minor."[11]

Dinu's interpretation of Chopin's music is very personal. He approaches the great Polish composer of the Romantic School with a classical conception. No matter how paradoxical such a union may seem, we must admit that the integration of specifically romantic material within a classical discipline does not lead to a lowering of its artistic value but, on the contrary, emphasises it. Many pianists try to express Chopin's emotions in an exaggerated manner, while others, more reticent go to the other extreme. Lipatti achieves a unique equilibrium, revealing the emotional world of Chopin's works with nobility, simplicity and purity, stressing in this way its profound essence. At the same time he invokes Bach's polyphony with pre-classical precision, the purity of Mozart and even Beethoven's dramatic power. This does not imply a deviation from romantic feeling but a more complete and philosophical perception. The recording of Chopin's Nocturne No. 8 in D flat, Op 27, the only one left by Lipatti, is considered in all annotated discographies as the finest available. With exquisite artistry the pianist reveals the ideal traits of the soul passing from intimacy to drama, from tenderness to reverie. The complete set of recording of the Chopin Waltzes represents one of the most valuable achievements in the musical discography. By recording the Waltzes in a different order from the composer's own chronology, Lipatti aimed at complementing one Waltz with the next through the similarity or contrast between tonal planes and emotional climates. A unity is achieved in this way and they become a musical poem dedicated to the waltz. His interpretation, so different from the traditional one, is endowed with a classical and pure soberness which recreates Chopin's own austere principles, so often forgotten today.

The recording of the Sonata in B minor has been unanimously acclaimed as a landmark in the interpretative art of our time. Prodigiously structured, the Sonata has a unity never equalled before. The purity of the melodic line with its sincere *élan*, discreet *rubato*, polyphonic clarity, the dramatic feelings framed within an impetuous rhythm, all serve to enhance the presence of the interpreter. This recording was chosen unanimously by the Jury of the Charles Cros Academy for the Grand Prix du Disque, 1949.

H. L. de la Grange comments: "This is not the moment to make an analysis of Lipatti's Chopin recordings, nor to show in detail those qualities and refinements which conquer and move the listener... Everything appears simple, alive and natural... The works are played in a lyrical and intimate atmosphere of chamber music, thus, offering us moments of beauty which we have never known before or have forgotten..."[12]

We must not omit to mention the posthumous recording—in the series released by Columbia—of the Chopin Piano Concerto in E minor, Op 11. This is a re-edited recording which requires some discussion. According to the laconic note on the cover, the recording was made in 1948, but there is no mention of any orchestra or conductor, nor is there any commentary about the interpretaion. During 1947 Lipatti had recorded the Grieg Concerto with Alceo Galliera and the London Philharmonic Orchestra; only one month previously he recorded the Schumann Concerto with Herbert von Karajan and the same orchestra. This proves that he was in a good period of artistic activity which was being followed with great interest by the musical world. How is it possible, therefore, that until now there has been no explanation for the failure to identify the orchestra and conductor of this Chopin Concerto? (See *Appendix 1*)

Whatever the reasons, one thing is certain: Dinu Lipatti would never have agreed to the release of this particular recording knowing his serious and scrupulous attitude towards his art. It is possible that the recording was made, without Lipatti's knowledge, during a rehersal when an artist does not expand his complete emotion and sensitivity. How can one overlook the dozens of versions which Lipatti tried out before making any final and decisive recording? And one must not forget Lipatti's many reservations, expressed in letters to his family and teachers, about records which were considered summits of contemporary interpretation. Can it be mere coincidence that, during this time, there is no mention in any of Dinu's letters about recording Chopin's Concerto while all his other recordings are described in detail?

These considerations would be of little importance if the quality of the interpretation could have reached the high standard established by Lipatti himself. To our deep regret this is not so. We do not find the same imposing sound in the bass which constituted Dinu's harmonic foundation: we do not find the leonine amplitude of chords and the clarity of polyphonic texture, nor the amazing sonorous palette whereby the modulations were defined while the brio of the technical passages with their fine filigree work is absent. At the same time one misses a certain grandeur in the structure of the work and his unique end of phrases which always had a stillness born from an inner necessity and one cannot find the 'Lipattian touches' with its characteristic sonarities. At the same time one cannot deny certain qualities which might have made many pianists proud of this recording; a sustained accuracy, a sober rendering which avoids any facile slip into cheap romanticism.

Considering the above points we wonder whether, in order to popularize certain stages of an artist's realization, though justified by its documentary or pedagogical value, such an act may not also constitute an unjust indiscretion, a crude intrusion into the sublime effort of artistic creation. How would one judge an exhibition of sketches that had been thrown away into the wastepaper basket by a dissatisfied artist? Ultimately, there can be only one supreme judge—the *Music Lover*, and all these considerations are addressed to him.

Among the recordings of pieces with an atmosphere of intimacy and lyricism one must include those by Liszt, Brahms and Schubert. Liszt's *Sonnet 104 by Petrarch*, the *Cadenza* in Grieg's Concerto and *Alborada del Gracioso* by Ravel are probably the very finest records of Lipatti's interpretative art. It is quite possible that the affinites of this great pianist, difficult to define because of his versatility with many different styles, inclined towards Liszt, the eagle of the Romantic era.

The *Petrarch Sonnet* brings out all the characteristics of Lipatti's pianism and achieves a superb balance in fluctuations of tempi, a most difficult feat to attain. While the *Etude de Concert No 2: Gnomenreigen* is an unedited recording from Bucharest's Radio-Television Documentary Records Library, it reaches a standard which can only be compared with Rachmaninov's recording. The speed of the piece demands a Lipatti to perform it as there are successive sonorities which surpass the limits of the audibility of consecutive sounds. This forced Lipatti to find special means for its execution. He actually transformed the *appogiaturas* and the melodic intervals of 32nds into harmonic intervals as in Example 9, returning gradually and unobtrusively to the melodic intervals where the *tempi* permit.

Lipatti aims at a sonorous projection of the score, not its visual aspect, and brilliantly illustrates the basic principle of any creative interpretation which is to put "the spirit" before "the letter" of a text.

In the Brahms Intermezzi (recorded in Paris, in 1936 at the Ecole Normale de Musique) we can hear Lipatti during the period of his apprenticeship. Certain changes occur in the score, possibly imposed by the short length of the record, which are carried out so that they become an organic part of the agogic dynamic shape of the interpretation, and would pass unnoticed unless one paid scrupulous attention to the score. The interpretation can be described as enjoying great agogic freedom. The metric rhythm is sacrificed in favour of an inner rhythm and phrasing which flow with an admirable musical logic, at times nostalgic, at other times impetuous. Dinu does not yet possess the depth of his later achievements but speaks with all the sincerity and poetry of his nineteen years. Brahms's seven Waltzes op 39 and *Liebeslieder Waltzer* op 52 (with vocal quartet) played as a Duet for 4 hands on one piano by Dinu Lipatti with Nadia Boulanger, also during his studies in Paris, are another example of an admirable collaboration between the two artists—teacher and student—in the service of music.

The two Schubert Impromptus, recorded during Lipatti's last Besançon recital, are played with an unbelievable assurance and power of expression considering the state of his health at the time. It is a moving coincidence that the Impromptus, written during the last years of Schubert's life, could not have been better understood by any artist other than Lipatti. When he gave his last recital his rendering of the Impromptu in G flat, full of torment and suffering, reminds us of his poignant confession to Madeleine shortly before he died, that he gained in sensitivity during his illness which is why he did not regret it...

In concerto-playing, the integration of the piano with the instruments of the orchestra is so complete that it is inopportune to speak of the interpreter's knowledge as to when to be in the limelight and when to withdraw. The piano becomes an organic part of the whole and is never separate from the orchestra. Even the Cadenzas are not isolated but continue to be part of the structure of the work. The conception is so well crystallized, the interpreter so poised and in command of his ideas, that every passage is realised in the exact and intended climate, yet each moment retains its own character. As an example, the *Andante Espressivo* in the First Movement of Schumann's Piano Concerto leading to a *tempo primo* which, in most interpretations, does not maintain its character because the player anticipates the dynamics of the mood of the following passage:

When referring to the amplitude of Lipatti's sonorities it is no longer a question of his art or knowledge of how to make use of the qualities of the instrument but of the consequence of the psychological tension created by his conception of a work. The Finale of the Schumann Concerto illustrates this point very well for it is unlike other interpretations which exaggerate its intensity without achieving the same result.

In the second part of the Concerto one is aware of a certain inner agitation tending towards a faster tempo. As compensation for this tendency, which cannot be realized because the orchestra implacably maintains a slower tempo, the soloist allows himself some agogic freedom by bringing in some extra *arpeggios* to round out the flow of the melodic lines; or an occasional dynamic insistence to involve the orchestra which is quite unusual for Lipatti. A letter written by Lipatti at the time of the recording reveals, with 'his' usual modesty, this divergence with regard to the conception of the interpretation: "Alas! I did not count on an unexpected factor, a remarkable but superclassical conductor who, instead of helping my timid romantic *élans*, put a brake on my good intentions."[13] Similar remarks regarding the tempo have been made by some critics when discussing the Concerto in D by Mozart, played in Lucerne with the same conductor. (See *Appendix 2*)

Critics have often mentioned the 'saving' of the Grieg Concerto by Dinu Lipatti's masterly interpretation. His exceptional realization consists in his having conceived and recreated at a very high level the entire artistic potential of this work. He approached the work in all its simplicity, "as it is", without making it artificial by adding too much weight or by treating it too lightly, but by bringing to it spontaneity, robustness and complete sincerty. One must mention the Cadenza in the First Movement, one of the most beautiful moments in contemporary pianistic art, through its unity of structure, gradual emotional tension and integration within the whole of the Concerto. In the dynamic climaxes one has the impression that the steely fingers of the pianist have become incandescent. The realization of this Cadenza is of such a high artistic standard that one holds one's breath in case it cannot be maintained. But it is, and encountered again in other aspects. The tumultuous and dramatic Lipatti of the First Movement becomes serene in the *Adagio*, reaching an Olympian calm. Dynamic inflexions are very rich, with *crescendi* and *descrescendi* which only the human voice can achieve, and a masterly control of the various planes. The *Finale* integrates incisive rhythm with lyricism, calm with vitality. In the middle section there is an open romantic tendency which had been unnoticed before. It is more than sentiment, a true spiritualisation transcending the affect.

The only composer of the French School recorded by Lipatti is Ravel. *Alborada del Gracioso* was one of 'his' pieces and together with *La Vallée des Cloches* became part of many recital programmes. The realization of *Alborada del Gracioso* is perhaps the most characteristic example of his orchestral colouring. One can hear sounds suggesting the guitar, string instruments, castanets, tambourines, or wind instruments with certain staccato effects. This is possible through the Dinu's profound knowledge of all the expressive possibilities of the piano, and of the orchestra.

Thus, when the composer indicates a *mordent* demanding the first note to be held, he probably had in mind a *vibrato* effect of the mandoline, and this is achieved by repeating the third note with a very discreet nuance. This does not reflect any technical deficiency but, on the contrary, a desired effect.

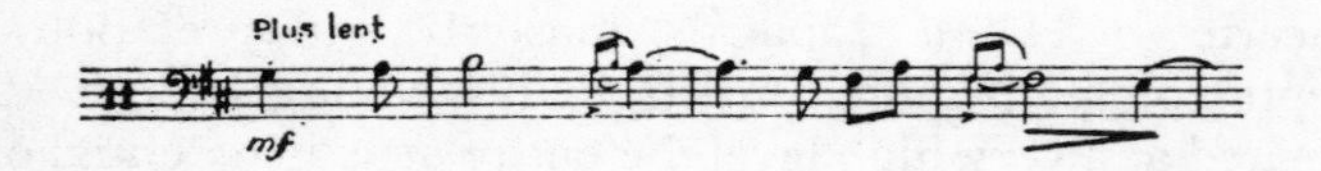

What is amazing is the variety of sonorous planes with distinct timbres, with stereophonic effects and extraordinary changes of moods occurring sometimes in very short fragments, the whole creating a kaleidoscopic image of rare diversity within its unity. The *glissandos* in fifths and thirds reach an uncanny technical perfection with an infinitesmal dynamic gradation and fluidity, while the repeated notes give a *vibrato* effect by their intensity.

Associating these musical impressions, together with the composer's programme indications about the title of the piece *El Gracioso*, a grotesque picture of a buffon is to be seen furtively 'riding' on an *ostinato* rhythm which becomes, with malicious irony, the leit-motif in a variety of landscapes and personages belonging to the Iberian world.

Whenever taking part in Rumanian musical festivals at home or abroad, Dinu Lipatti always included pieces by Rumanian composers in his programmes—Georges Enesco,

Mihail Jora, Mihail Andricu, Paul Constantinescu, Sabin Dragoi, Marcel Mihalovici and others. Unfortunately, only very few recordings of Enesco's works remain, and only a few of his own pieces.

During his studies in Paris Dinu made a recoding of the Second Movement, *Presto vivace*, of Enesco's Sonata No 1 in F sharp minor. Although only a matrix made in modest technical conditions, one can appreciate the pianist's masterly conception of the work with its gradually developing dramatic intensity framed by an impeccable rhythmic discipline.

His understanding of Enesco's style is even more evident in the *Bourrée* (Suite No 2 in D, Op 10). His execution and masterly interpretation combine to make a perfect fusion.

In the Sonata No 3 in D, Op 24, Lipatti covers a complex series of wide-ranging problems, from the clarity and simplicity of the pre-classics to contemporary tonal polyvalence and rhythmic intensities, surpassing ordinary pianistic tones to obtain a rich and authentic orchestral palette, as in Ravel's *Alborada*. The varied timbres achieved by dynamic contrasts and pedalling effects suggest the sounds of a 'caval' (a long pipe played by shepherds), cow-bells, alphenhorn, *pizzicato* effects, many kinds of bells with high and low registers which are organically integrated within the rhythmic and melodic structure of the work. The First Movement has almost Scarlattian sonorities adapted to Rumanian folkmusic. In his technical execution one detects an impressionistic climate coupling with the same feeling for folkmusic.

Only Enesco's Sonatas Nos 2 and 3 for violin and piano remain from Dinu's period as a chamber-music player, with the two great artists performing together. Their collaboration in the Sonata No 2 in F minor gives an impression, not only of perfect synchronisation, but of a wonderful fusion of intention, inner rhythm and spiritual and affective climate. In the well-known Sonata No 3, with its Rumanian popular style, the above characteristics become even more pronounced; at moments it becomes difficult to identify the instruments without consulting the score. This is due not only to the musical structure in which both instruments are alternately playing the component parts of a phrase, but to the art in the realization of nuances and the manner of stressing each tone;

there is a true reciprocal and 'continual substitution' in which the two instruments become 'one' with new sonorities. A characteristic example appears to the last page of the Second Movement when an authentic Rumanian atmosphere is created and the sounds of the 'caval' can be heard:

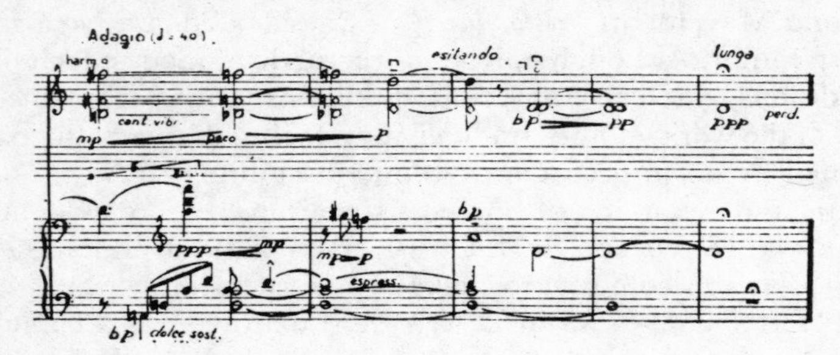

We can hear Lipatti playing his own compositions only in two recordings: *Sonatina for Left Hand* where polyphony and a varied sonorous colouring is superbly achieved with one hand; and the *Concertino in Classical Style* where the classical eloquence and soberness in the First and Second Movements combine happily with the modern humour of the Third Movement, and the infectious optimism of a popular dance in the Fourth Movement.

It is said that no one understands the meaning of a work better than its creator. In Lipatti's case one is confronted with a 'self-portrait' in which his pianism, ideas and ideals come to the fore. His whole being is revealed. The foundation and structure of his compositions, together with the unity of his interpretations, show his equilibrium and sense of order. The variety of different emotional climates reflects his complex personality and a profound grasp of fundamental musical values. At the same time, the humorous moments touching on the grotesque, particularly in the Concertino, show an optimistic, happy side of his disposition, occasionally tinged by an unmalicious irony. A lively atmosphere, coloured by popular vigour, as sketched in the Concertino and fully developed in the Sonatina indicates, once again, Lipatti's attachment to his native soil, his people, and the place of his childhood.

Thus we can say that through his recordings, Lipatti has left us his autobiography. It is up to us to understand it.

6 The Composer

I shall always maintain that his renown as an interpreter should not overshadow his image as a composer
Georges Enesco

From his earliest years Dinu Lipatti showed a special aptitude for composition. As Ernest Ansermet remarked, "for him to compose was just as natural as to play the piano, and Dinu possessed that rare gift of the born composer who does not sit down at his desk in order to 'search', but in order to 'find'."[1] Very early on he succeeded in 'finding' the right sonorous progressions on the piano to express musically various family scenes or portraits of family friends. Guided with care and understanding, his creative talent did not stop at the stage of an *enfant prodige* but developed harmoniously towards artistic fulfilment until illness sapped his strength and prevented his finding a clearly defined individual style and a unified conception in his compositions.

PIANO COMPOSITIONS

It was only natural for Dinu Lipatti, the pianist, to relate directly to the piano in his compositions. One third of his works are written exclusively for this instrument, while more than half of his entire output has the piano participating, either in chamber music or as an accompanying instrument.

Lipatti's first compositions date from the age of three, and by the time he was five he had completed his first "opus". Each piece bore a suggestive title—*A Quarrel in the House*, *Spring*, *Cradle Song*, etc., and these pieces were written down just as Dinu played them by a teacher, Paschill, at his fathers request. This first manuscript illustrates the budding talent of the very young Dinu before he could even read music. He appeared as

"composer and improviser," playing some of these pieces for the first time in 1922, at a charity concert.

Looking through one of these early manuscripts, now kept in the Rumanian National Library, one notices an attractive diversity of subject-matter as well as a great sense of harmony, modulation, phrasing and form. *A Song for Granny* is full of tenderness, written in binary form (molto andante-allegretto) and the harmonies are remiscent of some of Schumann's pieces in the *Album for the Young*. Here is a short fragment:

The *March of the Urchins* has an A B A form (as well as the tonal plan: G-E minor-G) and has a Polka rhythm with evident folk elements. This is a fragment from the B section:

Particularly interesting because of its inspiration from folk music is the piece *For my Nannie, Surcea*, with its syncopated rhythm and asymmetric structure of phrasing. At the end of the manuscript is the opening of a little *Valse*, pencilled in by Dinu himself. In this childish and clumsy writing one can already see a clear conception of an introduction, *Vivace*, followed by a *tempo di valse*, which are melodious and well harmonised. There are even quite well-placed indications for pedalling.

The first serious work was the *Sonata for Piano Solo* (1932) written while Dinu was still studying with Mihail Jora. A promising work, it bears a suggestive but naive motto—"Music is the language of the Gods". The piece did not escape the influence of those most admired Romantic composers, Chopin and Liszt, and it obtained First Mention at the 1932 Enesco Competition. Thereafter Dinu started to write for other instruments, attempting new musical styles. With Jora's encouragement he turned towards Rumanian folk music. Later on, while attending the Ecole Normale de Musique, he wrote *Nocturne* (1937) on a Moldavian theme, a composition of small proportions, yet representative of a young student's search for his identity. According to Rodica Oana-Pop,[2] a musicologist from Cluj, the *Nocturne*, still in manuscript in the possession of his friend, Miron Soarec, is written in a contemporary style combining classical polyphonic elements with impressionistic harmonies. Though still under the influence of Enesco's music, Lipatti was making a conscious effort to find his own individual language. Here is the theme based on a Christmas Carol from the Piatra Neamtz region (where Miron Soarec spent his childhood) as it appears in the first measure:

Three Dances for Two Pianos, composed in the same year and dedicated to Madeleine Cantacuzino, goes further in the blending of comtemporary idiom with specific Rumanian motives which often reappear and are absorbed into the musical langage.

The first *Dance* begins with an *ostinato* on the second piano imitating the sounds of the *tzambal* (zither). Over this base Piano I presents the first theme, a very rhythmical dance:

One must note the recurrent pattern of E, D, C, a device which often occurs in Lipatti's music. This theme, together with the more sprightly second one, reappears in modified rhythms and both are developed in motivic divisions and then return to the initial stage. The second section of the *Dance* introduces a new theme in arpeggios over a repeated D in the bass (pedal point), with a timbre which recalls the 'cimpoiu' (an instrument of the bagpipe family) similar to that in the *Andante* of Enesco's Sonata No 3 for Violin and Piano (from bar 11 onwards...). Before the tonal end of the *Dance* another musical idea is brought in with a pronounced modal character, over an ostinato bass in thirds and fourths in Prokofiev style.

The second *Dance* is written in ternary form with a characteristic atmosphere of liveliness and excitement. Here and there one senses the influence of Enesco's pianistic writing, while in the second section, *doppio movimento*, a clear idea develops as a vocal recitative with echoing imitations.

The third *Dance* is not in the manuscript in the Rumanian National Library, though the title on the cover is written in by the composer himself. The *Three Dances* were first performed and played by the composer and Smaranda Athanasof at a recital at Ateneu on 16 December 1939.

With this work Dinu began a series of compositions for two pianos, a combination which particularly appealed to him. In 1938 his *Suite for Two Pianos* used the dances again, with the addition of some elements from *Burlesque*, a sketch for a ballet. In *Two Romanian Folk Dances* (1939), the popular element is clearly stated in the title and constitutes the direct source of inspiration.

Lipatti's three *Nocturnes* for piano (1939) show obvious French influences. He actually referred to them as "French" and they express the composer's sensitivity, lyricism and inclination towards meditation. Only one of the *Nocturnes* is still known, that in F sharp minor, published by Salabert. It has ostinato patterns and some characteristic imitations, but the pianistic structure is rather heavy.

Fantasia for Piano (1940) appears as Lipatti's most developed pianistic composition, a work with real substance. In the introduction to the booklet, *Hommage à Lipatti*, his wife remarks that the *Fantasia* is "an important work which the composer hoped to develop into a symphony". In the original manuscript there are some notes regarding the orchestration of the work, and the length of the piece confirms this suggestion.

The *Fantasia* has five parts, all very different in structure and character. The first, *Andante Malinconico*, begins with a free introduction in an Enescian atmosphere. A *Vivace* follows which does not show anything new in the composer's development: a freely contoured polyphony based on richly decorated and undulating themes. The second part—*Molto Tranquillo* contains a fine example of heterophony.[3]

The central section, *Presto*, is reminiscent of Prokofiev. A series of great sonorites lead to a climax, and and is followed by a long resolution of the tension, after which the initial episode reappears enriched by a figuration of sixteenths (semiquavers) in sequences. The third part, also *Presto*, is a lively and developed Scherzo. The fourth, *Allegretto Cantabile*, has a discreet Rumanian flavour with the calm development of a continuous melody treated in a classical manner. The last part, after an agitated *Allegro* with great dynamic outbursts, ends with a *Maestoso* regaining the serene tranquility of the beginning. Here are the first few bars:

Fantasia for Piano represents a step forward in Lipatti's pianistic creation, although it has an uneven structure and a certain lack of proportion. This is how the composer described the work in an interview in 1941: "In the introduction one notices two generating elements for the entire piece. The first has a nostalgic character while the second is passionate, daring and tormented. Two movements follow which, together with the introduction, constitute the first part. The Finale is in sonata form and leads to the expressive development of the two basic elements".[4] This work received its first performance by the composer at a concert of Rumanian music on 12 May 1941 in which Georges Enesco also took part.

Sonatina for Left Hand was written to commemorate two anniversaries: Enesco's 60th and Jora's 50th birthdays. It is inspired by folk music, "purely Rumanian themes and with much *brio*", as Lipatti described it.[5] The *Sonatina* has three movements of modest proportions. The first and third, in sonata form, present no ample development. The second, based on a simple and nostalgic *cantilena* with true Rumanian characteristics (asymmetric rhythms, appoggiaturas, major-minor parallelisms, etc) seem to be telling again an old story:

The pianistic writing exploits the qualities and resources of the instrument and the interpreter has to cope with unusual difficulties of technique and expression. The recording of this *Sonatina* by the composer himself is a valuable testimonial. Composer and interpreter meet in creating a true masterpiece. With tendencies towards neo-Classicism in the treatment, the *Sonatina for Left Hand* represents the composer's statement about the inspiration of folk music, with its conciseness and richness of sentiment expressed in all its simplicity.

The *Sonatina for Left Hand* appears for the first time in the programme of a Chamber Music Concert of Rumanian Music given by Silvestri and Lipatti, on 27 February 1942, with no mention of its being a first performance. At the same concert Dinu also performed the *Three Nocturnes* and *Sonatina* for violin and piano with the violinist Al. Teodorescu.[6]

In 1943 Lipatti composed the *Rumanian Dances* for two

pianos, dedicatd to Ernest Ansermet, an important achievement showing, once again, his constant interest in Rumanian folk music.

The *First Dance* is entirely based on 'geampara,' a dance in assymetric rhythm usually performed after the wedding feast. There is only one theme, freely varied with intense chromaticisms moving through ingenious rhythmic and melodic changes and daring modulations. At one moment the two phrases of the theme appear superimposed with symmetrically opposed chromatic modulations, moving step by step:

First Piano—second phrase, C-B-B flat
Second Piano—first phrase, A-B-C

Beginning with a contrasting chord in *p*, the *Second Dance* has subdued sonorities. The first idea, on an ostinato bass, is written in the Lydian Mode with a lowered seventh:

A second idea follows, a slow dance which, together with new altered motives, moves to a resounding climax. In a short ending the mood of the beginning is recaptured with the same ostinato accompaniment.

The *Third Dance* reflects a happy village atmosphere. The theme of the first section is a 'dance for two', with superimposed bi-tonality:

Occasionally this is accompanied by a figuration imitating the 'tzambal' (zither). The central section introduces a contrasting theme developed in a conventional manner which, at the same time, becomes the subject in a short exposition of a four-part fugue. This is followed by a recapitulation of a free variant of the first section.

As in previous works, Lipatti makes use of folk and modal

themes, treating them in the style of the French school of composition. He introduces freely-developed harmonies and polyphony using sonorous blocks, richly chromaticized, creating polytonal and polymodal colouristic effects. While following a broad modal line it does not integrate itself into actual modal harmonies. Here it is important to note the unity of the structure: a gradual transition from one dance to another through anticipating the mood or the themes and through a development of the form: monotematic (Dance I), binary (Dance II), ternary (Dance III). This is the style of the artist's period of maturity, with remarkable realizations, but also with certain limitations which he will try to overcome, perhaps, in his later work *Aubade for Wind Instruments*.

Two years later Lipatti wrote a new version of the *Dances* for piano and full orchestra which we shall discuss later on, under the section 'Instrumental Works'.

His last composition, in strictly chronological order, and the last piece written for the piano, is a 'joke' for four hands dedicated to Dr. Dubois-Ferrière, his doctor: *Henri's March* (1950). Written in a moment of temporary relief from illness, it draw its inspiration from folk music and appears as a tribute to that "very dear part of his life", as a composer.

Among Lipatti's works for the piano we also find a few transcriptions, a version of Albeniz's *Navarra* (1940), in the Manuscript Library of the Bucharest Academy, and *Pastorale for Organ* by Bach (probably 1942), which Dinu often performed at his recitals. Then we have the Cadenzas to Haydn and several Mozart concertos. The last are true recreations, bringing out the personality of the composers while respecting the style of the concertos.

INSTRUMENTAL AND CHAMBER MUSIC WORKS

Sonatina for Violin and Piano (1933) establishes a decisive moment in Lipatti's artistic creation. When he analysed his first compositions influenced by his favourite Romantic composers, particularly his Piano Sonata, Mihail Jora, his teacher, advised him to try to express himself through a more personal idiom, drawing on Rumanian folk music. This is what Lipatti achieves in the *Sonatina*. The 16-year-old composer realized which path he had to follow and he began to explore the richness of the Rumanian folklore with great sincerity.

The *Sonatina* enjoyed great success from the beginning. At the Enesco Competition in 1933 it was awarded Second Prize—though it was considered the best work—and received its first public performance on 25 April at a Chamber Music Concert organised by the Society of Rumanian Composers, with the violinist Anton Sarvas and the composer at the piano.

The first part, *Allegro Moderato*, written in free sonata form, begins with a simple, yet inspired, theme played by both instruments in unison;

The second, very sprightly theme dominates the development and the short impetuous Coda. *Andantino*, the second movement, is a theme with variations. The noble slow tune is surprisingly concise for a composer searching for a new means of expression;

Harmonies and structure are somewhat heavy. The variations bring in new rhythms, those of the 'Hora' and other dances, modal changes and modulations while the fifth variation is also the Finale of the work. This Finale begins with a melodic *tessitura*, more like an improvisation, and after a broad development, it reaches an interesting conclusion when the two themes of the first movement re-appear in inverted order. In spite of some naive touches and limitations, the *Sonatina* is a very deserving work. It marks the inauguration of a chain of works inspired by Rumanian folk music with its modes, rhythms, specific developments and cadences which are integrated in a simple and original way into classical form. The return in the second and third movements to motives from the first part stresses the cyclic and unified character of the *Sonatina*. These are qualities which justify the unanimous appreciation and the award conferred on this work.

Lipatti also composed two Piano Trios; *Fantasia for piano, violin and cello* (1936) and *Improvisation for violin, cello and piano* (1939). The first work, at first entitled *Trio*, was commissioned by Mihail Jora and was often performed by Lipatti with the violinist Lola Bobesco and the cellist Antonio Janigro during his stay in Paris.

In five parts, with a repeat of the first, the *Fantasia*, which Lipatti liked to call 'cosmopolite', achieves an interesting and gradual transition from the descriptive, modal manner of previous compositions of folk music inspiration to the use of contemporary technique. The first theme, taken from folk music, is presented by the piano:

When compared with the final theme in the fifth section, Grave:

one notices for the first time in Lipatti's music some daring modulatory inflections using chromatic progressions, asymmetric rhythms (particularly in the fourth section), polytonalities, and other techniques which will find fuller usage in later works—as in the *Aubade for Wind Instruments*.

Improvisation is a shorter work. The original manuscript belonging to Miron Soarec, consists of only three pages with the inscription "*Première Improvisation (sur commande!) pour violon, violoncello et piano, dédiée à Soarec et Co. avec ma solanelle benediction.* Dinu Lipatti, Bucharest, 1939." This has been included with the "Nocturne" in the book "My Friend Dinu Lipatti" op. cit.

Written with a marked sense of proportion *Improvisation* shows the usual French influences. An introduction with the character of an exposition creates a meditative atmosphere, using a repeated rhythmical pattern in eighths played by the piano against the long lines of the violin and cello. The basic thematic element is presented by the two stringed instruments. A crescendo leads to the climax of the work marked by a short but expressive entry of the piano in the 'parlato' style favoured by Enesco. There is a happy blending of the sounds of the lower register of the violin with those of the high register of the cello. *Improvisation* ends with some subtle sonorities which suggest a return to the first motive of the theme.

In the *Concerto for Organ and Piano* (1939) Lipatti uses an unusual combination of instruments. In the Library of the Rumian Academy there are three original manuscripts of this illustrating the different stages of its composition. The first version shows Lipatti in 'the heat of creation'—a first manuscript filled with corrections and erasions. The second is a transcription of the first in the usual orderly manner of the composer, with certain sketches for orchestration added later at the top of the pages. The third version, without title, is unfinished, with only the piano part and with space left for the organ and orchestral instruments. This work is dedicated to Nadia Boulanger.

In this *Concerto* Lipatti tried to achieve a combination of the two instruments in an original and remarkable blending.

His main preoccupation was to combine the contemporary devices with the neo-classical tendencies of the French School and Rumanian folk music. In the first movement, *Allegretto*, there are some chromatic modulations of the first theme and the theme of the *Andante*, with its modal structure, is developed through rhythmical transformation of the motive in the first bar, a frequent device in his compositions

In the third movement a Scherzo enlivens the mood and the *Trio* is reminiscent of Debussy's music. The finale, *Risoluto*, based on two themes of a classical nature, is interestingly structured in sonata form with a fugue on the initial theme as development.

In the *Concerto for Organ and Piano* the composer is attempting various techniques inspired by different sources, and at the same time he is taking liberties with regard to form. In general, however, the work lacks the simplicity and unity which the composer would have wanted.

In June of the same year Lipatti wrote his first composition for a wind instrument, *Introduction and Allegro for Solo Flute*, inspired by folk music. The introduction, a *Doina* which moves along in an expressive *parlando rubato* on a freely stylized melody avoiding any fixed tonality, is reminiscent of the *melopée* for flute in the *Aubade for Wind Instruments*. The next section, *Con Brio*, is based on '*Cimpoiul*' (Bagpipe), a 'Hora' dance from Muntenia, and is written in the Mixolydian Mode.

In the following year the composer turned to Domenico Scarlatti's music for harpsichord and transcribed *Six Sonatas for Wind Quintet* (flute, oboe, clarinet, bassoon, horn) in a very original manner. In fact, this was a return to a similar transcription he wrote in 1938. In both these transcriptions he retains the atmosphere of the original version while emphasizing their true intentions and characteristic polyphony.

The last work in this group is *Aubade for Wind Quartet* (1949), dedicated to the conductor, Paul Sacher. This is a work of Lipatti's mature period where a concise form and musical language are interwoven with profound musical thought. The composer's search for an individual style, after having absorbed valuable contemporary influences, is evident, and here again the source of inspiration derives from folk music.

The first movement, *Prelude*, begins in an *improvvisando* manner with the solo flute playing a free *Doina*. Three motives appear throughout the work: (a) lively dance (b) slow and modulating (c) a slow motive again which Lipatti had already used in the Finale of the *Sonatina for Left Hand* (the second theme, which begins at bar 40).

It is an interesting introduction and worthy of what follows, presenting us with the composer's ideas on the use of folk melos. From the start his style is more clearly defined than previously and achieves an organic integration of folk-elements with a clear musical language. From the first bars, certain inflexions create a special modal ambiance, quite daring at times, as in the (b) motive reminiscent of Bartok's technique in the step-by-step fluctuations (G-G sharp in measures 1, 4, 5, and 6). G. Firca, the musicologist, remarks in *The Modal Basis of Diatonic Chromaticism*,[7] that this latest compositional technique creates an oscillation in seconds and subsequently varied thirds (measures 2 and 4), as well as the appearance of a diminished octave—essential elements in the definition of 'diatonic chromaticism' so frequently met with in the contemporary music of Stravinsky, Bartók, Enesco, etc. Motive (c) contains Messiaen's 'inverted chromatic formula' due to the same oscillation in seconds.

The writing is polyphonic, the composer being mainly interested in the linear development of the musical discourse. The harmonies are dissonant, polytonal, with Bartókian resonances, emphasizing clashes of seconds and minor ninths or enharmonic augmented octaves. Occasionally he uses chords found in Stravinsky's music *Threni* (The Symphony in three movements), and related to Bartók's major-minor (*E-G-C-E flat*). Lipatti's chord is constructed of two superimposed thirds, one major and one minor: *D-F sharp–D sharp–F sharp*, in bar 25, or, *E flat–G-E natural–G* in bar 30, etc.

The second part, *Dance*, is in ternary form. The theme of the opening section presented in unison by all the instruments is a *Sârba*, a dance full of vitality, with syncopated and lively rhythms, changes of time signatures and expressive alterations creating augmented intervals, in particular the Lydian fourth.

The tune of this dance is known in many parts of Rumania, (around the Bran Castle region, for instance, we find it under the name of *Breaza*), and Lipatti develops it by using some of the devices mentioned above. The instruments join successively in groups of two or three, with contrasting ideas and polymodal or polyrhythmical moments of great intensity. One also notices, among others, the use of certain Bartókian rhythmic progressions which enliven the development of the polyphonic passages.

The third part, *Nocturne*, is influenced by 18th century serenades, and actually contradicts the title *Aubade* which means a work performed early in the morning. The *Nocturne* is also in ternary form moving over an *ostinato* bass, an influence of the French School frequently met with in Lipatti's music. The principal melody has a distinctly Rumanian flavour, while the dissonant central section begins suddenly and *fortissimo* on the same *ostinato* bass. At the climax the polyphonic structure reaches a perfect symmetry which can be traced around an axis through the oboe and clarinet parts. Here is a graphic representation (bars 67 and 68):

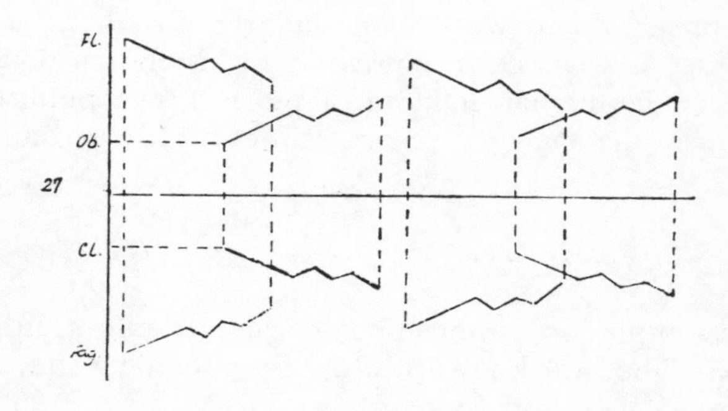

The resolution of the tension in the middle section, marked *diminuendo*, begins with bar 76 and forms the 'golden section' of the entire movement (124 bars). Here again the composer uses a Bartókian device.

The last part of the *Aubade*, *Scherzo*, has a very lively tempo, *presto vivace*, and the orchestration shows a wide range of color. It is classical in style and in structure and with regard to melodic lines of the themes and the tonal planes, which are more stable than in the two previous movements.

Dinu Lipatti's profound dedication to composition is perhaps most noticeable in this work. Here he succeeded, more than in any of his previous works, in reaching a synthesis of popular inspiration with contemporary compositional techniques. From Enesco he had learnt a certain instrumental colouring, an organic assimilation of chromaticism in thematic development, the relationship between polyphony and monody, and of unison, but did not master the 'heterophony' (which he had attempted in the *Fantasia for Piano*).

From Bartók he learned the asymmetry in structure, daring modulations, rythmic freedom, certain elements of modal chord progression, polymodalism moving towards a diatonic chromaticism. This was metioned before and noticed in earlier works: *Fantasia for piano, violin and cello, Improvision for violin, cello and piano*, and *Rumanian Dances* (1945). At the same time the construction of the work is classical in structure and there is thematic unity within the movements. In this respect the same compositional technique as in the *Aubade* is used. The *Nocturne*, especially the *Scherzo*, does not fall into this category but shows a return to the style of earlier works which was never clearly defined before. Yet, *Aubade for Wind Quartet* seems to be Lipatti's most representative work, particularly in the first two movements, and is a clear expression of his chosen path well-anchored in Rumanian folklore. This work was published in New York in the *Study Score Series*, Rongwen Music Inc. 1958.

SYMPHONIC COMPOSITIONS

Lipatti's symphonic compositions consist of only a fifth of all his works. The best known are the Symphonic Suite, *Şatrarii* ('Gypsies') (1934) and *Concertino in Classical Style*. (1936).

The *Şatrarii* is the first composition of ample dimension which received the 'Hononary Prize' at the Georges Enesco National Competition for Composition in 1934, the third and most important award. Two years later, on 23 January 1936, Mihail Jora conducted the first performance of his distinguished pupils work at the 'Ateneu'. Subsequently the *Suite* was performed either in fragments or as a whole at different concerts in Rumania or abroad.

Written for large orchestra, *Satrarii*, is of popular inspiration with well-defined programme music presented by the composer in the suggestive titles of the three parts which evoke episodes in the life of gypsy nomads. It shows Lipatti's definite ideas as a composer as well as a search for varied and personal solutions with regard to the orchestration. The influence of Mihail Jora and Georges Enesco is certainly felt but the jury was convinced that the seventeen-year old composer deserved the award.

The first part, *The Gypsies are Coming—Allegro Maestoso*—is in free sonata form and describes the arrival of the gypsies at Floreasca, a suburb of Bucharest. The first theme, *Cantabile*, has specific Rumanian melodic intervals and a syncopated rhythm which is reminiscent of Jora's *Dance of Olteni* in his ballet *At the Market*.

The second theme, played by wind instruments in the high register, in lively and picturesque colours, has oriental inflexions suggesting the vivid atmosphere of the moment.

The second part, *Idyll at Floreasca—Andantino*—is in a meditative mood. Two basic slightly contrasting sections alternate and there are varied retakes.

The Finale of the *Suite*, *Merriment with Gypsy Players,—Allegro*—of ternary structure, is more unified than the other two parts and is developed over a discreet ostinato, very rhythmical and well suited to Rumanian folk dance.

Both themes of this movement are modal with oriental inflexions. An ample well-proportioned development continually maintains the robust atmosphere of a popular *fête*.

The Suite *Satrarii* is the only large-scale symphonic work by Dinu Lipatti and it emphasizes the composer's strong links with the native folklore. He gives the work a descriptive and picturesque treatment making use of popular chromatic modes, stressing intentionally the oriental character of certain elements, all within an atmosphere of popular humour. This work brings Lipatti close to other composers of the time: Mihail Jora, with whom he shares similarities in the use of thematic material, Theodor Rogalsky, Filip Lazar and others. Occasionally Lipatti attempts altered modal harmonies while the developments are chromatic and non-modal. The variety of treatments and the orchestral effects vividly illustrate the subject-matter but diminish the unity of the work through the cyclical use of certain motives. The younger composer broadens the techniques used in his *Sonatina for violin and piano*, but the work would have gained from a more economical treatment. The Second Movement is much too long. Yet the work stands as one of true merit and an important point of departure in a composer's promising career.

The *Concertino in Classical Style for piano and chamber orchestra* (1936) is from Lipatti's first year of study in Paris. In spite of various influences, the composer retains his personality and succeeds in creating an original fusion between classical and contemporary devices in which a neo-Classical orientation is dominant. It was Lipatti's first published composition (Universal Editions, Vienna) and was first performed on 5 October 1939 in Bucharest at the opening of the season of Symphonic Concerts at the 'Ateneu', under George Georgescu's baton with the composer as soloist.

At first the work was named *Classical Suite*, at Nadia Boulanger's suggestion. It is written in four movements and the composer adopted the Concerto Grosso form, adding a *Scherzo* before the Finale. The first movement, *Allegro Moderato*, presents the character of a prelude written in triplets with a calm atmosphere reminiscent of Bach's well-known *Chorale in G* ('Jesu Joy of Man's Desiring') so often played by the composer. Against this background the oboe, fluently and persistently, brings in the only theme of the movement:

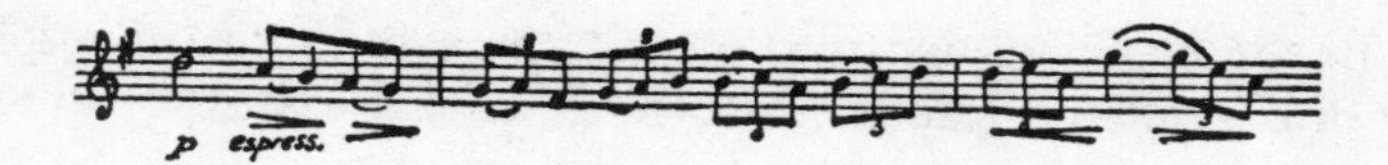

The piano first appears as an obligato instrument in the orchestral ensemble, but comes into its own in the divertimento section.

The second movement, *Adagio Molto*, in B minor, the favourite key of the cantor of Leipzig, reminds one of the clear writing of two-part inventions, and of the melodic sinuosities and rhythmical fluctuation of certain instrumental parts in oratorios; and, also, of the restrained meditative mood in the *Andate* of the *Italian Concerto*. A violin solo, like a classical aria, dominates this movement with the piano developing a cadenza towards the end. The Swiss music critic, Aloys R Mooser,[8] states that this "restrained and intimate climate is occasionally penetrated by a painful agitation which seems to reiterate the composer's credo, 'Music is a serious thing.'"

The third movement, *Allegretto*, is actually a *Scherzo*. The piano accompanies the theme enhancing it by a fine sonorous filigree of semiquavers (sixteenths). The *Trio*, in complete contrast, brings in with great humour a dialogue between oboe and piano on an ostinato orchestral accompaniment. The influence of contemporary composers like Stravinsky and Prokofiev can be felt, and occasionally there is allusion to jazz.

The Finale, *Allegro Molto*, is in sonata form. The first theme (first measure in the piano part) is borrowed from the Finale of Haydn's Sonata in G. The orchestra ingeniously brings in certain inflexions of popular dance:

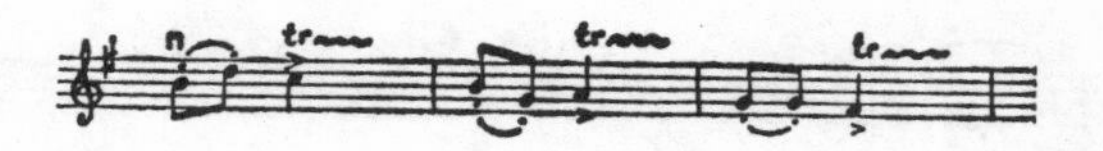

while the second theme, dreamy and lyrical, has a discreet modal flavour:

The Coda, in a long diminuendo, presents a broad resolution of previous sonorous climaxes—a characteristic treatment in Lipatti's music, as mentioned earlier.

This work has enjoyed a well-deserved popularity. With melodic freshness, and maintaining a classical form without verging on *pastiche*, it presents interesting and often original ideas. Aloys R Mooser thought that the *Concertino in Classical Style* confirmed Lipatti's creative talent as a composer, and the recording made with the composer as soloist, accompanied by the Berlin Chamber Music Orchestra under Hans von Benda, is a worthy testimonial.

Two years later Lipatti wrote a new orchstral work *Symphonie Concertante* for Two Pianos and String Orchestra (1938), dedicated to Charles Munch, who conducted it on 3 July 1939 at the Salle Pleyel with Clara Haskill and the composer as soloists. The very first performance of the work had taken place on 10 May 1939 under the conductor Patin. This is not a work of large dimensions, as might be expected from the title. After *Satrarii*, Lipatti avoided the full orchestra preferring to search for new means of expression in simpler forms, (the first two movements are in ternary form with an attempted free sonata form in the third movement). *Symphonie Concertante*, unlike the *Concertino*, strongly illustrates the influence of contemporary French music, as does *Three Dances for Two Pianos* composed a year earlier.

Here is the theme of the Introduction in the first movement, *Molto Maestoso*, appearing as a classical aria, richly altered and undulating:

Three motives constitute the material for this movement, imitating each other and treated with capricious rhythmical variations and polytonal clashes. A central episode brings in a welcome contrast through its poly-rhythmical passages.

The second movement, *Molto Adagio*, with alternate time signatures of $\frac{3}{4}$ and $\frac{2}{4}$ has a lyrical and poetical atmosphere, and a musical idea of a *Doina* adds a discreet Rumanian flavour.

The Fïnale, *Allegro con Spirito*, is very rhythmical and with accents of humour and irony. Several motives from folk dances are evident in the dialogue between the two pianos and orchestra. The development of the thematic material is free, leading to an extremely lively and happy closure.

As to Lipatti's *Three Symphonic Sketches* mentioned in his correspondence, no trace of any manuscript remains. For several years he gave up attempting other symphonic works, but in 1945 he decided to transcribe The *Rumanian Dances for Two Pianos* for full orchestra and one piano. This work and *Satrarii* are his only compositions for full orchestra.

The second version of *Rumanian Dances* received its first performance by the Suisse Romande Orchestra, under Ernest Ansermet, on 10 October 1945, with Lipatti as soloist.

Aloys R Mooser wrote in La Suisse:

> The *Rumanian Dances* are noticeable for the freshness and expressive character of the folk themes, the asymmetric movement of their capricious and bouncy rhythms which do not conform to any traditional metres, and a richness of the harmonic cloak with which the composer has enveloped the work. At every moment he offers us unexpected relationships, bringing them together with charm or with clashes which do not hurt the ear but keep it continuously on the alert through their innovation and vitality. Treated by the expert hand we have come to know, the piano has the most important role, yet the composer admirably resists the temptation to abuse this privilege.[9]

Among Lipatti's future projects we find from letters (written to Paul Sacher from Montana)[10] reference to two symphonic works: *Symphonia de Camera*, of which three-quarters had been sketched out in 1949; and a *Concerto for Piano and Chamber Orchestra* which, in the same year, Lipatti declared himself unable to begin until he was fit enough to play it himself.

VOCAL COMPOSITIONS

This last chapter of Lipatti's creative out-put is rather limited. It consists of two Lieder cycles. The first, set to poems by Verlaine, contains *Five Songs* for Tenor. (1941). It is refined and inspired music reflecting the composer's artistic maturity. Sometimes the vocal part is a recitative with a free improvisatory character, at other times it is a simple melody as and where the text demands such treatment. The accompaniment with impressionistic harmonies is closely linked to the voice, either anticipating or moving parallel with it, or imitating it like an echo. Occasional independent chromatic passages add a certain colour expressing the mood of the poem. The influence of Debussy, Duparc and, particularly in the last song of Spanish character, of Ravel is obvious. Here is an inspired fragment from the fourth Lied, *A Forgotten Aria*, in which the composer evokes a longing for the beloved in the rhythm of an old *Sicilienne*:

The second cycle, *Four Songs for Voice and Piano* (1945) is set to poems by Rimbaud, Eluard and Valéry. The original manuscript, for tenor and piano, is in the Library of the Rumanian Composers' Union. In these songs Lipatti achieves a greater simplicity and conciseness. The recitative is close to the intonation of speech, the accompaniment is most economial and without any pianistic displays, expressing in characteristic passages the fundamental ideas of the poems.

The two Lieder Cycles, greatly influenced by the French School through its poetic sources, achieve a unity through the structure, dimensions and similar motives. The quality of the poems is brought out with a discreet sensitivity.

In some of his letters Lipatti talked about another *Seven Melodies*, among his future projects, without mentioning the names of any poets; and *Prière de St François* for alto and string orchestra which he planned to combine with his *Chorale for Strings* composed in Pratteln in 1944—but none of these were ever finished.

At the end of this review of Dinu Lipatti's compositions, we can affirm that for him composition was not of secondary importance to his prodigious activity as performer and interpreter, but a demanding and continuous necessity. He suffered deeply from his inability to satisfy this inner need, and in one of his letters to Mihail Jora (Paris, 26 April 1935) he even affirmed that the moments when he greatly regretted being a pianist were not rare. There is seldom a letter in which Lipatti does not mention how much time the piano takes up, thus making it impossible to devote himself to composition, "this very dear chapter" in his work and life.

On the other hand, his extreme scrupulousness often made him abandon quite successful attempts of which we only know about from his letters: an unfinished Piano Sonata in 1937; a Toccata in E major for two flutes, two oboes and strings, (1936) which would have had three movements, though only two were completed, *Prelude* and *Intermezzo*, both greatly praised by Stravinsky; several choral works with orchestral accompaniment (1937); an unfinished Wind Quintet (1938) whose manuscript is now in the Library of the Rumanian Academy, and others.

In general we can speak of four main directions in Lipatti's music:

1. *A neo-Romantic orientation*—influenced by Schumann, Chopin and Liszt—in some of the early compositions: the Píano Sonata (1932) and an unfinished Piano Sonata.

2. *Rumanian orientation*—influenced by the Rumanian School of composition, i.e. Enesco, Jora, Lazar, etc. This is evident in some early works: *Sonatina for violin and piano*, the Suite *Satrarii*, *Nocturne on a Moldavian Theme, Fantasia for piano, violin and cello, Introduction and Allegro for flute, Two Dances in Rumanian Folk Style for two pianos, Fantasia for Piano, Sonatina for Left Hand, Rumanian Dances*, and *Aubade for Wind Instruments*.

3. *Neo-Classical orientation*—the strong influence of Bach's music during Lipatti's studies in Paris. *Concertino in Classical Style*, *Suite for String Orchestra*, several Cadenzas for piano concertos by Haydn and Mozart, *Toccata for Wind Instruments and Strings* (unfinished) and some other compositions.

4. *Modern and contemporary orientation*—influence of the French School, in particular Dukas, Debussy and Ravel: *Improvisations for violin, cello and piano*, *Three Nocturnes*, *Lieder*. Lipatti next followed the path traced by Stravinsky: *Concertino*, (*Trio* in the third movement), *Three Dances for Two Pianos*, the unfinished *Wind Quintet*. Finally he drew on elements from both directions: *Symphonie Concertante*, *Concerto for organ and piano*, *Suite for Two Pianos*, *Fantasia for Piano*, *Rumanian Dances*, *Aubade for Wind Instruments*.

It is obvious that such a definition is not, and cannot be, absolute. There were interweaving of other orientations as well, but it is interesting to note that most of Lipatti's compositions with Rumanian orientation remain his more permanent works. Moreover the Rumanian influence is felt even in compositions with different orientations. In Lipatti's later period he admitted to two basic orientations—Rumanian and contemporary, with the aim of creating a fusion between the two. On one side, indigenous, melodic and rhythmic elements; on the other, the tendency to use polyphony with its resulting chromatic harmonisation, dissonances, and rich modulations leading to polytonality, polyrhythms, while still achieving a desired simplicity and conciseness in expression. The fusion is evident in *Three Rumanian Dances* (1945) and in *Aubade for Wind*

Quartet (first and second movements). This last work indicates the direction which Lipatti would have taken, reaching beyond any influences while adopting a certain severity which was curbing his drive and originality.

It is perhaps appropriate to emphasise the optimistic character of Lipatti's compositions. A robustness stemming from the use of folk music is often combined with a discreet humour and programatic tendencies. In Lipatti's music we do not meet accents of profound sadness without their being followed by a serene mood. It is even more significant to find this flow of vitality in the work of an artist whose life was so tragic and so short.

Although destiny took him away too soon and thus deprived us of the mature works which he was preparing, Dinu Lipatti remains part of Rumanian music as a sincere and authentic composer whose works are a permanent contribution to the general appreciation of the richness of Rumanian folklore—'pure Rumanian gold'.

7 Dinu Lipatti—The Teacher

by Jacques Chapuis

It is not easy to talk about Dinu Lipatti—the Teacher. One has to talk about the supreme musician, the pianist of unique qualities, the composer, and above all about the man with a generous and noble personality, subtle humour and great abnegation. From 1944 to 1949 he held a 'Cours de Perfectionnement' at the Generva Conservatoire and I was one of the few privileged selected to study with him.

Lipatti never intended to be 'a pedagogue', He believed in stimulating and developing the understanding of the great works of piano literature and the musicianship of those who came to him for guidance, helping them to attain their ideals. To do so he planned to write a 'Study on Interpretation' in collaboration with his teacher and mentor, Nadia Boulanger. *Hélas*, the project never materialized but what is left is Lipatti's 'Artistic Credo' which he formulated in a letter to a young pianist who asked his advice on how to work and what principles he should follow.

Here are a few excerpts which sum up his philosophy and his attitude to his work as a teacher.

> What can I tell you about interpretation? I can only recapitulate, perhaps very imperfectly, the method which I believe guides us, in stages, to the TRUTH.
>
> First, one should try to discover the complete emotional content of a work by playing it a great deal in various ways before ever starting to play it 'technically'. When I say 'playing it a great deal' I think above all playing it 'mentally' as the work would be performed by the most perfect of interpreters. Having lodged in our mind the impression of perfect beauty given by this 'mental'

interpretation—an impression continually renewed and re-vivified by repitition of this performance in the silence of the night—we can go on to the actual technical work, by dissecting each difficulty into a thousand small units so that we can eliminate every physical and technical obstacle. This process of dissection must not involve the whole work played from the beginning to the end but each single detail must be dealt with separately. The study must be done with a clear head and one should beware of injecting any sentiment into it.

Finally comes the last phase when the piece, mastered technically throughout, must be built up architecturally into its overall lines and played right through so that we can view it in its perspective. And the cold, clear-headed, detached being who has conducted the practice work on the material of which the music is made takes part in this complete performance together with the artist, full of emotion, of spirit, of life and warmth. It is the artist who has recreated it in his mind and who has now discovered a new and greater power of expression. Forgive me for expressing myself so badly about something so solemn.

Lipatti's approach to teaching had the same extraordinary maturity which he brought to everything he did, always giving of his best. When he first took up his post as Piano Professor he felt rather nervous as he considered himself unprepared for such a task. But his complete dedication to music and his desire to help younger musicians soon dispelled his nervousness. He was very demanding, expecting the same dedication and complete involvement from his students. As the same time he felt great responsibility towards them and he was reluctant to miss lessons when his engagements kept him away for several weeks at a time. Each lesson brought new revelations, whether on a point of interpretation or a technical problem for everything became clear as soon as he illustrated them in his inimitable way.

Working with Dinu Lipatti was a question of what he called 'musical conscience', a search for the 'truth'. He instilled in us the importance of *deciding right from the first stage* of studying a work what that particular work should sound like and to have a complete vision of it *as a whole*. Then, and only then, were his students encouraged to play it and this had to be done with extreme care and organisation so that each phrase would become an integral part of the work. *If you hear in your imagination what a musical phrase should sound like, you have already created in your mind the physical movements which will express those sounds*— Lipatti often told us. Indeed, Lipatti possessed one of the most perfect means of expressing his musical intentions, a piano technique which served him totally.

When I asked him how the famous Chopin Etude in Thirds ought to be approached, he simply smiled and said that he had practised it for at least six months, every morning, slowly, with each hand separately, listening intenely to every tone, studying every movement of his arms, hands, fingers and his body involvement to be sure that these 'mirrored' exactly his musical ideas. Only then did he dare play it in public. I must add that I don't think I have ever heard anyone giving a performance of this Etude to equal Lipatti's. Sometimes he thought that instead of explaining 'how to practice' a certain passage, it would be better to illustrate it. The student could learn more by watching that extraordinary co-ordination between the music, as he perceived it and the movements needed to express it. Lipatti liked to tell the famous fable of the ant and the centipede when one of us asked too many questions.

> The ant had been watching for days the centipede walking, moving all those legs with such perfect co-ordination and elegance until one day, in awe and admiration, she plucked up her courage and asked him:
>
> 'Monsieur Centipede, how can you move all those legs so beautifully, how can you walk so simply and elegantly?' 'Well, I don't know' replied the centipede, 'I just walk.' 'Oh, surely you know exactly what to do, at every moment, otherwise you could not move your legs in such perfect order.'
>
> Flattered by this remark, the centipede promised to think about it and explain it to the ant the following day. The ant arrived early, very excited, and waited and waited, but the centipede never appeared. Rather worried, she went to look for him in the wood, and after a time found the centipede lying exhausted at the foot of a tree. 'I've been trying so hard to work out how to walk. I got more and more confused and now, here I am... I don't know what to do, I can't walk anymore.'

Lipatti believed that, like the centipede, the pianist must allow natural co-ordination to function freely without any interference or unnecessary analysis. Indeed, he believed in a detailed analytical study of the works performed, but he insisted that there should be a total fusion between the musical thought—the harmonic and rhythmic structure, the melodic lines, the emotion—and the pianistic realisation. Above all, the interpreter must allow his spontaneity to take over in performance. Whenever one of us had to appear in public, he gave the following advice: 'Now that you have worked well and you have studied your programme in its minutest detail, and you also *know how you would like it to be performed, play it exactly as you feel. Think only of the music and not of what I have told you or of how* ***I*** *want you to play it.'*

I often think of the time I spent at Lipatti's course which was run as a Master Class, with all the students present, for he insisted that it was very important for us to listen to one another. In this way we would learn to listen intently to our own playing. Not all his students were highly gifted, but he worked with each one with the same seriousness and interest, no matter what problems were encountered. If finger technique was not adequate he did not recommend studies for finger agility but, instead, he demanded that the student should work on *slow* movements of sonatas, nocturnes or other pieces requiring *cantabile tone* and a long *legato* line. Of course, all aspects of technique were thoroughly studied but always through the music. In my own case, when I joined his class, I was anxious to play with the exhuberance and temperament of an excited young pianist. He thought that I was too tense when playing and that my tone was rather harsh. With great patience he showed me how to use the arm weight, how to achieve a supple arm and wrist and how to develop my finger technique to obtain 'steel fingers in velvet gloves' as one critic so aptly described Lipatti's pianism. He made me realise that my strident tone was the result of a 'lack of unison' between my musical intentions and my physical gestures.

Lipatti—the Teacher—tried to pass on to us everything he knew, everthing he believed in. He insisted that the musical score should always be 'our Bible'. But, which score? He often remarked: 'Urtext? Yes, It is very important. But the "Urspirit" is even more important for a true interpretation.'

It was a sad day when Lipatti's failing health forced him to leave the Geneva Conservatoire. For myself and for my colleagues—among them artists like Bela Siki, Fred Weiss, Fernanda Kayser, Aimé Leonardi and a few others—those years remain as a unique experience on many levels of consciousness. Lipatti's *Artistic Credo*, the noble and inspiring letter to a young pianist in which he put as much of his art which is communicable in writing, will always be a testament for his pupils who, in their turn, will strive to pass it on to their own students. Thus, Lipatti's art remains with us.

Footnotes

Abbreviations

AL	Anna Lipatti
CFJ	Collection Family Jora
CFM	Collection Family Musicesca
DL	Dinu Lipatti
DT	Dragos Tanasescu
FM	Florica Muzicescu
MJ	Mihail Jora
MC/ML	Madeleine Cantacuzino/Madeleine Lipatti
MS	Miron Soarec

1: First Steps

1 Photo in the collection of Captain Costinescu, Bucharest

2: Years of Apprenticeship

1 DT. *Dinu Lipatti*. Collection *Viata in Imagini*, Bucharest, ed. Muzicala, 1962, p4. (Jora talked to the author)
2 Unsigned article, 'Festivalul Societatii Principele Mircea', Bucharest, May 15 1928. (Newspaper unknown)
3 From authors interview with FM
4 *Enescu despre Lipatti*. In *Revista Muzicala*, Bucharest, No. 2, 1928. An unsigned interview
5 From authors interview with FM
6 AL. *La vie du pianiste Dinu Lipatti ecrite par sa mere*. Paris, ed. La Colombe, 1954
7 Alexandrescu, Romeo. *Academia Regala de Muzica. Productia clasei de orchestra*. In *Universul*, Bucharest, June 1932

8 Sym. *Productia clasei de orchestra*. In *Adevarul*, No. 148, 12 June 1932
9 Correspondence with MS. Bucharest, 24 December 1932. (MS Collection)
10 Sym. *Filarmonica*. In *Adervarul*, Bucharest 11 February 1933.
11 Breazul, G. *Pianistul Dinu Lipatti*. In *Cuvintul*, Bucharest, 13 February 1933
12 *Filarmonica*. In *Universul*, Bucharest, April 1933.
13 Letter to MS. Vienna, 26 May 1933. (Collection MS)
14 2 June 1933. See MS *Marturii inedite despre Dinu Lipatti*. In *Studii de Muzicolgie*, Bucharest Vol. XII, ed. Muzicala, 1976.
15 Ibid
16 There were two other Rumanian participants, Sofia Cosma and Virgil Gheorghiu
17 MS. Op. cit. Letter from Vienna, 13 June 1933
18 Two undated press notices
19 Letter to FM. 31 August 1934. (CFM)
20 Paris, 5 February 1935. (CFJ)
21 Bucharest, 22 August 1939. (Collection Professor DT)
22 Letter to Professor DT. Paris, 17 November 1957
23 Letter to MS. 13 December 1934. (Op. cit.)
24 AL. *Dinu Lipatti. La douleur de ma vie*. Geneva, ed. Perret-Gentil 1967, p 40
25 Ibid p 53
26 Nicoara, Adriana. *De vorba cu Dinu Lipatti*. In *Universal Literar*, Bucharest 1941
27 Paris, 8 October 1934. (CFM)
28 Fragments from letters from Duingt, 16 July 1935; Paris, 6 November 1935 and 8 October 1934. (CFM)
29 Paris, 21 May 1935. (CFJ)
30 Paris, 19 November 1934. (CFJ)
31 Paris, 25 March 1935. (Collection MS)
32 Paris, 20 December 1934. (CFJ)
33 Ibid
34 Paris, 6 November 1934. (CFJ)
35 Ibid
36 Paris, 5 February 1935. (CFJ)
37 Ibid
38 To FM. Paris, 16 January 1935. (CFM)
39 Ibid
40 Paris, 5 February 1935
41 AL. *Dinu Lipatti. La douleur de ma vie*. Geneva, ed. Perret-Gentil 1967, p 43
42 To FM. Paris, 27 March 1935. (CMF)

43 Ibid
44 To MJ. Paris, 23 June 1935 (CJF)
45 From *La Revue Musicale*. Note sent to FM, 16 July 1935. Duingt
46 From his suite *Satrarii*
47 To FM. Duingt, 16 July 1935. (CFM)
48 To MJ. Paris, 26 April 1935. (CFJ)
49 Paris, 22 July 1935. (CFJ)
50 Paris 26 January 1936. (CFJ)
51 To FM. Paris, 24 March 1936. (CFM)
52 *Homage a Dinu Lipatti*. Geneva, Labor et Fides, 1951
53 Duingt, 22 July 1935; Paris 6 November 1935. (CFJ)
54 Letters to MS and FM. Paris, dated 25 March 1935 and December 18 1935 respectively
55 To FM. Duingt, 16 July 1935.(CFM)
56 To MS. Cannes, 21 September 1935. (Collection MS)
57 Cortot, A. Letter to Kiesgen, C. 12 February 1935. (Reproduced on the poster of the concert in Montreux)
58 Signed Amy-Ch, 30 October 1935.
59 Letter to FM. Paris, 6 November 1935. (CFM)
60 Ibid. Paris, 19 October 1935
61 From FM. Bucharest 22 August 1939 (col. D.T.)
62 ML. *Dedicace*, in *Homage a Dinu Lipatti*. Op. cit. p 12
63 Paris, 26 January 1936 (CFJ)
64 To FM. Paris, 5 March 1936. (CFM)
65 *Le Monde Musical*, No. 4, 30 April 1936
66 To FM. Paris, 24 March 1936 (CFM)
67 Paris, 19 June 1936 (CFM)
68 Ibid 24 March 1936 (CFM)
69 Paris, 1936 (CFJ)
70 Paris, 6 June 1936
71 To FM. 8 September 1936. (CFM)
72 To MJ. 23 August 1936. (CFJ)
73 20 September 1936 (CFJ)
74 Ciomac, Emanoil. *Pagini de Cronica Muzicala 1915–1938*
75 Ibid
76 Ciomac, Emanoil. In *Timpul*, Bucharest, 30 April 1941
77 Undated letter from the musicologist Constantin Brailoiu
78 Ciomac, Emanoil. *Pagini de Cronica Muzicala 1915–1938*, Op. cit
79 ML. *Souvenirs*, in: *In Memoriam Dinu Lipatti*. ed. Labor et Fides, 1970, p. 30
80 To MJ. 26 February 1937. (CFJ)
81 AL. *Dinu Lipatti. La douleur de ma vie*, p 49. ed. Perret-Gentil 1967
82 To MJ. Paris, 30 June 1937. (CFJ)

83 Rome, 29 January 1938
84 Paris, 5 February 1938 (CFJ)
85 Paris, 10 March 1938 (CFJ)
86 Paris, 5 February 1935 (CFJ)
87 To FM. Paris, 27 March 1935. (CFM)
88 From letters to MJ. 5 February and 10 March 1938 (CFJ)
89 Nicoara, Adriana. *De vorba cu Dinu Lipatti*. Op. cit
90 To MJ. Paris, 21 April 1938. (CFJ)
91 Paris, 18 July and 6 November 1938 (CFJ)
92 Paris, 24 December 1938 (CFJ)
93 To FM. Paris 17 January 1939. (CFM)
94 To MJ. Paris, 24 December 1938. (CFJ)
95 Gavoty, B-Hauert, R. *Clara Haskil, Les Grands Interprètes* Geneva, ed. Kister, 1962
96 *In Memoriam Dinu Lipatti*, Op. cit. p. 75
97 Excerpts from letters between Clara Haskil and Dinu Lipatti 1939–1943. (Collection Professor DT)
98 Excerpt from the speech given by Igor Markevitch in memory of Clara Haskil at the Vevey Theatre, 19 April 1961
99 Loo, Esther van. *Monsieur Dinu Lipatti* in *L'Art Musical*, Paris, 21 April 1939
100 Paris, 24 March 1939
101 To MJ. Bagnoles, 18 July 1938 (CFJ)
102 Geneva, 31 March 1947 (CFJ)
103 Paris, 28 December 1937 (CFJ)
104 DL. *Cronica artistica. Viata Muzicala la Paris*, in *Libertatea*, Bucharest, Nos, 10 and 11, 1939

3: Fame

1 To MJ. Glimbocata, 19 August 1939 (CFJ)
2 Bucharest, 29 August 1939 (Collection Professor DT)
3 FM to DL. Bucharest, 22 August 1939 (Collection Professor DT)
4 Bucharest, 17 March 1942 (DL's 25th birthday). Copy owned by Professor Corneliu Gheorghiu, Brussels
5 Gheorghiu Virgil in *Curentul*, Bucharest, 5 October 1939
6 MJ in *Timpul*, Bucharest, 16 October 1939
7 To MJ. Fundateanca, 2 June 1940 (CFJ)
8 According to the music review in the newspaper *Timpul*, Bucharest, 7 January 1941
9 *Universul Literar*, Bucharest, 3 May 1941
10 Excerpt from the programme of the concert given by the Radio Symphony Orchestra on 8 May 1941 at the Ateneul Roman

11 To MC. Fundateanca, 9 September 1941 (Collection Professor DT)
12 To FM. Fundateanca, 28 August 1941 (CFM)
13 Ibid
14 To MC. 7 September 1941 (Collection Professor DT)
15 *Timpul*, 15 October 1941
16 Alexandrescu, Romeo, *Spicuiri critice din trecut*. Bucharest, Ed. Muzicala, 1970
17 To MC. October 1941 (Collection Professor DT)
18 *Homage a Dinu Lipatti*, Geneva, Labor et Fides 1951, p. 78
19 *Timpul*, 16 February 1942
20 Dedication on the Manuscript (Museum of Rumanian Music, Bucharest)
21 Alexandrescu, Romeo. Op. cit
22 To MC. Berlin 22 March 1941 (Professor DT)
23 To MC Vienna, 26 March 1941 (DT)
24 To MC Rome, 4 April 1941 (DT)
25 Alexandrescu, Romeo. Op. cit
26 Ciomac, Emanoil, in *Timpul*, Bucharest, 23 November 1942
27 To FM. Berlin, 5 January 1943 (CFM)
28 Letter to parents. Stockholm, 20 September 1943 (Collection Professor DT)
29 14 September 1943
30 Unsigned review of 14 September 1943
31 A review whch also appeared in September 1943
32 To FM (CFM)
33 14 September 1943
34 To MJ. Versoix, 4 November 1943 (CFJ)
35 Ibid
36 Fragments from letters to FM. Montana, 28 February 1944 (CFM)
37 Fragments from letters to FM and MJ at the end of 1943 (CFJ and CFM)
38 Ibid
39 Ibid
40 Ibid
41 To FM, Montana, 28 February 1944 (CFM)
42 From letters to his family, Spring 1946 (DT)
43 To FM. 1946 (CFM)
44 Montana, 9 August 1946 (CFM)
45 Geneva, 30 March 1947 (CFM)
46 Ibid
47 Letter to FM. Geneva (CFM)
48 ML. *Dedicace*, in *Homage a Dinu Lipatti*. Op. cit
49 Letter to FM from DL and ML, Geneva, 23 June 1947 (CFM)

50 To Popa, Costache. Geneva 11 July 1947 (Collection C. Popa)
51 Excerpts from letters to FM from DL and ML. Geneva, 17 September 1947 and Amsterdam, 11 October 1947 (CFM)
52 To FM. Geneva 16 May 1948 (CFM)
53 Geneva, 1 January 1948 (CFM)
54 Ibid
55 To FM. Paris, 19 June 1936 (CFM)
56 Geneve, 21 March 1948 (CFM)
57 Geneva, 16 May 1948 (CFM)
58 Ibid
59 Siki, Bela, in *Homage a Dinu Lipatti*, Op. cit. p. 86
60 To FM (CFM)
61 *In Memoriam Dinu Lipatti*. Geneva, Op. cit. p. 56
62 *Homage a Dinu Lipatti*, Op. cit. p. 81
63 To FM (CFM)
64 Geneva, 31 October 1948 (CFM)
65 From letters to his family at end of 1948 (DT)
66 Montana, 10 January 1949 (CFM)
67 To FM. Amsterdam, 31 January 1949
68 Fragments from letters to FM (CFM)
69 *Homage a Dinu Lipatti*. Op. cit. p. 81
70 Fragments from letters to FM (CFM)
71 From personal recollections of Henri Gagnebin to Grigore Bargauanu, Geneva, 1967

4: Finis Tragediae

1 The review entitled: "Au Victoria Hall la Rentrée de DL" in an unidentified newspaper, February 1950
2 *Ebauche d'un projet pour un cour d'interpretation au Conservatoire de Genève* (May 1950). In *Dinu Lipatti 1917–1950*. FC 491/5. "Album dedicated to the memory of DL, produced for Pathé-Marconi by the Société Nationale Mercure, Paris publishers, 2 December 1955, p. 23
3 *Hommage a Dinu Lipatti*, Geneva, Labor et Fides, 1951, p. 61
4 To FM from ML. August 1950 (CFM) *N.B.* The discs mentioned in the letter were also issued on 78, like all of DL's recordings
5 To AL. Geneva, 9 September 1950 (Collection Professor DT)
6 To FM. Geneva, 14 September 1950 (Collection Professor DT)
7 ML. *Dinu Lipatti. Son dernier recital*, In *Le Guide du Concert et du Disque*, Paris, No 177, 27 December 1957.
8 Chapuis, Jacques. 'Il aimait repétér cette phrase: Ne vous servez-pas de la musique, servez-la" In *Homage a Dinu Lipatti*, Op. cit. p. 41
9 Dr. Henri Dubois-Ferriere who died 20 years after Dinu Lipatti

initiated in 1970 "Fondation Dr H. Dubois-Ferriere—Dinu Lipatti pour la lutte contre la léucémie et les maladies de sang". The Foundation works in close collaboration with the Department of Hematology at the Cantonal Hospital in Geneva. Many types of books and records connected with DL are donated to the Foundation for further research

5: The Interpreter

1 *Ebauche d'un projet pour un cour d'interpretation au Conservatoire de Geneve* (May 1950). In *Dinu Lipatti 1917–1950*. Op. cit. p. 23
2 *Une lettre...* in *In Memoriam Dinu Lipatti*. Geneva, Labor et Fides, 1970, p. 107
3 *Homage a Dinu Lipatti*.Geneva, Labor et Fides, 1951, p. 32
4 *In Memoriam Dinu Lipatti*. Op. cit. p. 95–96
5 AL. *Dinu Lipatti. La douleur de ma vie*. Geneva, ed. Perret-Gentil, 1967, p. 43
6 Legge, Walter. *Dinu Lipatti enregistre a Geneve*, in *Revue musicale de la Suisse Romande*, Lausanne, December 1960, p. 224
7 *In Memoriam Dinu Lipatti*. Op. cit. p. 38
8 Une lettre... in *In Memoriam Dinu Lipatti*. Op. cit. p. 108
9 *In Memoriam Dinu Lipatti*. Op. cit. p. 79
10 Paris, Hachette, 1965
11 Guitton, Pierre, in Paris probably in 1947
12 *Lipatti interprete de Chopin*, in *Dinu Lipatti 1917–1950*. Op. cit. p. 22
13 To FM. Geneva 16 May 1948 (CFM)

6: The Composer

1 *In Memoriam Dinu Lipatti*. Op. cit. p. 39
2 Oana Pop, Rodica. *Compositie inedita de Dinu Lipatti*, in *Lucrari de Muzicologie*, Vol 3, Cluj 1967. Now published—together with *Improvisations for Violin, Cello and Piano*—in the book *My Friend Dinu Lipatti* by MS, ed. Muzicala, Bucharest 1981
3 *Heterophony* (From Greek *heteros*-another; *phone*-sound, voice). Musical structure of folkloric origin which extends beyond Europe, based on the flow of two or more voices (instruments) of the same melodic line, with deviations from this line in one or more parts, due to a degree of improvisation from the interpreter. From Sava Iosif and Vartolomei, Luminita. *Dictionar de Muzica*, Bucharest, ed. Stiintifica si Enciclopedica, 1979)
4 Nicoara, Adriana. *De vorba cu Dinu Lipatti*, Universul Literar, Burcharest, 1943
5 From letter to FM. Fundateanca, 28 August 1941 (CFM)

6 Anuarul Ateneului Roman, 1942, Bucharest 1943, p. 145
7 *Bazele modale ale cromatismului diatonic*, Bucharest, ed. Muzicala, 1966
8 R.-Aloys Mooser, *Dinu Lipatti—Concertino in Classical Style* (Geneva May 22, 1954). In *Aspects de la Musique Contemporaine (1953–57)*, Geneva, Ed. Labor et Fides, 1957 p. 48–50
9 R.-Aloys Mooser, *Dinu Lipatti—Danses Roumaines pour piano et orchestre*, in *Regards sur la Musique Contemporaine (1921–1946)*, Lausanne, Librarie P. Rouge, 1946, p. 414
10 *Hommage à Dinu Lipatti*. Op. cit. p. 80

Appendix 1

Chopin Concerto in E minor

TRANSLATORS' NOTE

Dinu Lipatti's recording of the Chopin Concerto in E minor was first issued by the EMI Company in 1965; in the USA on 'Seraphim' label, and subsequently it was published in many other countries (see Discography p.208). A note on the record-sleeve reads:

> This recording comes from a tape which EMI acquired, made at a concert in Switzerland in May 1948. Although there is no question but that the playing is of Dinu Lipatti, extensive enquiries have failed to establish the name of the conductor and orchestra...

Very suprising indeed. But, for Lipatti's admirers the record was a revelation since nothing was known about the existence of such a tape, which may have been done by an amateur during a rehearsal (see Discography at end of 'In Memoriam Dinu Lipatti' Op. cit.)

In 1981, when EMI issued a complete album of 'The Art of Dinu Lipatti', Robin Ray, in the BBC programme *Music Weekly* (8.3.81) made an extraordinary announcement. A certain music lover, Mr Michael C. Matthews, from Eastbourne, Sussex, claimed that the Lipatti's record was identical in all respects with that first issued in the early 1950's by the Czech company 'Supraphon', with the Polish Pianist Halina Czerny-Stefanska, as soloist, and the Czech Philharmonic Orchestra conducted by Vaclav Smetaček. Indeed, the BBC engineers' tests proved the claim to be correct. This astonishing discovery prompted Robin Ray to raise certain pertinent questions to which no answers were then available: How was the supposedly 'Lipatti Tape' discovered? Who had authenticated it? How was it that Dinu Lipatti's widow knew nothing of the recording? If EMI claimed that the tape had been made at a public concert, how can the absence of any audience noise be explained? Had Halina Czerny-Stefanska heard the so-called

Lipatti record? If the same pianist is soloist on both discs, who receives the royalties?

The world-wide publicity which surrounded this discovery brought forth a statement from Mr Peter Andry, the Director of EMI International Classical Division which is as surprising as Mr Matthews's original bombshell. We publish here some relevant excerpts from the EMI statement.

> In 1964, a Mr Kaiser, a great admirer of Lipatti, brought a tape of the Chopin Concerto, assuming that the soloist was Dinu Lipatti, to the EMI former distributor in Zurich, Hans Jecklin, who told Madeleine Lipatti about this great discovery. Mr Kaiser received the tape as a gift from a Mr Collins, an American collector of folklore music, for having been given a number of rare recordings of Swiss folkmusic. Both Mr Collins and Mr Kaiser were convinced that the tape was genuine and, indeed, when this was authenticated by Walter Legge, Ernest Ansermet *and* Madame Lipatti, EMI issued the recording. The company emphasises that there was no suggestion of any 'conscious deception' and the independent authentication by those best placed to recognise Lipatti's playing proves their good faith. Unfortunately, at the time of this incident, Walter Legge who was personally responsible for securing for posterity such few recordings of Dinu Lipatti which survive, and Ernest Ansermet, the great Swiss Conductor, who had been a close friend and collaborator of the artist, were both dead. Madame Lipatti was very ill in her Southern France home and could not give any explanation.
>
> It was thanks to the wide publicity in the European press that there was, if one may call it so, a happy ending to this disturbing situation.
>
> Apparently, early in 1960, a Dr Kaspar—known as an early radio pirate—came to Madeleine Lipatti offering her a tape of the Chopin Concerto, as played by Dinu Lipatti, to be turned into a gramophone record. But, when the company (at the time it was 'Columbia') made some enquiries as to how the musicians should be paid, Dr Kaspar disappeared, together with the precious tape.
>
> And now, a Dr Marc Gertsch—a friend of the Lipatti family and a great fan of Dinu's—produced what we consider to be a genuine tape. As a boy of 14 he got hold of a tape (probably the same one as Dr Kaspar had) which a Berne radio amateur had

recorded from a transmission on 7 February 1950, on a REVOX recorder. The young boy re-recorded it in 1951, with a hand-held microphone on a Webcor machine. The technical quality of the tape, of course, leaves a great deal to be desired, but, despite this, the playing of Lipatti is remarkable and of outstanding beauty. The tape has been pitch-corrected and re-transferred by EMI and forms the basis of a new EMI issue. The tape has been authenticated by Dr V. Hauser, Director of Schweitzerische Interpreten-Gesellschaft, as a true recording of the concert on 7 February 1950 by the Tonhalle Orchestra conducted by Otto Ackermann, a compatriot of Lipatti. The previous EMI recording has been withdrawn throughout the world and all those possessing a copy could obtain a free record of the newly issued one.

AUTHORS' NOTE

Listening to the authentic tape of the live performance of Dinu Lipatti (as soloist in the Chopin E minor Concerto, with the Tonhalle Orchestra of Zurich, conducted by the Rumanian born conductor, Otto Ackermann, and issued by EMI in 1981) one realizes immediately that the artist brings a new vision to this interpretation. This does not appear as an antithesis of a faithful rendering of the score, but on the contrary, it takes one on a higher plane, transending it. As in other performances, there is here also that specific clarity in the voicing of the lines in their various harmonic context, each one with its own colour or timbre as well as with noticeable dynamic contrasts of the different planes. This is an execution of great intensity and, at the same time, with subtle chiselling of the tonal palette in spite of the uneveness of the quality of the recording itself.

Throughout the concerto, a discreet acompaniment, even in the less inspired passages with the recurrent 'Alberti Bass', allows the melodic lines to gain in expressiveness and there are moments of unique refinement of nuances, as at the end of the second movement when there is a magical change of tonality from A flat to E (bars 101–103).

Lipatti allows himself certain fluctuations of tempo which bring new dimensions to the work—as in the first movement, with metronomical oscillations between 92 and 152. These are a direct result of the artist's need to emphasise the phrasing or to introduce a rubato, but these changes are so subtle and are executed with such sensitivity that they are noticeable only when studied under the scrutiny of the metronome. Only an artist and musician with a supreme control of the instrument can find the right balance to achieve that 'Chopinian rubato' which was praised even by Toscanini.

This recording of the Chopin Concerto was made in the last year of Lipatti's life, in the same month as the Schumann concerto under Ansermet, and it radiates a poignant, yet serene and resigned sadness.

TONHALLE ZÜRICH GROSSER SAAL

Montag, den 6. Februar 1950, 20.15 Uhr

ÖFFENTLICHE HAUPTPROBE

Dienstag, den 7. Februar 1950, 20.15 Uhr

7. ABONNEMENTSKONZERT

der Tonhalle-Gesellschaft

Leitung: **Otto Ackermann**
Solist: **Dinu Lipatti** (Klavier)
Orchester: **Das Tonhalle-Orchester**

PROGRAMM

F. MENDELSSOHN	**Sinfonie Nr. 4, in A-dur, op. 90 „Italienische“** Allegro vivace — Andante con moto — Con moto moderato — Saltarello
F. CHOPIN	**Klavierkonzert Nr. 1, in e-moll, op. 11** Allegro maestoso — Larghetto — Rondo
	PAUSE
F. CHOPIN	**Solostücke für Klavier** Nocturne in Des-dur, op. 27, Nr. 2 Etude in e-moll, op. 25, Nr. 5 Etude in Ges-dur, op. 10, Nr. 5
O. RESPIGHI	**Pinien von Rom, sinfonische Dichtung** Pinien der Villa Borghese Pinien bei einer Katakombe Pinien auf dem Janiculum Pinien der Via Appia

Konzertflügel Steinway & Sons (Vertreter: Hug & Co. und Pianohaus Jecklin)

Appendix 2

Two recordings were issued after the original book was published:

1 Bach Concerto in D minor, which Lipatti played with the Concertgebuow Orchestra under Eduard van Beinum on 2 October 1941 at the Concertgebuow Hall in Amsterdam. This was released only in 1977 from a private tape (see Discography p.203)
2 The Schumann Concerto in A minor with Ernest Ansermet conducting the Orchestre de la Suisse Romande on 22 February 1950 at the Victoria Hall, Geneva. It was released in 1970 by Decca (now EMI) from the tape found in the archives of the Radio Suisse Romande (see Discography p.216).

1 The recordings of the Bach concerto presents some aspects of interest to both performers and Bach scholars. This is the only Concerto by Bach recorded by Lipatti and shows not only his qualities as interpreter but also his ideas on how far a performer should respect the original text. He adopts from the Busoni edition certain variants when he believes that these underline the artistic value of the concerto but he rejects those which might diminish it. He was aware that it was not satisfactory to reproduce faithfully the harpsichord score when playing the piano. The harpsichord timbre stands out when accompanied by a string orchestra while the piano timbre is not favoured in similar situations. Again, when he senses that the piano transcription is not quite right he interrupts the musical discourse, allowing the orchestra to continue alone. This happens on several occasions: in the introductions and endings of the first two movements and in the development of the Finale.

From Busoni he takes octave passages or plays motives, when repeated, in thirds or in another register—suggesting the harpsichord or organ techniques. It should also be noticed how he uses the expressive qualities of the piano in crescendi and decrescendi of great refinement and tension as well as in occasional dynamic contrasts between phrases or even within one single phrase. There is an extra dimension added to the performance and a polyphonic clarity, specific to Lipatti, and these are emphasised by his effective pedalling.

The conception of this concerto represents a synthesis of Lipatti's ideas which he has already expressed in the sketch of the 'Cours d'Interpretation' which he had planned to give at the Geneva Conservatoir in collaboration with Nadia Boulanger. He also told his students that it was more important to be faithful to the 'Ur-spirit' than to the 'Ur-text'. A true respect of the authentic text does not consist in a formal rendering but in bringing to light its artistic meaning.

2 The second version of the Schumann Concerto was issued by Decca as late as 1970 (see Discography p.216).

As to be expected this recording cannot be as good technically as the first one which was done under optimum conditions, in the studio, with the Philharmonia Orchestra conducted by Karajan and issued in 1948. Yet, this second recording presents some qualities which cannot be found in the Karajan version. There is an intense depth of feeling and breath of emotion which pervades all through the three movements. One must also remember Lipatti's illness which took a turn for the worse in the two years which elapsed between the two performances, as well as Dinu's own words that these years of suffering have brought a more mature and more profound understanding of the music. From the first chords of the Introduction, the youthful enthusiasm of the first version gives way to a slower, more dramatic and almost painful statement. The nostalgic, almost light mood of the main theme receives a new accent of suffering and then dies slowly away towards the end. A wrong note in bar 66 of the exposition of the first movement (G instead of A)—an unheard-of occurence in Lipatti's playing—adds extra poignancy, making one think of the artist's physical frailness in this last year of his life which stands out in such contrast with the vitality of his interpretation.

The Ansermet version is also richer in nuances and provides a more subtle dynamo-agogic quality. One cannot help noticing the spiritual quality of the Cadenza of the first movement or the delicacy of the Intermezzo, this time played with more freedom and at a slightly faster tempo. Lipatti has assimilated the interpretation of this concerto to such an extent that it is perhaps true to say that he is expressing here his own psychological portrait.

Discography

Compiled with Notes by Grigore Bargauanu

This discography contains all known Lipatti recordings up to the present time. Composers are listed in alphabetical order and by their works. Most recordings were issued on 78 rpm and remade on *monaural-microgorve* after the death of the artist. (Exceptions: Schumann's *Concerto*, by Lipatti-Ansermet and several American re-issues on stereophonic recording made from the original monaural).

Only recording companies and institutions who issued the first releases of recordings are indicated with the serial number, matrix or catalogue number, names of makers and date of the first release, etc., and- for unedited recordings- where these may be found. The recording of Chopin's *Concerto No 1*, a special and unique case, is described in greater detail (see Appendix).

Lipatti's recordings have been reissued by many companies and under different labels. Apart from EMI Records of Gt Britain which include Columbia and His Master's Voice, and which owns the majority of recordings released practically world-wide, there are Decca (Gt Britain), Jecklin (Switzerland), Electrecord (Rumania). We must also mention: Angel, Everest, Monitor, Odyssey, Seraphim and Turnabout (USA), Déesse (France) and Melodia (USSR), Angel Records (Japan).

It can only be hoped that one day certain unedited recordings of great artistic value may be released; on the other hand the search for unedited Lipatti recordings continues and the future may well hold in store some beutiful and unexpected surprises...

Johann Sebastian Bach

1. *Concerto No 1 in D minor for piano and string orchestra* BWV 1052
(Allegro, Adagio, Allegro)
Amsterdam Concertgebouw Orchestra cond: Edward van Beinum
Amsterdam, 2 October 1947
Private recording of concert given at the Concertgebouw Hall

JECKLIN (Switzerland) 'Historische Tondokumente.Catalogue
No:. Disc 541
Release: 1977(33 rpm)
Note. This disc was issued by the Educational Media Associates, Berkeley and released with the *Liebeslieder* Waltzes Op. 52 by Brahms under the label:
OPUS Records (USA) Dave Music
Catalogue No:
MLG 80 (33 rpm)

2. *Chorale* 'Jesu, Joy of Man's Desiring' in G major, No 10, Finale of the Cantata BWV 147 (Herz und Mund und Tat und Leben-Festo Visitationis Mariae) transcription for piano by Myra Hess.

a. Bucharest 28 April 1941	RADIO ROMANIA Test record. Two unedited versions. *Disc* (25cm78 rpm) Library of Recordings, Radio Romania, Bucharest (Nos 3474/b,3475b) *Tape* Electrecord Archives Bucharest Radiodiffusion Rumania, Bucharest.
b.(1) London 20 February 1947	COLUMBIA (Gt Britain) Producer: Walter Legge Balance Engineer:Charles Anderson
(2) London 4 March 1947	unedited Producer: Walter Legge Balance Engineer: Douglas Larter
(3) London 24 September 1947	Matrix No 1 CA 20314 Producer: Walter Legge Balance Engineer: Harold Davidson Released: 1947 (78 rpm, rep. 33 rmp) *Note* This is the best test, among many others, which received the temporary approval of Lipatti.
c. Geneva 10 July (1950) (Studio 2 Radio Geneva)	COLUMBIA (Gt Britain) Matrix No CZ 2188 Producer: Walter Legge' Balance Engineer: Anthony Griffith Release: 1951 (78 rpm, reissued 33 rpm) *Compact Disc* EMI Records CDC 74517-2 Released: 1986 (Digital remastering)

3. Two *Chorale Preludes*: 'Ich ruf zu Dir, Herr Jesu Christ' in F minor BWV 639 from *Orgelbüchlein* and 'Nun komm'der Heiden Heiland' in G major,BWV 659 from the *Achtzehn Choräle von verschiedener Art* (Leipzig). Piano transcription by Busoni.

a. Geneva, 10 July 1950 (Sudio 2 Radio Geneva)

COLUMBIA (Great Britain)
Matrix No:CZX 266 ('Ich ruf...)
CZX 265 ('Nun komm...)
Producer: Walter Legge
Balance Engineer: Anthony Griffith
Release: 1951 (78 rpm, reissue 33 rpm)
Compact Disc: ibid. Bach 2c.

Note The company DACAPO (EMI Electrola – R.F.A.) issued a version dated 'September 1947' without any other mention (see the records of the series 'Unvergänglich-Unvergessen' and the album 'Dinu Lipatti 1C 197-53780/86M). There must probably be a confusion of dates as the EMI archives in London have no trace of this version and if one compares it with the recording of July 1950 there is no difference in the interpretation. Therefore it must be a copy of the recording mentioned above.

4. *Partita No 1 in B flat* BWV 825 (Prelude, Allemande, Courante, Sarabande, Minuet I, Minuet II, Gigue)

a. Paris, 25 June 1936
Fragments (Prelude, Sarabande, Allemande) performed on the harpsichord.
N.B. The end of the record contains a brief improvisation on the *Toccata in C major* motif by J. S. Bach-Busoni.

ECOLE NORMALE DE MUSIQUE (France)'
Trial disc. unedited
Record (25 cm. 78 rpm). Library of the Rumanian Academy.
Tape Electrecord Archives, Bucharest
Note The Ecole Normale de Musique no longer possesses these recordings which were destroyed during the war.

b. Geneva, 9 July 1950 (Studio 2, Geneva Radio)

COLUMBIA (Gt Britain)
Matrix No: CZX 271–4
Producer: Walter Legge
Balance Engineer: Anthony Griffith

Release: 1950 (78 rpm, reissued 33 rpm)
Compact Disc: ibid. Bach 2c.

c. Besançon, 16 September 1950
Public broadcast of the last recital, Salle du Parlement. N.B. The broadcast cover the soloist's entrance on to the platform and an improvised extended *arpeggio* in B flat major before the opening of the *Partita*.
Note see J. S. Bach 3

RADIO DIFFUSION FRANCAISE
COLUMBIA 'His last recital'
Recording transferred to EMI (Gt Britain)
Matrix No: XLX 543
Release: 1957 (33 rpm)

5. *Siciliano* in G minor, second movement of the *Sonata No 2 in E flat major* for flute and harpsichord BWV 1031, transcription for piano by Wilhelm Kempf.
a. Geneva, 6 July 1950 (Studio 2, Geneva Radio)
Note see J. S. Bach 3

COLUMBIA (Gt Britain)
Matrix No: CZ 2187
Producer: Walter Legge
Balance Engineer: Anthony Griffith
Release: 1951 (78 rpm, reissued 33 rpm)
Compact Disc: ibid. Bach 2c.

Béla Bartók

1. *Concerto No 3 for piano and orchestra*
(Allegretto, Adagio religioso, Allegro vivace)
Südwestfunk Orchestra, Zurich
cond. Paul Sacher
– Baden-Baden, May 1948

SÜDWESTFUNK (R.F.A.)
unedited
Note The recording was never issued because the conductor did not consider it satisfactory

Johannes Brahms

1. Two *Intermezzi*: B flat minor, Op 117 No 2 and E flat minor, Op 118 No 6.
– Paris, 25 June 1936

ECOLE NORMALE DE MUSIQUE (France)
Trial record: unedited
Record (25cm, 78 rpm) Library of the Rumanian Acadamy,
Tape Electrecord Archives Bucharest Radio Romania, Bucharest
Note. See J. S. Bach 4a

2. Two *Intermezzi*: A mior. Op 116 No 2 and E flat major, Op 117 No. 1 – Bucharest, 1941(?)

Trial Record (Rumania)
unedited
Private collection.
Tape Electrecord Archives, Bucharest Radio Romania, Bucharest.

3. *Liebeslieder* op 52, Waltzes for Piano Duet and Vocal Quartet ad lib (verse from *Polydora* by Daumer)
Nos 1–6
Nos 7–13
Nos 14–18 &1
Interpreters: Dinu Lipatti -Nadia Boulanger with Marie Blanche, Comtesse de Polignac, Iréne Kedrof, Paul Dérenne(Nos 1–3, 17, 18, 1
Hugues Cuénod (Nos 5, 6, 8–12, 14–16),
Doda Conrad.
Paris, 20 February 1937
(M.2LA 1538–9)
12 March 1937
(M.2LA 1594–5,1555)
22 January 1938
(M. 2LA 2378)

LA VOIX DE SON MAITRE (France)

Matrix No:2LA 1538-9
Matrix No:2LA 1595 & 2378
Matrix No:2LA 1555 & 1594
Published: 1938 (78 rpm reissue 33 rpm)
Note. This recording was reissued on 33rpm by the Educational Media Associates, Berkeley, and released with the Concerto in D minor by J.S. Bach under the label:
OPUS Records (USA)
Calalogue No: MLG 80
Issued 1977 (33 rpm)

4. Seven *Waltzes* op 39 for two pianos, in the following order:
No. 6 in C sharp, No 15 in A, No 2 in E, No 1 in B,
No 14 in A minor, No 10 in G, No 5 in E, No 6 – repeat
Interpreters: Dinu Lipatti-Nadia Boulanger
Paris 25 February 1937

LA VOIX DE SON MAITRE (France)

Matrix No: 2LA 1559

Matrix No: 2LA 1560

Released: 1938 (78 rpm reissue 33 rpm)

Frederic Chopin

1. *Barcarolle in F sharp major*, op. 60
London 21 April 1948
(Studio 3 Abbey Road)

COLUMBIA (Gt Britain)
Matrix No: CAX 10237–8
Producer: Walter Legge
Balance Engineer: Robert Beckett
Release: 1951 (78 rpm, reissued 33 rpm)

Compact Disc EMI Records (Gt Britain) CDC 7 47390 2
Release: 1986 (Digital remastering)

2. *Concerto for piano and orchestra No 1 in E minor*, Op. 11 (Allegro maestoso, Romance-Larghetto, Rondo-Vivace). Zurich Tonhalle. Orchestra, cond. Otto Ackermann –Zurich 7 February 1950
Private recording of concert given at the Tonnhalle.

EMI Records (Gt Britain)
Private recording: Dr Marc Gertsch
New Matrix No: 2 XEA 7274–5
Tapes remastered by Keith Hardwick
Release: August 1981 (33 rpm)

Note: A recording of Chopin's Concerto in E minor distributed between 1966 and 1981, was attributed to Dinu Lippati in error. In order to avoid any further confusion arising the main releases of this apocryphal recording are listed as presently identified: (The orchestra, conductor and place or recording being unknown).

Concerto for piano and orchestra No 1 in E minor, Op.11
Dinu Lipatti and orchestra (or: Dinu Lipatti. X) –May 1948.

I. COLUMBIA (EMI, Electrola – RFA)
Unvergänglich – Unvergessen, Folge 211
Catalogue No: C 80934
Matrix No: XAX 2972–3
Release: 1966 (33 rpm)

II. SERAPHIM (USA)
Catalogue No: 60007
Matrix No: XAX 2972–3
Release: 1966

III. HIS MASTERS VOICE (EMI – Britain)
"Dinu Lipatti plays Chopin"
Catalogue No: HQM 1248 (IE 053. 01238 M)
Matrix No: 2XEA. 4265–6
Release: 1971

IV. DACAPO (EMI. Electrola – W. Germany)
"Unvergänglich – Unbergessen"
"Dinu Lipatti 6"
Catalogue No: C 80934
(1C 049–01 716 M)
Matrix No: XAX 2972–3
Release: 1976

V. HIS MASTER'S VOICE
(EMI – Britain)
"The Art of Dinu Lipatti"
(album of four records – Chopin *Conerto* third record)
Catalogue No: RLS 749
Matrix No: 2XEA.4265–6
Release: 1980

VI. DACAPO (EMI Electrola – RFA)
"Dinu Lipatti"
(album of seven records – Chopin *Concerto* sixth record)
catalogue No: 1C 197–53 780/86 M
Matrix No: XAX 2972–3
Release: January 1981

Concerto No 1 in E minor for piano and orchestra, Op. 11
Halina Czerny-Stefanska Piano
Czech Philharmonic Orchestra, cond Vaclav Smetaček
Prague, 24–26 August 1955

SUPRAPHON (Czechoslovakia)
Ariola – Eurodisc (RFA)
Catalogue No: 203 729–250
Producer: Dr Ladislav Sip
Balance Engineer: Miroslav Svaton
Release: Prague, 1955, Munich, 1981

Note The true identitiy of this recording was discovered in 1981 when it was immediately re-released with the following declration: "Recording erroneously attributed to Dinu Lipatti" (See Appendix 1, p. 197)

3. *Etude No 5 in G flat Majow*, Op. 10 "Black Keys"

a. Bucharest, 28 April 1941

RADIO ROMANIA
Trial recording: unedited
Record (25 cm, 78 rpm) Record Library of Radio Romania, Bucharest (No. 3476/b)
Tape Electrecord Archives, Bucharest. Radio Romania, Bucharest

b. Zurich, 7 February 1950
Encore at the end of the Tonhalle concert

JECKLIN (Switzerland)
'Historische Tondokumente'
Histroical Sound Archives
Private recording:
Dr Marc Gertsch
Release: 1977 (33 rpm)

4. *Etude No 5 in E minor*, Op 25 – Zurich, 7 February 1950 Encore at the end of the Tonhalle concert	JECKLIN (Switzerland) 'Historische Tondokumente' Private recording: Dr Marc Gertsch Release: 1977 (33 rpm)
5. *Mazurka No 3 in C sharp minor*, Op 50 No 3 –Geneva, 11 July 1950 (Studio 2, Radio Geneve)	COLUMBIA (Gt Britain) Matrix No: CZX 277 Producer: Walter Legge Balance Engineer: Anthony Griffith Release: 1950 (78 rpm, reissue 33 rpm) *Compact Disc* EMI Records (Gt Britain) CDC 7 47390 2 Release: 1986 (Digital remastering)
6. *Noctrurne No 8 in D flat major*, Op 27, No. 2	
a. London, 20 February 1947 (Studio 3, Abbey Road)	COLUMBIA (Gt Britain) Matrix No: CA 20315–6 Producer: Walter Legge Balance Engineer: Charles Anderson Release: 1947 (78 rpm, reissue 33 rpm) *Compact Disc* EMI Records (Gt Britain) CDC 7 473902 Release: 1986 (Digital remastering)
b. Zurich, 7 February 1950 'Encore' at the end of the Tonhalle concert	JECKLIN (Switzerland) Private recording: Dr Marc Gertsch, Release: 1977 (33 rpm)
7. *Sonata No 3 in B minor*, Op 58 (Allegro maestoso. Scherzo-molto vivace, Largo Finale-presto non tanto) –London, 1 and 4 March 1947 (Studio 3, Abbey Road)	COLUMBIA (Gt Britain) Matrix No: CAX 9838–43 Producer: Walter Legge Balance Engineer: Douglas Larter Release: 1947 (78 rpm, reissue 33 rpm)

Note This record was awarded the *Charles Cros Academy's* Grand Prix du Disque in Paris, 1949

8. *Waltz No 2 in A flat Major* Op 34 No1

a. Bucharest, 28 April 1941	RADIO ROMANIA Trial recording unedited *Record* (25 cm, 78 rpm) Record Library of Radio Romania (No 3476/a) *Tape* Electrecord Archives, Bucharest. Radio Romania, Bucharest.
b. London, 24 September 1947 (Studio 3, Abbey Road)	COLUMBIA (Gt Britain) Matrix No: CAX 10027 Producer: Walter Legge Balance Engineer: Harold Davidson Release 1947 (78 rpm, reissue 33 rpm)
c. Geneva, 3 – 12 July 1950 (Studio 2, Radio Geneva)	COLUMBIA (Gt Britian) See: 14 Waltses – Chopin (9)
9. *14 Waltzes*, in the following order:	COLUMBIA (Gt Britain)
No 4 in F major, Op 34 No 3 Mo 5 in A flat major, Op 42 No 6 in D flat major, Op 64 No 1 No 9 in A flat major, Op 69 No 1 No 7 in C sharp minor, Op 64 No 2 No 11 in G flat major, Op 70 No 1 No 10 in B minor, Op 69 No 2 No 14 in E minor Op posth.	Matrix No: XAX 108
No 3 in A minor, Op 34 No 2 No 8 in A flat major, Op 64 No 3 No 12 in F minor, Op 70 No 2 No 13 in D flat major, Op 70 No 3 No 1 in E flat major, Op 18 No 2 in A flat major, Op 34 No 1	Matrix No: XAX 109
Geneva, 3–12 July 1950 (Sudio 2, Geneva Radio)	Producer: Walter Legge Balance Engineer: Anthony Griffith Release: 1950 (78 rpm, reissue 33 rpm) *Compact Disc* EMI Records (Gt Britain) CDC 7 473902 Release: 1986 (Digital remastering)

10. *13 Waltzes*, in the following order:
Nos 5, 6, 9, 7, 11, 10, 14 –
Nos 3, 4, 12, 13, 8, 1 –
–Besançon, 16 September 1950
Public broadcast of the last recital, Salle du Parlement.

RADIODIFFUSION FRANCAISE
Matrix No: XLX 545
Matrix No: XLX 546
COLUMBIA 'His last Recital' recording transferred to EMI (Gt Britain)
Release: 1957 (33 rpm)

Note. Waltz No 2 in A flat major Op 34, No 1 was not performed.

Georges Enesco

1. *Bourrée from Suite pour le piano No 2 in D major*, Op 10.
– Bucharest, 2 March 1943
(Studio of the Rumanian Broadcasting)

ELECTRECORD (Romania)
Historical recording
Catalogue No: ECE 0766
Original recording 78 rpm on DISCOTECA label, reissued 33 rpm.

Note. This recording was made at the request of the Rumanian Folklore Archives. Enesco recorded the slow movements of his *Suite No 2* (Sarabande and Pavane) and Lipatti the rapid movements (Toccata and Bourrée). Lipatti's recording of the Toccata has been lost. A recording of Enesco's Suite' Impressions d'Enfance' is known to have been made but it has not been found.

2. *Sonata in F sharp minor for piano* Op 24, No 1. Second Movement, Presto Vivace.
– Paris, 25 June 1936

ECOLE NORMALE DE MUSIQUE (France)
Trial record: unedited
Record (25 cm, 78 rpm) Library of the Rumanian Academy, Bucharest.
Tape Electrecord Archives, Bucharest, Radio Romania, Bucharest.
Note. See J. S. Bach 4a

3. *Sonata in D major for piano*, Op. 24 No. 3 (Vivace con brio, Andantion cantabile, Allegro con spirito)
–Radio Bern, October 1943

COLUMBIA (Gt Britain)
Matrix No: XZX 19
Release: 1956 (33 rpm)

4. *Sonata No 2 in F minor for piano and violin*, Op 6.
(Assez mouvementé, Tranquillement, Vif).
Interpreters; Dinu Lipatti – Georges Enesco
– Bucharest, 13 March 1943

ELECTRECORD (Romania)
Historical Recording
Cataloge Nos: ECD 61
ECD 0767
Original recording 78 rpm, released under DISCOTECA label, reissued on 33 rpm.

5. *Sanata No 3 in A minor for piano and violin*, Op 25,
"in popular Rumanian style".
(Moderato malinconico, Andante sostenuto e misterioso, Allegro con brio ma non troppo mosso)
– Bucharest, 11 March 1943

ELECTRECORD (Romania)
Historical Recording
Catalogue Nos: ECD 95
ECE 0767
Original recording 78 rpm, released under DISCOTECA label, reissued on 33 rpm.

Note Enesco wrote in the French original: "dans le caractère populaire roumain"

Edward Grieg

1. *Concerto in A minor for piano and orchestra*, Op 16
(Allegro molto moderato, Adagio, Allegro moderato molto e marcaio – Andante maestoso). The Philarmonia Orchestra, cond. Alceo Galliera

London, 18 and 19 September, 1947
(Abbey Road Studios)

COLUMBIA (Gt Britain)
Matrix No: CAX 10041–7
Producer: Walter Legge
Balance Engineer. Robert Beckett
Release: 1947 (78 rpm, reissue 33 rpm)

Dinu Lipatti

1. *Concertiono in classical style for piano and chamber orchestra*, Op 3
(Allegro maestoso, Adagio molto, Allegretto, Allegro molto).
Berlin Chamber Orchestra, cond. Hans von Benda
– Berlin, 14 January 1943

ELECTRECORD (Rumania)
Historical Recording
Catalogue Nos: ECD 1278
ECE 0766
Original recording 78 rpm, released under DISCOTECA label reissued 33 rpm.

2. *Sonatina for left hand alone*
(Allegro, Andante expressivo, Allegro).
– Bucharest, 4 March 1943
(Studio of Rumanian Broadcasting)

ELECRECORD (Rumania)
Historical Recording
Catalogue Nos: ECD 1278
ECE 0766
Original recording 78 rpm. released under DISCOTECA label, reissued 33 rpm.

Franz Liszt

1 *La Ronde des Lutins*, ('Gnomenreigen') Etude de Concert No 2 Bucharest, 28 April 1941

RADIO ROMANIA
Trial record unedited
Record (25cm, 78 rpm). Record Library Radio Romania, Bucharest. (No 3474/a)
Tape Electrecord Archives, Bucharest. Radio Romania, Bucharest.

2 *La Leggierezza*, "Caprice poetique" Etude de Concert No 2 – London, October 1946

COLUMBIA (Gt Britain)
unedited
Matrix No: CAX 9708–1
Produced: Walter Legge

Note. This recording has been made from the recordings done by Lipatti in Zürich during the summer of 1946 and they were damaged on the way to London. The release was not possible because of the faults on the matrix which, ultimately, was destroyed. The recording of Chopin Valse (No2?) had probably the same fate. According to Walter Legge's testimony, this recording should have completed the verso of the disc.

3. *Sonetto del Petrarca* No. 104 "Pace non trovo" *Années de pélérinage*, 2nd year, Italie No 5 (14)

a. London, October–November 1946

COLUMBIA (Gt Britain)
unedited No: CAX 9707–1
Producer: Walter Legge

b. London, 24 September 1947 (Studio 3, Abbey Road)

COLUMBIA (Gt Britain)
Matrix No: CA 20498–9
Producer: Walter Legge
Balance Engineer: Harold Davidson
Release: 1948 (78 rpm, reissue 33 rpm)
Note see Franz Liszt 2

Wolfgang Amadeus Mozart

1 *Concerto No 21 in C major* for piano and orchestra, K.V. 467 (Allegro maestoso, Andante, Allegro vivace assai). Cadenzas by Lipatti, Lucerne Festival Orchestra conducted by Herbert von Karajan.
–Lucerne, 23 August 1950
Public broadcast of the concert given in the Kunstaus.

COLUMBIA (Gt Britain)
Matrix No: XZ 9003–4
Release: 1961 (33 rpm)

2. *Sonata No 8 in A minor* K.V. 310 (Allegro maestoso, Andante cantabile con expressione Presto)

a. Geneva, 9 July 1950 (Studio 2, Geneva Radio)

COLUMBIA (Gt Britain)
Matrix No: CZX 267–70
Producer: Walter Legge
Balance Engineer: Anthony Griffith
Release: 1951 (78 rpm, reissue 33 rpm)
Compact Disc: ibid. Bach 2c.

b. Besançon, 16 September 1950 Public broadcast of the last recital. Salle du Parlement. N.B. The original recording contained a short improvisation before the *Sonata's* attack, marking the passage from the key of Bach's *Partita* (B flat Major) to that of Mozart *Sonata* (A minor)

RADIO DIFFUSION FRANCAISE
Matrix No: XLX 544
Release: 1957 (33 rpm)
COLUMBIA 'His last Recital' recording transferred to EMI Records (Gt Britain)

Note. The company DACAPO (EMI Electrola – RFG) issued a version dated 'January 1950' without any mention. In our opinion, this must be a copy of the recording of July 1950, as for some works by J. S. Bach.
Note: see J. S. Bach 3.

3. Mozart-Busoni. *Duettino concertante for two pianos.* Interpreters:: Madeleine Cantacuzène-Lipatti –Bucharest, 1940–41 (?)

Trial disc (Romania)
Private collection (Prof D Tanasescu, Bucharest) Disc in deteriorated condition.

Maurice Ravel

Alborada del gracioso (*Mirroirs* No 4)
London, 17 April 1948
(Studio 3, Abbey Road)

COLUMBIA (Gt Britain)
Matrix No: CA 20740–1
Producer: Walter Legge
Balance Engineer: Robert Beckett
Release: 1948 (78 rpm, reissue 33 rpm)

Domenico Scarlatti

1. *Sonata in G major* L. 387 (KK.14) –Bucharest, 28 April 1941

RADIO ROMANIA
Trial record: unedited
Record (25 cm, 78 rpm) Record Library of Radio Romania Bucharest (N0 3475–a)
Tape: Electrecord Archives Bucharest. Radio Romania Bucharest

2. *Sonata in D minor*, "Pastorale" L.413 (KK.9)
– London, 20 February 1947
(Studio 3, Abbey Road)

COLUMBIA (Gt Britain)
Matrix No: CA 20313
Producer: Walter Legge
Balance Engineer:
Charles Anderson
Release: 1951 (78 rpm, reissue 33 rpm)
Compact Disc: ibid. Bach 2c.

3. *Sonata in E major* L. 23 (KK.380)
–London, 27 September 1947
(Studio 3, Abbey Road)

COLUMBIA (Gt Britain)
Matrix No: 20504
Producer: Walter Legge
Balance Engineer:
Harold Davidson
Release: 1951 (78 rpm. reissue 33rpm)
Compact Disc: ibid. Bach 2c.

Franz Schubert

1. Two *Impromptus*: G flat major, Op 90 No 3 (D.899,3) and E flat major, Op 90 No 2 (D899,2)
Besançon. 16 September 1950
Public broadcast of last recital, Salle du Parlement.

RADIODIFFUSION FRANCAISE
COLUMBIA
'His Last Recital' Recording transferred to EMI Recording (Gt Britain)
Matrix No: XLX 544
Release: 1957 (33 rpm)

Robert Schumann

1. *Concerto in A minor for piano and orchestra*, Op.54 (Allegro affetuoso, Intermezzo-Andantino grazioso, Allegro vivace).

a. The Philharmonia Orchestra, cond: Herbert van Karajan
London 9 and 10 April 1948

COLUMBIA (Gt Britain)
Matrix No: CAX 10206–13
Producer: Walter Legge
Balance Engineer: Robert Beckett
Release: 1948 (78 rpm. reissue 33 rpm)

b. Orchestre de la Suisse Romande, cond: Ernest Ansermet
Geneva, 22 February 1950
Public recording of concert given at the Victoria Hall, released by courtesy of Radio Suisse Romande

DECCA (Gt Britain)
"Ace of Diamonds"
Stereophonic recording made from the original monaural
Release: 1970 (33 rpm)

2. *Etude Symphonique No 9*, Op 13
Bucharest, 28 April 1941

RADIO ROMANIA
Trial record: unedited
Record (25 cm, 78 rpm) Record Library Radio Romania, Bucharest (No 3476/b)
Tape Electrecord Archives, Bucharest Radio Romania, Bucharest.

Dinu Lipatti's Compositions

1 **Little Dinu Lipatti's Compositions:** 'transcribed from his own playing' by Joseph Paschill, May 1922.

1 Le Printemps
2 Chanson pour Grand-Mere
3 Dorelina
4 Triste Separation
5 March of the Urchins
6 Regrets
7 Doux Souvenir
8 A ma bonne Surcea

Dedicatee: No 6-'Mother'
Unpublished: Ms in Rumanian Academy Library
First Performance: Bucharest, May 1922. Pianist: the composer.

2 **Piano Sonata** (2nd Jan, 1932)
I Allegro moderato
II Andante
III Allegro

Motto: 'Music is the language of the Gods'
Unpublished: Ms. Library of Union of Rumanian Composers
Awards: 1st Mention in the National Competition for Composition 'George Enesco' (1932)
First London performance (1st Movt) 1 August, 1987; John Ogdon.

3 **Sonatina for Violin and Piano Op 1** (Fundateanca, 20 Sept 1933)
I Allegro moderato
II Andantino
III Allegro maestro

Motto: 'National music is the crown of feeling of a nation'
Dedicatee: 'A Monsieur Mihail Jora'
Publisher: Editura Muzicala, Bucuresti, 1970.
First Performance: Bucharest, 25 April 1934: Anton Adrian Sarvas with the composer at the piano.
Awards: 2nd Prize 'George Enescu' (1933)
Transcription for Two Pianos (1933) See No 3 bis.

3bis **Sonata in E minor for Two Pianos** – Transcription of op cit No 3.
Unpublished.

4 **Satrarii; Symphonic Suite, op 2** (1934)

I	Allegro maestoso	('The Gipsies are coming')
II	Andantino	('Idyl at Floreasca')
III	Allegro	('Ivresse')

Unpublished.
First Performance: Bucharest, 23 January 1936, Orchestra Filarmonica conducted by Mihail Jora.
Awards: 1st Prize (Honorary) 'George Enescu' (1934)
Silver Medal of the French Republic (1937)

5 **Cadenzas for Mozart Piano Concerto in D minor** K.V.466(1936)
Unpublished.

6 **Concertino in Classical Style for Pianos and Chamber Orchestra op 3** (1936)

I Allegro Maestoso
II Adagio molto
III Allegretto
IV Allegro molto

Dedicatee: 'Fraulein Florica Musicesco gewidmet'
Edited by: Universal Edition, Vienna, 1941 (U.E.11.296) out of print
First Performance: Bucharest, 5 Oct 1939; the composer with Orchestra Filarmonica, conducted by George Georgescu.
Note: Originally titled 'Suite in Classical Style'

7 **Fantasia for Violin, Violoncello and Piano** (1936)

I Allegro molto
II Andante
III Presto
IV Allegretto
V Grave
(VI Repeat of 1st Movm.)

Dedicatee: 'A mon maitre Alfred Cortot'
Unpublished.

8 **Suite in Classical Style for String Orchestra** (1936)
Unpublished.

(This composition whose manuscript is not known, is briefly mentioned in several letters and appears in a list of Lipatti's compositions in some of the concert programmes)

9 **Toccata for Chamber Orchestra** (1936) -unfinished
I Prelude
II Intermezzo

Unpublished: Ms. Library of Union of Rumanian Composers.
Note: Last movement was supposed to be a Fugue.

10 **Romantic Sonata for Piano in D** (April 1937) -unfinished.
I Allegro Appassionato
Unpublished

11 **Nocturne for Piano** (November 1937)
Moderato (theme moldave)

Dedicatee: 'A mon maitre Michel Jora'
Edited by Editura Muzicala, Bucuresti, 1981 (added to the book: *My Friend Dinu Lipatti* by Miron Soarec)
First Performance: Paris 16 Febr 1938; at the piano, the composer

12 **Three Dances for Two Pianos** (1937)

Dedicatee: 'A Madeleine Cantacuzène'
Unpublished: Ms. Rumanian Academy Library
First Performance: Bucharest, 16 Dec. 1939; Smaranda Athanasof and the composer.
Note: The Ms has only the first two Dances.

13 **Symphonie Concertante for Two Pianos and String Orchestra op 5** (Paris 11 April 1938)
I Molto maestoso
II Molto adagio
III Allegro con spirito

Dedicatee: 'A mon Maitre Charles Munch'
Publisher: Editura Muzicala Bucuresti, 1984
First Performance: Paris 10 May 1939; Clara Haskil with the composer; conductor Ionel Patin.

14 **Wind Quintet** (Paris 18 Sept 1938) -unfinished.
I Grave – Allegretto grazioso (unfinished)

Dedicatee: 'A Monsieur Roger Cortet'
Unpublished: Ms. Rumanian Academy Library

15 **Cadenzas for Two Piano Concerto** in Eb K.V.365 by Mozart (Paris, 19 Oct 1938)

Unpublished: Two ms. Rumanian Academy Library.

16 **Two Piano Suite** (Paris, 2 Nov 1938)

Unpublished:
First Performance: Paris, 19 Jan 1939; Nibya Bellini and the composer.
(Private performance: Paris 17 Jan 1939, Clara Haskil with the composer)

17 **Two Sonatas for Wind Quintet** – transcription of Scarlatti Sonatas (1938)

I C major
II G major

Unpublished.

18 **Introduction and Allegro For Solo Flute** (Paris, 11 June 1939)

I Rubato
II Con Brio

Dedicatee: 'A Monsieur R. Cortet'
Unpublished: Ms. Rumanian Academy Library.

19 **Concerto for Organ and Piano** (Fundateanca, 7/18 August, 1939)

I Allegretto
II Andante cantabile
III Allegro grazioso
IV Risoluto

Motto: 'J'ai composé cette histoire – simple, simple, simple, Pour mettre en fureur les gens – graves, graves, graves...' (Charles Cros)
Dedicatee: 'A Mlle Nadia Boulanger'
Unpublished: Three mss. Rumanian Academy Library
First Performance: Bucharest, 8 Dec 1970. Horst Gehan and Corneliu Gheorghiu.

20 **Two Dances in Rumanian Style For Two Pianos** (1939)
Unpublished.

21 **First Improvisation for Violin, Cello and Piano** (Bucharest 1939)
Dedicatee: 'dédiée a Soarec & Co avec ma solennelle bénédiction'
Editors: Ed. Muzicala, Bucuresti 1981 (Added to the book: 'My Friend Dinu Lipatti' by Miron Soarec)

22 **Trois Nocturnes Française for Piano op 6** (1939)
Nocturne in F sharp minor
Dedicatee: 'Dedié a Clara Haskil'
Publishers: Editions Salabert, Paris 1956 (E.A.S.16644)
First Performance: Bucharest, 16 Dec 1939 with the composer at the piano.

Note: Only this Nocturne of the three composed in 1939 is known although the others are mentioned in letters and programme notes and it appears that Lipatti had composed several and often performed three.

23 **Six Sonatas for Wind Quintet** – transcription of D. Scarlatti (1939)
- I Allegro marciale
- II Andante
- III Allegro ma non tropo
- IV Allegretto
- V Allegro moderato
- VI Allegro molto

First Performance: Paris, 1939, Philharmonic Quintet. *Unpublished*

24 **Fantasia for Piano op 8** (Fundateanca, 31 May 1940)
- a
  - I Andante malinconico – Vivace
  - II Molto tranquillo – Presto – Molto tranquillo
  - III Presto
- b
  - IV Allegretto cantabile
  - V Allegro – Maestoso

Dedicatee: 'Dedié à Madeleine Cantacuzène'
Unpublished: Manuscript, Library of Union of Rumanian Composers
First Performance: Bucharest, 12 May 1941; at the piano – the composer.

25 **Navarra by I. Albeniz**; piano transcription by D Lipatti (June 1940)
Unpublished: Ms in the Rumanian Academy Library

26 **Sonatina for Left Hand** (Fundateanca, August 1941)
- I Allegro
- II Andante espressivo
- III Allegro

Publishers: Editions Salabert, Paris, 1953 (E.A.S. 15589)
First London performance August 1987

27 **Three Symphonic Sketches, op 4** (1937–1941)
Unpublished
Note: See No 8 and no 28

28 **Concertino in French Style for Piano and Orchestra, op 7** (1939–1941)
Unpublished.
Note: No details of this composition available, but Lipatti included it in the list of his works.

29 **Pastorale in F for Piano** – transcription of the organ work of J. S. Bach, BWV 590 (1942? and August 1950)
- I Andantino tranquillo
- II Allegretto grazioso
- III Andante cantabile
- IV Allegro deciso

Publishers: Schott & Co Ltd, London, 1953 (5748)

30 **Rumanian Dances for Two Pianos** (Fundateanca, 17 July 1943)
I Vif
II Andantino
III Allegro vivace

Dedicatee: 'Dediées au Maître Ernest Ansermet'
Publishers: Editions Salabert, Paris, 1954 (E.A.S.15.711)
First London performance August 1987, John Ogdon/Brenda Lucas
Transcription for Piano and Orchestra (1945). See No 37

31 **Cadenzas for Haydn Concerto for Piano And Orchestra in D** (Hob. XVIII/II) (1944)

32 **Cadenzas for Mozart Concerto for Piano and Orchestra in Bb** (1944) *Unpublished*

33 **Chorale for Strings** (Pratteln 1944)
Unpublished.
Note: This work is mentioned only in Lipatti's correspondence. He hoped to include in this composition a vocal piece for alto ('Priere de St Francois')

34 **Cadenzas for Mozart Concerto for Piano and Orchestra in C** (K.V.467) (Montana 22 January 1945)
Publishers: Editura Muzicala, Bucuresti, 1971 (added to the book *Dinu Lipatti* by Dragos Tanasescu and Grigore Bargauanu)

35 **Five Songs on poems by Verlaine, op 9 for tenor and piano** (Fundateanca, 14 July 1941; Geneva, 20 March 1945)
1 A une Femme
2 Green
3–4 Deux Ariettes oubliées
I Il pleure dans mon coeur
II Le piano que baise une main frêle
5 Serenade

Unpublished: Ms Library of Union of Rumanian Composers
Note: From his correspondence we learn that Lipatti had written six Songs during 1941. He went several times over the manuscript but in the final version there were only five. This explains the two different dates at the end of the original manuscript.

36 **Four Melodies for Voice and Piano on poems by Rimbaud, Eluard, Valéry (for tenor and piano)** (June 1945)
1 Sensation (Rimbaud)
2 L'Amoureuse (Eluard)
3 Capitale de la Douleur (Eluard)
4 Les Pas (Valery)

Dedicatees: No 1 'A ma mère'; No 2 'A Madeleine' No 3 'A Marie Sarasin'; No 4 'A Germaine de Narros'

Unpublished: Ms Library of Union of Rumanian Composers
Note: Melody No 4, 'Les Pas' has been published, in a limited edition,

during the IV International Festival 'Georges Enesco'. Ed. Muzicala, Bucuresti, 1967.

37 **Rumanian Dances (Second Version) for Piano and Orchestra** (Merimont, 5 August 1945)
- I Vif
- II Andantino
- III Allegro Vivace

Dedicatee: 'Dediées au Maitre Ernest Ansermet'
Publishers: Editions Salabert, Paris, 1954 (E.A.S. 15.711) as a Two Piano score. Complete score, for Piano and Orchestra, on hire from the publishers.
First performance: Geneva, 10 October 1945; the composer with Suisse Romande Orchestra, cond. Ernest Ansermet.

38 **Aubade for Woodwind Quartet** (1949)
- I Prelude (Lento, Vivo, Lento)
- II Danse (Allegretto grazioso)
- III Nocturne (Andante espressivo)
- IV Scherzo (Presto)

Dedicatee: 'A Paul Sacher'
Publishers: Rongwen Music, Inc. New York, 1955 (R.M.2034) Contemporary Composers – Study Score Series No 17.
First performance: London, 5 March 1951

39 **La Marche d'Henri**
A Musical Joke for Piano Duet (one piano) (20 March 1950)

Dedicatee: 'A Henry Dubois-Ferrière'
Unpublished:
Note: Primo has the mention 'Gabrielle', while Secundo has 'Henri'.

40 **Two Piano Studies** – transcriptions of two Chorales from the Cantata BWV 208 ('Was mir behagt') by J. S. Bach (Sept 1950)
- I Allegro ('Weil die wollenreichen herden')
- II Andantino ('Schafe können sicher weiden')

Publishers: Schott & Co Ltd, London, 1953 (5747)

41 **Continuo from** *Musical Offering* BWV 1079 by J. S. Bach, realized by D. Lipatti (finished by Nadia Boulanger) (1950)
Unpublished: Manuscript, Library of Union of Rumanian Composers.

Selected Bibliography

Books and Albums

1 *Dinu Lipatti (1917–1950)*
Commemorative Album of Columbia recordings – FCX 491/5. "Album consacré à la memoire de Dinu Lipatti realisé pour Pathé-Marconi par la S. N. Mercure, editeur à Paris, le 2 Decembre 1955". It contains the following texts:

Handman, Dorel	*Avant-propos* p. 2
	Dinu Lipatti p. 5
Lipatti, Madeleine	*Dinu Lipatti et le Piano* (Paris 19 Sept 1955) p. 9
Legge. Walter	*Dinu Lipatti enregistre* p. 17
Grange, H. L. de la	*Dinu Lipatti interprète de Chopin* p. 20
Lipatti, Dinu	*Ebauche d'un projet pour un Cours d'Interpretation au Conservatoire de Genève* (May 1950) p. 23
Lipatti, Dinu	*Projets de travail* etablis par Dinu Lipatti quelques mois avant sa mort. Une Journée de travail de Lipatti. p. 24

2 *Dinu Lipatti. Son Dernier Recital* Columbia Album – FCX 698/9, Paris, Ed. Mercure, October 1957. It contains the following essays:

Rostand Claude	*Le dernier Recital de Dinu Lipatti à Besançon*
Lipatti, Madeleine	*Dinu Lipatti, son dernier recital*

3 Lipatti, Anna
La Vie du Pianiste Dinu Lipatti ecrite par sa mère. Paris, Ed. La Colombe 1954

4 Lipatti, Anna
Dinu Lipatti – la Douleur de Ma Vie. Geneva, Ed. Perret-Gentil, 1967

5 Lipatti, Madeleine (Edited)
Hommage a Dinu Lipatti. Geneva, Ed. Labor et Fides, 1951. It contains tributes, letters, accounts by: Madeleine Lipatti (*Dedicace* p. 11), E. Ansermet, W. Backhaus, Brigitte V. Barbey, Nadia Boulanger, C. J. Burckhardt, J. Chapuis, A. Cortot, P. Ducotterd, G. Enesco, E. Fischer, H. Gagnebin, A. Honegger, H. van Karajan, R. P. Laval, W. Legge, N. Magaloff, R. Manuel, I. Markevitch, F. Martin, R.-A. Mooser,
P. Sacher, B. Siki.

6 Lipatti, Madeleine (Edit.)
1970 in Memoriam Dinu Lipatti 1917–1950. Geneva, Ed. Labot et Fides 1970. It contains memoirs, letters, tributes by: Madeleine Lipatti (*Souvenirs* p. 7), E. Ansermet, W. Backhaus, Nadia Boulanger, G.-J. Burckhardt, J. Chapuis, A. Cortot, Dr H. Dubois-Ferrière, G. Enesco, E. Fischer, P. Fournier, H. Gagnebin, B. L. Gelber, M. Gendron, A. Honegger, A. Janigro, H. v, Karajan, R. P. J. Laval, W. Legge, N. Magaloff, I. Markevitch, F. Martin, Y. Menuhin, R. A Mooser, R Manuel, P. Sacher, Hedy Salquin, B. Siki, R. Weisz.

7 Tanasescu, Dragos
Dinu Lipatti. Collection 'Viata in Imagini' Bucuresti Ed. Muzicala 1962 (Rumanian and Hungarian language)

8 Tanasescu, Dragos
Lipatti. Bucuresti Ed. Meridiana 1965 (Rumanian, French, English and German languages)

9 Tanasescu, Dragos & Bargauanu, Grigore.
Dinu Lipatti Bucuresti, Ed. Muzicala, 1971 (Preface: Henri Gagnebin. Addenda: *D. Lipatti*. Cadenza to Mozart Concerto in C, K.V.467)

10 Soarec, Miron
Prietenul meu Dinu Lipatti, Bucuresti Ed. Muzicala 1981 (Addenda: *D. Lipatti-Nocturne* for Piano, 1937; *Premiere Improvisation pour Violon, Violoncelle et Piano*, 1939

Footnote: Nos 1, 3–9 contain a Discography and List of Lipatti Compositions

Essays

1 Bargauanu, Grigore
Dinu Lipatti Interpret. In *Muzica*, Bucuresti, No 1, January 1964

2 Bargauanu, Grigore
Dinu Lipatti Compozitor In *Muzica*, Nr 5–6 May/June 1964 (The essay comprises a Discography and a List of compositions)

3 Bargauanu, Grigore & Tanasescu, Dragos.
Aspects Inedits de l'activité d'interprète de Dinu Lipatti In *Nouvelles Musicales de Roumanie*, Bucuresti, No 1 January 1970

3a Bargauanu, Grigore & Tanasescu, Dragos.
Dinu Lipatti Compositeur In *Revue Musicale de Suisse Romande*, No 4, March 1986

4 Gheciu, Radu *Arta Pianistica a lui Dinu Lipatti* In *Muzica* No 12 December 1956

5 Gendre, André
Une amitie artistique: Dinu Lipatti et George Schwob. In *Revue Musicale de la Suisse Romande* Lausanne, No 5 December 1980 (It contains 16 letters from D. L. written between 1946 & 1950)

6 Hoffman, Alfred
Un mare Interpret Romin al Muzicii lui Chopin – Dinu Lipatti. In *Studii si Cercetari de Istoria Artei*, Bucuresti Ed. Academiei R. P. R No 2 1960; also in the Archives of the Congress "Chopin", Warsaw 1960.

7 Oana-Pop, Rodica
O Compozitie Inedita a lui Dinu Lipatti.. In *Lucrari de Muzicologie*, Cluj, Music Conservatoire 'Gh. Dima' Vol 3, 1967

8 Tanasescu, Dragos
Dinu Lipatti critic muzical si pedagog. In *Muzica* Bucuresti No 12 December 1964

9 Tanasescu, Dragos & Bargauanu, Grigore.
Aspecte Inedite ale Artei lui Dinu Lipatti (Noi vestigii cu privire la interpret. Ultima compozitie a lui D. L: Aubade for Wind Quartet) In *Muzica*, No 11, November 1967

10 Tanasescu, Dragos & Bargauanu, Grigore.
Interferente stilistice in Creatia lui D. L. In *Muzica* No 1 January 1971

11 Tanasescu, Dragos & Bargauanu, Grigore.
O Inregistrare Inedita a lui Dinu Lipatti: Concertul in Re minor de J. S. Bach. In *Muzica* No 3 March 1975

12 Tanasescu, Dragos & Bargauanu, Grigore.
Dinu Lipatti Ispolnitel (Dinu Lipatti Interpret) In: *Straniti istorii ruminskoi muziki* (Pages from History of Rumanian Music) A selection of articles and essays edited by Rufina Leites, Moscova, Muzika, 1979. (This is a translation in Russian of the chapter *The Interpreter* from the book *Dinu Lipatti*, Bucuresti, Editura Muzicala, 1971)

13 Tanasescu, Dragos & Bargauanu, Grigore.
Dinu Lipatti et ses Maitres Roumains. In: *Nouvelles Musicales de Roumanie, Muzica*, Buc. No 12, December 1980.

14 Vancea, Zeno.
Dinu Lipatti. In: *Muzica*, Buc. No 2, Feb. 1976

Articles and Other Excerpts

1 Alexandrescu, Romeo.
Dinu Lipatti. Impressions et Souvenirs In: *Nouvelles Musicales de Roumanie, Muzica*, Buc. No 6 Iunie 1972

2 Balan, Theodor.
Cu Florica Musicescu despre Dinu Lipatti la o Jumatate de Veac dela nasterea muzicianului. In *Muzica* Buc. No 3 March 1967

3 Barbier, Jean-Joël.
Le dernier Recital de Dinu Lipatti. In Journal Musical Français, Paris No 64, 20 Jan. 1958.

4 Bargauanu, Grigore.
Pe urmele lui Dinu Lipatti – impresii de calatorie la Geneva. In: *Muzica* No 11, November 1967

5 Bargauanu, Grigore.
Dinu Lipatti. In: *Müvelödes* Buc. No 12 Dec 1975 (Hungarian language)

6 Bargauanu, Grigore.
Chronique du Disque (Lipatti: *Tziganes, Symphonie Concertante pour deux pianos et orchestre a cordes*. Orchestre Philharmonque de Cluj. Direction: Emil Simon; Pianos: Sofia Cosma et Corneliu Gheorghiu. Disque Electrerecord, STM-ECE 01120). In *Nouvelles Musicales de Roumanie. Muzica* Buc. No 3 March 1976.

7 Bargauanu, Grigore & Tanasescu, Dragos.
Dinu Lipatti. In: *Nouvelles Musicales de Roumanie. Muzica* Buc No 1 Jan 1971 (The article contains a List of Compositions, a Discography, Lipatti's appreciations on music and musicians, the sketch of the project for an Interpretation Course at Geneva Conservatoire, reminiscences on Dinu Lipatti, music reviews).

8 Bargauanu, Grigore & Tanasescu, Dragos.
Considerations sur l'activité d'Interprete de Dinu Lipatti. In: *Nouvelles musicales de Roumanie. Muzica*. Buc. No 11 Novemb, 1971. (It contains the Preface to the book *Dinu Lipatti* op. cit. by Henri Gagnebin.)

9 Brezianu, Barbu.
Sase ani dela moartea lui Dinu Lipatti. In *Muzica* Buc. No 12, Dec 1956

10 Burckhardt, Carl J.
Dinu Lipatti. In: *Begegnungen* Zurich 1958. Reprinted in: *Diener der Musik* edited by M. Müller and W. Mertz, Tübingen, 1965.

11 Cresta, Michel.
Discographie (at the end of the article: *Le Prince Lipatti* by A. Lompech) In: *Le Monde de la Musique* Paris, No 49 Oct. 1982

12 Ekiert, Janusz.
Dinu Lipatti. In: *Wirtuozi*, Warsawa, Centrala Handlowa przemyslu muzycznego, 1957

13 Enesco, Georges
Mon ami Lipatti. In: *Journal des Jeunesses musicales de France* Paris No 4,13 Dec. 1950

14 Fladt, Hartmut.
Lipatti-Hickhack. In: *Neue Musikzeitung*, Regensburg, Oct–Nov 1981.

15 Gagnebin, Henri.
Le souvenir d'un grand pianiste. Dinu Lipatti l'idole du public. In *La Tribune de Genève*, 29/30 April 1967

16 Gheorghiu, Corneliu.
Rasfoind Albumul dedicat lui Dinu Lipatti. In: *Scinteia*, Buc. No 6820 3 Dec. 1975

17 Ghircoiasu, Romeo.
Permanentele virtuozitatii lui Dinu Lipatti. In *Scinteia* No 7285 19 March 1967.

18 Goléa, Antoine.
Dinu Lipatti. In *Disques*, Paris No 32, 25 Dec 1950

19 Hoffman, Alfred.
Actualitatea artei lui Dinu Lipatti. Cu prilejul impliniri a zece ani dela moartea sa. In: *Muzica* No 12, Dec 1960.

20 Jora, Mihail.
Ginduri despre Dinu Lipatti. In: *Contimporanul* No. 49 2 Dec 1960

21 Josar.
Un botez... artistic. In: *Curierul Artelor* Buc No 79/84 1921

22 Laszlo, Ferenc.
Scandal Chopin in lumea Discului. In: *A Hét*, Buc. 15 Oct 1982 (In Hungarian)

23 Legge, Walter.
Dinu Lipatti. In *Gramophone*, Stanmore, Middx. Feb. 1951. Reprinted in *The Gramophone Jubilee Book.* London 1973.

24 Legge, Walter.
Dinu Lipatti enregistre a Genève. In *Revue Musicale de la Suisse Romande*, Lausanne, Dec. 1960.

25 Leites, Rufina.
Jizn, podosnaia komete In: *Sovetskaia Muzika* Moscow, No 8 August 1969.

26 Lipatti, Madeleine.
Dinu Lipatti. Son dernier Recital. In: *Le Guide du Concert et du Disque.* Paris No 177, 27 Dec. 1957.

27 Lompeck, Alain.
Le Prince Lipatti, followed by *Un Phare pour les Jeunes Pianistes* (Interview with François-René Duchable). In: *Le Monde de la Musique* Paris No 49 Oct. 1982

28 Meyer, Martin.
Wirklichkeit und Legende. In: *Fonoforum*, Köln, No 6 June 1978 (it contains a discography).

29 Mooser, R.-Aloys.
Dinu Lipatti – Danses Roumaines pour piano et Orchestre In: *Regards sur la musique Contemporaine 1929–1946.* Lausanne, Librairie P. Rouge, 1946.

30 Mooser, R.-Aloys.
Dinu Lipatti – Concertino en style classique. In: *Aspects de la Musique Contemporaine 1953–1957.* Geneva, Ed Labor et Fides, 1957.

31 Nicoara, Adriana.
De vorba cu Dinu Lipatti. (Interview) In: *Universul Literar* Buc. 1941.

32 Normand, Gilles.
Un Pianiste Inspiré – Dinu Lipatti. In: *Musica-disques*, Paris, No 90, Sept. 1961.

33 Panigel, Armand.
Discographie (end of article by Antoine Golea) in: *Disques*, Paris, No 32, 25 Dec 1950.

34 Rattalino, Pierro.
Genio e Regolatezza, carriera, mito e stile del pianista Dinu Lipatti. In: *Discoteca*, Milan, Dec 1976.

35 Ripeanu, Valeriu.
Virsta Vesniciei. In: *Gazeta Literara*. Buc. No 21, 16 March 1967.

36 Sava, Iosif.
Florica Musicescu despre Dinu Lipatti. In: *Scinteia Tineretului* Buc. No 5307, 11 June 1966.

37 Sava, Iosif.
Dinu Lipatti – jumatate de veac. Interviu cu Corneliu Gheorghiu. In: *Scinteia Tineretului* Buc. No 5546 19 March 1967.

38 Siki, Bela.
Dinu Lipatti. In: *Recorded Sound*, London, No 15, 1964..

39 Sperantia, Eugeniu.
Dinu Lipatti. In: *Steaua*, Cluj, Dec. 1957.

40 Soarec, Miron.
Dinu Lipatti in lumina unor scrisori inedite. In: *Lucrari de Muzicologie*, Cluj, Conservatorul de Muzica "G. Dima", Vol 4, 1968.

41 Soarec, Miron.
Marturii inedite despre Dinu Lipatti. In: Studii de Muzicologie, Vol XII, Ed. Muzicala, 1976.

42 Tanasescu, Dragos.
Zum Vierzigsten Geburtstag Dinu Lipattis. In: *Rumänische Rundschau*, Buc. No 2, 1957.

43 Tanasescu, Dragos.
Senzatie in Lumea Discului. In: *Contemporanul* Buc. April 1983.

44 Tanasescu, Dragos and Bargauanu, Grigore.
O prestigioasa colaborare artistica: George Enescu – Dinu Lipatti. In *Ateneu*, Bacau, No 8, August 1971.

45 Tanasescu, Dragos and Bargauanu, Grigore.
Dinu Lipatti – Sonatina pentru Vioara si Pian, Patru melodii pentru Voce si Pian, Trei Dansuri Rominesti pentru doua Piane, Improvizatie pentru Vioara, Violoncel si Pian. Interpreti: Cornelia Bronzetti – Victoria Stefanescu; Valentin Teodorian – Lisette Georgescu; Suzana Szörenyi – Hilda Jerea; Stefan Gheorghiu – Radu Aldulescu – Miron Soarec. On Record Sleeve of Electrerecord ECE 0628, Buc. Febr. 1972.

46 Vancea, Zeno.
Un muzician de celebritate mondiala. In: *Romania Libera*, Buc. No 6973, 19 March 1967.

47 X X X
EMI et le Mystere Lipatti. In: *Harmonie*, Paris, No 11 July/Aug. 1981.

Various

1 Aguettant, Robert.
Catalogue commenté et discographie critique. In: *Chopin*, Paris, Hachette, 1965.

2 Alexandrescu, Romeo.
Spicuiri critice din trecut. Buc. Ed. Muzicala, 1970.

3 Baker, Theodore. *Baker's Biographical Dictionary of Musicians*. New York, Ed. Slonimsky, 1958, 1971, 1978.

4 Bennqitz, Hanspeter.
Interpretenlexikon des Instrumental Musik. Bern und München, Francke Verlag, 1964.

5 Borba Tomás et Lopes Garcia, Fernando,
Dicionário de música. Lisbon, Ed. Cosmos, 1963.

6 Bourniquel, Camille.
Chopin. Cap. Discographie, Paris, Ed. du Seuil (Collection Microcosmos, "Solfèges"), 1957, 1980.

7 Breazul, George.
Dinu Lipatti. In: *Die Musik in Geschichte und Gegenwart,* Kassel, Bärenreiter Verlag, Vol. VIII, 1960.

8 *Britannica Book of Music*, 1980.

9 *Bulletin du Conservatoire de Musique de Genève*. (Nouveaux Professeurs, p. 1) Genèva, No 8. April 1944.

10 *Bulletin d'Informations* Ed. Salabert, Paris No 6, 1953.

11 Ciomac, Emanoil.
Pagini de Cronica Muzicala 1915–1935. Buc. Ed. Muzicala, 1967.

12 *The Concise Encyclopedia of Music and Musicians*. Edited by Martin Cooper, Hutchinson, London, 1975.

13 Cosma, Viorel, *Muzicieni Romini, Compozitori si Muzicologi. Lexicon.* Buc. Ed. Muzicala, 1970.

14 Delavrancea, Celia.
Scrieri. Buc. Ed. Eminescu, 1982.

15 *Diapason. Dictionnaire des Disques.* Paris. Robert Laffont, 1981.

16 *Dizionario Ricordi della Musica e dei Musicisti.* Milano, Ricordi C. 1959

17 *Encyclopedie van de Muziek.* Amsterdam, Brussel, Elsevier, 1957.

18 *Entiklopediceskii muzicalnii slovar.* Editor: B. S. Steinpress & I. M. Iampolski, Moscow, Ed. Sevetskaia Enticlopediia, 1966

19 Ewen, David.
Encyclopedia of Concert Music. London, Peter Owen Ltd 1959.

20 Frank/Altman.
Kurzgefasstes Ponkunstler-Lexikon. Vol 2. Wilhelmshaven, Heinrichshofen's Verlag, 1978.

21 *Das Grosse Lexikon der Musik.* Editors: Marc Honegger and Günther Massenkeil, Vol 5. Freiburg, Basel, Wien, Herder, 1981.

22 Hanszewska Mieczyslava.
1000 Kompozitorow. Cracow, Polski Widawnictwo Muzyczne, 1963.

23 *The International Cyclopedia of Music and Musicians.* Chief Editor Oscar Thompson, New York, Toronto, Dood Mead & Co. London J. M. Dent & Sons Ltd, 1975.

24 Jacobs, Arthur.
A New Dictionary of Music. Harmondsworth, Middx. Penguin Books, Ltd. 1970, 1974.

25 Jora, Mihail.
Momente Muzicale. Bucuresti, Ed. Muzicala, 1968.

26 Kingdon Ward, Martha.
Dinu Lipatti. In: *Grove Dictionary of Music and Musicians.* London, Macmillan & Co Ltd. 1954.

27 Monsaingeon, Bruno
Mademoiselle. Entretiens avec Nadia Boulanger Paris, Ed. Van de Velde, 1980.

28 *La Musica*. (Dictionary edited by Guido M. Gatti) Vol. 2, Torino, Unione Tipografico – Editrice Torinese, 1971,

29 *Musikkenns Hvem Hvor*. Copenhagen, Politikens Forlag, 1950, 1961.

30 Nanquette, Claude.
Anthologie des Interprètes Paris, Stock/Musique, 1979.

31 *The New College Encylopedia of Music*. New York, W. W. Norton & Co. Inc. 1976

32 Onnen, Frank.
Encyclopédie de la Musique. Bruxelles, Ed. Sequoia, 1964.

33 Pâris, Alain. *Dictionnaire des Interprètes*. Paris, Robert Laffont, 1982.

34 Prieberg, Fred, K.
Lexikon des Neuen Musik. Freiburg-München, Verlag Karl Alber, 1958.

35 *Riemann Musik Lexikon*. Mainz, B. Schott's & Sohne, 1961 (Editor Wilibald Gurlitt) ibid. Ergänzungsband, 1975 (editor Carl Dahlhaus)

36 Schäffer, Boguslav.
Leksykon Kompozytorów XX wieku. Vol. 1. Cracow, Polski Wydawnictwo Muzyczne, 1963.

37 Schönberg, Harold C.
Great Pianists

38 *Schweitzer Musiker-Lexikon*. Zurich, Atlantis Verlag, 1964.

39 Seeger, Horst.
Musiklexikon, Vol. 2, Leipzig, VEB Deutscher Verlag fur Musik, 1966.

40 Shawe-Taylor, Desmond.
Dinu Lipatti In: *New Grove's Dictionary of Music and Musicians*, Vol 11, London, Macmillan & Co. Ltd. 1980.

41 *Sohlmans Musiklexikon*. Vol 4. Stockholm, Sohlmans Forlag AB, 1977.

42 Spycket, Jérôme.
Clara Haskil. Lausanne, Ed. Payot, 1975.

43 Weiss, Marcel.
Dinu Lipatti. In: *Larousse de la Musique* (edited by Antoine Golea-Marc Vignal) Paris, Librairie Larousse, 1982.

44 Worbs, Hans Christoph.
Grosse Pianisten einst und jetzt. Berlin, Rembrandt Verlag, 1964.

Two Cadenzas by Dinu Lipatti

The Mozart Piano Concerto in C Major (K467)

CADENCES
POUR
LE CONCERTO EN UT MAJEUR K.467 DE MOZART
I
DINU LIPATTI
p espress.
mp
poco rit.
p dim.
a tempo
pp
leggiero
poco a poco cresc.

f
mp
cresc.
f
dim.
dolce
p legato
senza rigore
più dolce

a tempo poco a poco
cresc.
risoluto
f
legato
legato
espress.
dim.
p
poco cresc.

sf
p legg.
senza Ped.
stacc. e leggiero
stacc.

stacc.
cresc.
tr
m.g.
f
tr
m.g.
tr
tr
m.g.
Cresc.
più f

poco rit.
Tutti
Tempo

II

grazioso
poco rit.
mp
p dolce
Ped.
a tempo
poco a poco
p
poco cresc.
senza Ped.

tempo primo
tr
tr
mf
dim.
(senza ritenuto)
8
Tutti
pp
8
Montana, le 22 Janvier 1945

Index